THE HIDDEN FACE OF LOCAL POWER

MIRYA R. HOLMAN

THE HIDDEN FACE
OF LOCAL POWER

Appointed Boards and the Limits of Democracy

TEMPLE UNIVERSITY PRESS

Philadelphia • *Rome* • *Tokyo*

TEMPLE UNIVERSITY PRESS
Philadelphia, Pennsylvania 19122
tupress.temple.edu

Cataloging information is available from the Library of Congress.

Names: Holman, Mirya author
Title: The hidden face of local power : appointed boards and the limits of
  democracy / Mirya R. Holman.
Other titles: Appointed boards and the limits of democracy
Description: Philadelphia : Temple University Press, 2025. | Includes
  bibliographical references and index. | Summary: "Develops a framework
  for understanding how cities use appointed boards and commissions"—
  Provided by publisher.
Identifiers: LCCN 2025003014 (print) | LCCN 2025003015 (ebook) | ISBN
  9781439926703 cloth | ISBN 9781439926710 paperback | ISBN 9781439926727 pdf
Subjects: LCSH: Municipal government—United States—Citizen participation
  | Citizens' advisory committees—United States | Municipal officials and
  employees—Selection and appointment | Democracy—United States
Classification: LCC JS391 .H65 2025 (print) | LCC JS391 (ebook) | DDC
  352.140973—dc23/eng/20250508
LC record available at https://lccn.loc.gov/2025003014
LC ebook record available at https://lccn.loc.gov/2025003015

The manufacturer's authorized representative in the EU for product safety is
Temple University Rome, Via di San Sebastianello, 16, 00187 Rome RM, Italy
(https://rome.temple.edu/).
tempress@temple.edu

9 8 7 6 5 4 3 2 1

CONTENTS

SECTION III DO BOARDS MATTER?

Acknowledgments

This book is dedicated to my academic coven. Someone once said that my research agenda is a combination of "No one thinks about that" and "That's hard to study." Yes. This book is that! But here's the thing: Once I started talking about this project, friends, colleagues, and supporters quickly bought in to the idea that they should be thinking about boards and told me how much they wanted to read this book. Emily Farris is my ride or die and I'm so thankful that I have her enthusiasm and support in my life. I am particularly thankful for the support of Tiffany Barnes, Justin de Benedictis-Kessner, Andrea Benjamin, Peter Burns, Salil Benegal, Anna Mahoney, Heather Ondercin, Jessica Trounstine, and Christina Wolbrecht. Random people online told me that this was interesting—I don't know if y'all understand how those small exchanges kept me going at various points during this process. I owe Peter Burns a particular debt of gratitude: he is why I am in this career and continue to think that questions about local politics are interesting and important. My MHAWS bebes are a constant source of joy and support. My morning writing group is amazing: Christina Xydias, Bethany Albertson, and Shannon McGregor are such a positive influence in my life. The online community created by Sara Angevine is amazing, as is the support from the FAFO group. Aaron Javsicas is a great editor—offering feedback, remaining enthusiastic about the project as I wrote other books instead of finishing this one, and agreeing to publish yet another of my books! Thanks to Temple University Press and Aaron in particular for their support of my research broadly and this project specifically. A MEE-centered writing retreat in Atlantic City forcefully pushed this book forward (one of SIX books to come out of that retreat!). I am so thankful that I met Kelly Clancy—her editing is a major reason this is a done book and not just floating around in a drafts folder somewhere. All errors are mine, but a lot of the good here is due to her diligence and support.

Archivists and librarians were very helpful in my research process. I knew I wanted to write a book that included a deep discussion of the history of boards and how we got here. The thing is, I wasn't sure how to do that! I read a lot of examples and work on archival methods and then kind of jumped in. I was lucky to have archivists and librarians who caught me when I jumped. Information about the development of boards and commissions in Los Angeles came from a variety of sources, including the University of Southern California "LA as Subject" archive, the Online Archive of California, the Huntington Museum, and the Thomas and Dorothy Leavey Center for the Study of Los Angeles. Sometimes the best thing a librarian can tell you is that the material isn't at a place! I spent too much time at the Los Angeles City Archives and Records Center—Michael Holland was so helpful in identifying sources, aided me as I sifted through records, and was patient with my seemingly never-ending requests. All the archivists at the New Orleans Public Library did the same thing for me, setting aside a desk so I could come in and work through boxes and boxes of mayoral correspondence, meeting minutes, and board rosters. City managers and clerks provided board rosters to me, sometimes going well beyond my simple requests by sending along handbooks, old rosters, and funny stories.

I started writing something about boards in 2017; by 2019, I worked in earnest on this for the summer. The book I set out to write was descriptive: What boards exist? Who sits on them? (Boring!) A visiting position at Australian National University over the summer of 2019 helped convince me that I had a more interesting story to tell about these boards. A talk there and several other talks in that year helped my thinking enormously. I appreciate Katrine Beauregard, Zoe Sullivan, Jana von Stein, and Keith Dowling for their very helpful conversations about the ideas in the book. Another talk at Texas A&M University was very helpful: Diana O'Brien, David Fortunato, and Paul Kelstedt gave particularly useful comments. At Tulane, J. Celeste Lay, Casey Love, Chris Fettweis, Menaka Philips, and the Polichix provided a great level of support. Working with Christina Wolbrecht, Lakshmi Iyer, and the United WE organization helped me keep at this project and gave me new perspectives to consider as I developed a related research agenda with them. I am particularly thankful for Wendy Doyle's work at United WE for helping me think about women's civic engagement through boards.

Part of the reason I wrote this book was purely for career advancement: I was repeatedly told by senior people at a previous employer that I needed this book in order to be promoted—that the 70+ articles, book, grants, edited volume, and textbook I had written were not enough. A senior administrator told me that, because I work on lots of different projects and have a lot of coauthors, "People might say that you don't have a distinctive research agenda." Well, here's a distinctive research agenda. I am so thankful that I don't work there anymore. For those who feel trapped: change is possible.

I continue to be quite surprised that I managed to finish this book. It turns out that what I needed was a semester off from teaching and to be out of a toxic department. I appreciate the Hobby School at the University of Houston for providing both of those for me. I am especially thankful to Jim Granato for trusting his faculty to do their jobs. "Happy faculty are productive faculty"—yes sir. Here's what I do when I am happy and can just do my job (again, errors my own).

The research in this book cost approximately $18,000, between trips to archives, a small team of research assistants, and paying participants for their time. Many people do not have access to resources like that, and I'm very thankful that I worked at institutions that had funds available. I also spent a lot of my own money traveling while I worked on this book. I wrote this book all over the world: the first words were written on a solo writing retreat in Folegandros, Greece, with additional work in Waiheke Island, Canberra, Budapest, Vienna, Reykjavik, Munich, Sibenik, Krakow, Prague, Paris, Oxford, and Playa del Carmen. Time in a writer's cottage at my dad's house, at a townhouse in Houston, and by the pool in New Orleans rounded it out. Some of these trips connected to conferences. Others were the result of me feeling restless. I am luckier than I deserve in so many ways, but that I can work all over the world is up there. I often think back to being a sad teenager in Cave Junction, Oregon, and how I would yearn to get out, to see more of the world, to leave that small town and small life behind. My life is so much better and bigger and brighter than I ever dreamed.

My family and friends have been a bit bewildered and a lot supportive about this project (honestly, that's true about most things I do). Zach, the love of my life, is always there for my nerd pursuits. From giving me rides to archives to supporting any trip I want to take to gently rolling his eyes at my purchase of a thousand weird books to ready companionship for celebrating each step of the way, Zach undergirds all of this. Friends patiently listen to my stories. Family members pretended like they understood. My dad, upon hearing that this book would be published, asked, "What's next?" What a great question. I am my father's daughter, so there are six books planned. Nola, Lambeaux, Marx, and Maggie are the best pit crew. I am surrounded by people and creatures who believe that I'm smart and funny and if I choose to write a book about local boards, then it simply must be interesting. They are the best.

THE HIDDEN FACE OF LOCAL POWER

1

Local Appointed Boards

In the late spring of 2020, amid a global pandemic, a Minneapolis police officer murdered George Floyd. A recording of Mr. Floyd's death rocked Minneapolis and the United States, with subsequent widespread Black Lives Matter protests, racial uprisings, and a refocusing on policy tools to address police violence and racism. In conversations on social media, calls for reform often focused on creating commissions for police oversight. Alexandria Ocasio-Cortez (@AOC), a member of the House of Representatives, tweeted to her more-than-one-million followers, "A lot of ppl are asking abt policy solutions. Here are a few: 1. Ask your mayor and city council for strong Citizen Review Boards. 2. Budgets. They're powerful. Find your city's police budget. Compare that to the school & housing budget. More $ in fmr → school-to-prison pipeline."[1] A month later, her tweet had been liked by 39,000 people and retweeted more than 10,000 times. Yet, at the point of AOC's call, most large U.S. cities already had a police oversight commission.[2] Indeed, Minneapolis already had both a Police Conduct Oversight Commission and a Police Conduct Review Panel; the latter of these was created "For the purposes of (1) assuring that police services are delivered in a lawful and nondiscriminatory manner, (2) providing to the public meaningful participatory oversight of the police and their interactions with the citizenry and (3) investigating complaints of misconduct."[3] This was not the first time that police violence and killings elevated calls for civilian oversight: AOC's call echoed efforts by the ACLU and the NAACP, following high-profile police killings and violence in the 1960s and 1970s, that "there should exist somewhere, separate from the police department itself, an independent, impartial tribunal of carefully selected, outstanding citizens from the community at large" (Gross and Reitman 1966, 2).

In New Orleans, residents are less enthusiastic about the idea of an appointed board as the salvation for policy issues. The Sewerage and Water Board (S&WB) of New Orleans was created in 1899 to oversee the construction of systems to provide clean drinking water, sewage removal, and stormwater drainage for the city (Behrman 1914; Earl 1903). Today, the S&WB continues to provide those services to the city. The 11 members of the board oversee an agency that operates more than 280 miles of canals and 24 pumping houses, and provides drainage for the City of New Orleans and surrounding areas (SWBONO 2021). Well, kind of. The S&WB also has recently faced storms regularly overwhelming the pumping system,[4] a dated electric system to power pumps,[5] allegations of corruption,[6] an aging billing system,[7] investigations by auditors and the FBI,[8] a secret sex room,[9] and various contaminations of the city's drinking water ranging from brain-eating amoeba to lead.[10] The problems with the system are not new, nor are the recent calls to reform and restructure the system, to dissolve the board, or to place the management under a city department (Stein 2023c). And yet, the appointed board continues to oversee the city's essential public works systems.

The Sewerage and Water Board of New Orleans and the City of Minneapolis's police oversight board are but a narrow glimpse into the many bodies of appointed individuals who engage in deliberation and decision-making over a local government policy in the United States. Even though every city in the United States uses appointed boards, we know little about the origins, functions, or consequences of these commonplace governing mechanisms. Why do cities create these boards? What do these appointed boards do? And are these boards good for democracy? This book asks and answers these questions.

A "Strong Boards, Weak Boards" Theory of Local Boards

In this book, I develop and test a "strong boards, weak boards" framework for understanding how cities use appointed boards and commissions. In short, I argue that cities create, fill, and support boards strategically. For cities, *strong* boards generate policy, including in controversial areas; make decisions that consolidate power; and make choices that defend the interests of business, the wealthy, and white residents. Cities use another set of boards, *weak* boards, not to generate policy but to pacify agitation from marginalized groups, including women, racial minorities, and poor people; to give the appearance of inclusivity and redistributional policymaking; and to pretend like they have democratic deliberation.

I argue that critical junctures in the political development of cities led to the development of strong boards with extensive power to regulate land use, finances, and civil service. Cities and their white residents use these boards to create and reinforce segregation and to centralize those individuals involved in real estate development in local politics (Logan and Molotch 1987; Trounstine 2018). Later, neoliberal shifts in economic development policy (Weaver 2021) led cities to create a new set of strong boards: those in charge of offering and approving incentives to attract businesses and development to that city.

Weak boards, in comparison, are created during points of political strife as a tool of distraction. These boards emerged from a variety of pressures on cities. A requirement by the federal government in the 1950s and 1960s that cities create representative boards if they wanted federal funds pushed the creation of a variety of civilian advisory councils. The post–civil rights re-enfranchisement of Black voters pushed cities to desegregate boards. The second wave of feminism activated women to demand representation and policy change from local governments. But instead of expanding access for these groups to the instruments of governance, cities responded by creating weak boards to maintain the distribution of power in the hands of rich white men. The disparate power of these boards continues through to today, with path dependency and status quo contributing to the continued power and prestige of boards that relate to development, public spaces, and finances and the limited power of boards that advise on poverty, identity politics, or criminal justice reform.

Cities preserve this strong board–weak board dichotomy through policymaking power, institutional design, and who serves on the boards. As a result, cities design strong boards to have broad policymaking power and to make decisions with agility. The choices that these boards make are focused on the consolidation of resources for political and economic insiders. These decisions often reinforce economic and racial inequality. The membership of these boards includes those who already have access to power, those who have held political office, white people, the wealthy, men, and those with business and economic backgrounds.

In comparison, weak boards have few independent powers and serve as advisory boards. Cities design weak boards to maximize representation and deliberation: they are large boards with diverse memberships. Weak board membership includes those without traditional avenues of access to power, including the politically inexperienced, women, residents of color, the poor, and those without connections to economic power. While these boards and their members might aim to disrupt the status quo and change power distributions in their city, their institutional design, dependence, and lack of resources make the boards toothless.

The institutional design and practices of weak and strong boards translate into whether these boards affect policy. Cities fill weak boards with individuals who engage in earnest deliberative policymaking with few real policy consequences. Because of their limited institutional design and disconnected membership, weak boards are ineffective. "Status of Women" (SOW) boards do not actually increase the status of women. Boards that target sources and consequences of poverty, such as affordable housing boards, rent control boards, and social service advisory councils, do not produce equitable changes in the amount of affordable housing, the current rental rates, or the cost or availability of mobile homes. In short, these boards do not produce the policy changes that the public, or even members of the board, think they are producing. Strong boards, on the other hand, are able to change policy but do so largely without deliberation.

These strong and weak boards fulfill two different antidemocratic goals: providing a veneer of democracy and undercutting democratic accountability. Weak boards allow cities and political leaders to appear as though they are responding to constituent demands and democratizing the voices of those who create policy. At the same time, strong boards allow cities to bypass democratic accountability, pushing decisions out of the public eye and consolidating the power and policymaking of economic elites.

Cities and Their Boards

My view of boards is a marked departure from how cities themselves frame these institutions. According to cities, boards and commissions represent opportunities for deliberation, offering citizens the chance to immerse themselves in learning about, debating, and making decisions in a policy arena, with few, if any, barriers to entry. In a flyer from Gonzales, Texas, the city asks residents (in both English and Spanish) to "Please speak for your community!" noting that "this exciting opportunity" would provide residents with the chance "to continue to shape and improve [their] community." Tacoma, Washington, recruits citizens to join boards with the tagline "Wanted: Passion, Skills and Experience!" Other cities use similar language: "The American democratic experience is built upon the foundation of concerned and caring citizens becoming actively involved in local government." Others ask residents to "please give serious consideration to becoming more involved in helping make our city the best city possible by applying to serve on a board or commission of your choice." Appeals to residents include that boards "provide opportunities for you to serve your community and shape our city" and that a board member's work "raises issues, concerns, and proposes meaningful change important to the well-being of the community at large."

Scholars also point to these boards as positives, often arguing that deliberative bodies like boards produce various benefits, including increasing transparency, creating strong democracy, and generating social capital in communities (Fung 2006; B. Barber 1985; Berry, Portney, and Thomson 1993; Stivers 1990; but see Shapiro 1999). Sonenshein (2006) notes in his overview of boards in Los Angeles, "The commissions are in effect charged with being the city's conscience on the issue." There are potential downstream effects as well: citizen participation can provide active residents with information about policymaking (including lessons about the complicated nature of policymaking) and may generate trust in public officials and accountability (Luskin, Fishkin, and Jowell 2002; Irvin and Stansbury 2004).

Within this view, participation of the population in decision-making processes improves both government and citizens' lives. Tocqueville (1835, 78) saw this component of local government as the true location of American democracy:

> Nevertheless, local assemblies of citizens constitute the strength of free nations. Town meetings are to liberty what primary schools are to science; they bring it within the people's reach, they teach men how to use it and how to enjoy it. A nation may establish a system of free government, but without the spirit of municipal institutions it cannot have the spirit of liberty. The transient passions and the interests of an hour, or the chance of circumstances, may have created the external forms of independence; but the despotic tendency that has been repelled will, sooner or later, inevitably reappear on the surface.

But scholars and observers of urban politics know that cities have always fallen short of ideal forms of local democracy. From early white men dominating political decisions, to political machines co-opting urban service failures and changing demographics to build corrupt systems that benefited themselves (Steffens 1904), to reformers invigorated by racism and business interests (Erie 1990) seeking to clean up government, to the redlining of the twentieth century (Trounstine 2018), cities have long used local political institutions to limit democracy. Today, only a small fraction of residents turn out to vote in local elections (de Benedictis-Kessner 2017; Trounstine 2013), white men from business backgrounds dominate urban political leadership (Kirkland 2020; Holman 2017), and populations express high levels of apathy and distrust in their local governments (Holman and Lay 2020; Crawford 2019). As Beierle notes, "Although a large cadre of citizens well-informed about . . . issues might fulfill a Jeffersonian ideal of public participation, such a vision is clearly not realistic" (1999, 82).

Deliberative bodies like appointed boards have also received their fair amount of criticism from scholars. In her foundational 1969 piece, Sherry Arnstein argues that on a "ladder" of citizen participation, institutions can range from manipulation, where, "in the name of citizen participation, people are placed on rubber stamp advisory committees or advisory boards . . . [this] bottom rung of the ladder signifies the distortion of participation into a public relations vehicle by powerholders," to citizen control, where "participants or residents can govern a program or an institution, be in full charge of policy and managerial aspects, and be able to negotiate the conditions under which 'outsiders' may change them" (Arnstein 1969, 218–22). Other scholars specifically point to local deliberative structures as "shallow"; these institutions can "delay decisions, increase conflict, disappoint participants, and lead to more distrust" (Yang and Pandey 2011).

The Hidden Face of Local Power uses boards to help us understand the development of urban political institutions in the United States, the allocation of power in local politics, and the persistence of inequality. In doing so, I contribute broadly to our understanding of the development and persistence of political institutions, race and racism, and how people use and live in urban spaces. This analysis offers a new view of the failures of local democracy.

My Contribution to Scholarship on Local Politics

Scholars of urban and local politics often focus on the role of institutions as a tool for understanding urban change, power in cities, and policy outcomes. Yet despite this focus, and despite the fact that boards and commissions exist as political institutions in every city in the United States, the role of boards and commissions remains a mystery, clouded in a lack of transparency and stymied by a lack of data and theory. The exclusion of boards from research is especially striking as stories of the importance of these bodies emerge in most of the foundational texts of urban politics. Instead of thinking of boards as an institutional feature worth being explored on its own, most urban politics scholars focus on elected officials OR on private actors, but rarely on the liminal space in between, where appointed boards exist.

A central proposition in this book is that white urban residents, including elected leaders, bureaucrats, and civilians, strategically used boards to institutionalize and reinforce racism. As political scientist Jessica Trounstine notes, "Segregation is not simply the result of *individual choices* about where to live. Neither racial antipathy nor economic inequality between groups is sufficient to create and perpetuate segregation. The maintenance of property values and the quality of public goods are collective endeavors. And like all collective endeavors, they require *collective action* for production and stability" (2018, 3, emphasis added). In short, racists are going to be racist, but they cannot use public institutions to institutionalize and enforce that racism unless they find other racists with similar goals. As the Kerner Commission (1968, 1) noted, "What white Americans have never fully understood—but what the Negro can never forget—is that white society is deeply implicated in the ghetto. White institutions created it, white institutions maintain it, and white society condones it." Here, I argue that boards provide one such convenient institution to create and maintain a racist state.

This book also provides a new view into how cities create and maintain land use policies. While cities lack control in many policy areas because of state and federal preemption and the free movement of individuals and capital across their borders (Paul E. Peterson 1981; Hirschman 1970), they do generally have broad jurisdiction over how land within their boundaries is used. Generally, state regulations in this area have focused on setting floors for things like building standards and affordable housing (Hatch 2017; Downs 1991) and allowing cities to make decisions about how far above these standards they would like to go (also see Goodman and Hatch 2023 for a discussion of preemption).

What cities look like, how people live in them, and how racial and economic inequalities are produced and reproduced all emerge out of land use regulations (Ihlanfeldt 2004; Glaeser, Gyourko, and Saks 2005; Bates and Santerre 1994). Researchers have repeatedly found that the outcome of board decisions is deeply important for quality of life. For example, the more stringent the municipal controls on land use, the higher the price of land and the lower the share of property occupied by low-income individuals (Ihlanfeldt 2004). Municipalities with a higher share of white residents (Donovan and Neiman 1992) and higher-income residents adopt more restrictive land use and zoning patterns; as such, racial and class-based segregation is exacerbated by restrictive land use regulations (Quigley, Raphael, and Rosenthal 2004; Lens and Monkkonen 2016). As a result, "The segregation of the rich . . . results in the hoarding of resources, amenities, and disproportionate political power" (Lens and Monkkonen 2016, 6). Appointed boards are a key institutional mechanism for this hoarding.

Early adoption of zoning laws varied across cities and was related to the presence of Progressive reformers, as well as larger budgets and higher property taxes (Trounstine 2018). The move to create zoning laws relates directly to desires by white leaders to reinforce social divisions and inequality, especially around race (Toll 1969; Stach 1989; Fischel 2004). The choices made by local boards and commissions perpetuated these forms of control—and continue to reinforce segregation in cities in the current era.[11] And yet, absent from this discussion is the fact that local zoning and planning boards are the site of these design reviews. Scholars of land use planning often gloss over the political nature of the zoning and planning boards that they place at the center of land use discussions. Nor do most scholars of urban land use consider that "ordinary" residents (often political amateurs) staff these boards. Thus, while scholarship on local land use and regulation identifies zoning and land use boards as central to segregation, inequality, and a wide set of quality-of-life issues, we know little about the politics behind the creation and implementation of these regulations.

My work builds directly on work on the (often unequal) deliberative and political structures of urban governance. Einstein, Glick, and Palmer (2019; 2019) also study boards from a different angle: who participates in contentious meetings by boards to approve new developments (particularly housing developments) in their communities. Einstein and colleagues find—over and over—that the public's participation in these boards is also unequal and undemocratic, in that participants are older, whiter, and less interested in building new housing than is the general population. Other scholars who examine inequality in electoral politics, from voter turnout to representation to interest groups (de Benedictis-Kessner 2021, 2022; Trounstine 2011, 2013; Anzia 2013; Benjamin 2017b; Benjamin and Carr 2022), also find that local "democratic" mechanisms are not actually democratic.

Like others before me, I draw on an American Political Development (APD) approach to help explain why some groups gain power and resources and other groups lose them in the shifts and stretches of city growth. As Megan Ming Francis notes, "APD scholars situate their analyses in a much longer time period than most political scientists" (2014, 12); this longer-time-period approach allows scholars to understand how institutions form, persist, and change. For example, Jessica Trounstine's (2008) work on changes in urban politics from political machines and reformers shows how reelection efforts often reduce accountability and the ability of voters to control their elected officials. In later work, Trounstine (2018) details how segregation policies put in place by local governments continue to produce racist outcomes today. Keneshia Grant's (2019) evaluation of the Great Migration examines how the movement of Black Americans from the South to urban centers transformed the politics of those places. Other work, such as evaluations of critical periods of change in Atlanta (Stone 1989), shows how government leaders rely on informal relationships with private enterprise to generate policy change or how the "neoliberal turn" occurred in urban development as national policies and parties shifted (Weaver 2016, 3). This scholarship is part of a much larger body of work that demonstrates the importance of evaluating not just the now of urban America but also how we got here, how institutions were created, and the factors that contribute to the stability and change of local political institutions.

Research on local democracy and urban politics regularly discusses the role of local boards as tools for policy change, patronage, and power consolidation. In their foundational work on the power of racial and ethnic minorities in local politics, Browning, Marshall, and Tabb note the following: "Appointments to commissions enabled elected officials to reward supporters, to give at least symbolic representation to groups, and to give ambitious activists to opportunity to gain visibility for future political candidacies" (1984, 156–57). Dahl's (1961) formative work on pluralism in New Haven, Connecticut, notes that appointments to committees worked as a tool for elected leaders to shore up their power and influence among supporters. In their book *Urban Fortunes*, Logan and Molotch (1987) discuss the role of appointments to local boards involving members of the rentier group, with the aim of shepherding or promoting local development. And Paul E. Peterson (1981) argues that boards are both a key resource in a spoils system and a way that elected and business leaders could cooperate to bypass local resistance to development. For example, when business leaders in Oakland, California, faced resistance to urban renewal, they convinced the mayor to "appoint a special committee called the Oakland Citizens Committee for Urban Renewal (OCCUR)" that gave the illusion of civilian involvement but was filled with business leaders (146).

I build on these foundational works by examining the creation and use of boards as political institutions. This departs from previous work that focuses on appointments to these boards or the use of these boards only as a tool of elected officials. I also differ from the other books on local boards. *Government in the Twilight Zone* by John Baker (2015) looks specifically at boards in small to midsize cities and uses surveys of board members, city managers, and elected officials to show that these institutions play a vital role in the governance of small towns in America. *Fields of Authority* by Jack Lucas (2016) examines the creation of "special purpose bodies" in Ontario, Canada. His work focuses on the development of these bodies in Canada as examples of institutional change, governance, and political authority. Like Lucas, I engage in a political development approach. But my work diverges in that I am less interested in the motivations of those who serve on these boards and broad institutional change and policy fields, and more interested in democratic outcomes and inequality.

My work integrates discussions of urban politics, democratic accountability, public administration, gender and politics, race and ethnic politics, representation, and deliberative theory. In doing so, I draw attention to the way institutions create more institutions to reinforce power, the persistence of path dependency in setting the rules for who gets to make decisions today, and the roles that transparency and deliberation play—or do not play—in promoting democracy.

Evidence

Understanding the purpose, role, and consequences of appointed boards in U.S. cities demands a multimethod approach. For the analysis in this book, I use a combination of methodological approaches, including case studies, archival research, observational quantitative analyses, qualitative surveys, observational data, and interviews, survey data, and experimental work.[12]

In the first section of the book, I trace the political development of boards across time in the United States. To do so, I use tools from APD and rely heavily on three in-depth case studies. I use the histories and experiences of Los Angeles, California, New Orleans, Louisiana, and Richmond, Virginia, as empirical cases to examine the deep processes of board creation, appointments to boards, and policy outcomes that emerge from a weak board–strong board framework. This approach is consistent with Orren and Skowronek's (2004, 11) view of political development that "at any given moment, the different rules, arrangements and timetables put into place by changes negotiated at various points in the past will be found to impose themselves on the actors of the present and to affect their efforts to negotiate changes of their own." Boards often have remarkable stickiness, spanning more than a century of use and power. And many boards today retain the powers and responsibilities given to them at the point of founding or major revision. These three cities routinely use boards as governing devices and have done so for more than 150 years. They provide an opportunity to evaluate not just the process by which cities created boards but also how cities and elected officials strategically use boards today to pursue political ends. Mapping their development thus requires understanding what happened in what order, recognizing the importance of "not just what, but when" (Pierson 2000).

In the second section of the book, I produce and analyze the largest (to my knowledge) dataset ever gathered on the presence, detail, and membership of appointed boards in cities in the United States, using the 100 largest cities in the United States (Large Cities Dataset) and all cities in California (California Cities Dataset). For each city, I gathered and coded information on the types of boards, their membership, and their descriptions, their initiating ordinances, and, in some cases, their meeting minutes and audio and video recordings. I also conducted interviews with board members, bureaucrats who handle board management, and elected officials. In evaluating the current era in each city, I use interviews, primary documents (including applications to serve on boards, board meeting minutes, city council meeting transcripts, and program documents), and participant observatory research to examine how these boards operate, what power they have, and how their membership is composed. I watched more than 350 hours of board meetings, both in person and online.

In the third section of the book, I turn to observational data on specific policies, surveys of the population, and a series of experiments. To evaluate the effect of boards on policy, I collected data from different cities on COVID and eviction policies, gender equality resolutions, and adoption of a slate of policies aimed at reducing and punishing sexual misconduct as well as Ban the Box policies. In the final empirical chapter, I use surveys and interviews with board members, and surveys and survey experiments conducted with the general public to understand when and how (and if) boards increase trust in local government and views of government legitimacy.

The Plan of the Book

To make my strong board–weak board argument, I ask three sets of questions across different sections of the book. In Section I, I focus on three questions: Under what conditions did cities create boards? How do critical junctures in urban history shape the creation, power, policymaking, and membership of boards? And how do boards contribute to inequality (particularly racial inequality) in cities? To answer these questions, I provide the first scholarly overview of the role of boards at key moments in urban political development. Using a political development approach as the grounding of the book, I first start with the view that the process and timing of institutional creation matters, in terms of democratic principles and practical implications. I engage in a roughly chronological discussion of urban history, documenting the major events that pushed cities to create boards, reinforced the power of boards, or revealed the importance of boards in the creation and maintenance of urban policy; a chronological approach highlights how boards represent the power of path dependency in the political development of the United States.

Section I of the book explores the emergence and persistence of boards in a series of chapters that focus on key points in urban American development. Chapter 2 takes us from the Colonial Era to the Progressive Era to the civil rights movement, examining how cities created and operated as their populations grew and as white leaders entrenched racism in local political institutions. Concentrating on the civil rights movement and post–racial insurgency efforts at urban renewal in Chapter 3, I take up the growth of boards from federal efforts and how white leaders in cities strategically used boards to obtain resources from the federal government's urban renewal funds while still shutting Black and poor residents out of any positions of power. In Chapter 4, I consider the rise of neoliberalism in cities, particularly following federal disinvestment in social services, as well as the modern board creation era. I end the chapter with the growth and renewal of police over-sight boards as a reaction to the Black Lives Matter protests and increased scrutiny of police misconduct and racism.

Section II of the book asks: What do boards look like today? Which boards and commissions exist today and what do they do? How do their powers, structures, and rules vary across weak boards and strong boards? And how representative are boards of the communities in which they serve? To an-swer these questions, I developed the first database of boards in the United States, including their issue areas, powers, and membership, and I investi-gate their institutional design, rules, and activities. In the Section II intro-duction, I discuss the data collection and analysis process for the quantita-tive results in the book. Then, in Chapter 5, I reintroduce weak and strong boards in the modern era and present issue area and membership as the pri-mary mechanisms for identifying the power associated with each board. Chap-ter 5 also asks: What forms of power do these boards have and how does that power differ for weak boards versus strong boards? The chapter examines the legal power and autonomy granted to boards and presents the first set of evi-dence that weak boards and strong boards differ in power and autonomy. I also evaluate the institutional design and membership of these boards, in-cluding the size of the board, decision-making rules, and membership re-quirements, showing that cities design strong boards to make decisions more quickly with small, homogenous memberships.

In Chapter 6, I ask: Who serves on boards and why? I argue that board membership is the consequence of strategic behavior by both elected officials and members of boards. Consequentially, white men are overrepresented on strong boards, a pattern that has persisted across time. In comparison, wom-en and people of color more often hold appointed positions than elected posi-tions, but the appointed seats they hold are concentrated on weak boards. Women of color are particularly likely to sit on weak boards. But it is not just that weak boards have less power than strong boards and that there are dif-ferences in who serves on these boards. These factors come together to re-inforce the power of strong boards and undercut the power of weak boards.

In Section III, I consider the consequences of these boards. Are these boards deliberative? Are they democratic in form or function? How and when do they influence policy in ways that represent more deliberative or demo-cratic impulses? In Chapter 7, I use policy case studies and observational, survey, and experimental data to probe the roles that boards play in making policy, encouraging deliberation, and supporting or subverting democracy. Chapter 8 examines whether and how boards shape policy. Using a combi-nation of qualitative and quantitative data, I examine the effectiveness of boards in generating policy during windows of opportunity, including dur-ing the COVID-19 pandemic and in response to the #MeToo movement. I show that the presence of weak boards does not influence policy. In comparison, women's representation on strong boards and in elected office does shape the adoption of policies. In short, weak power is not a substitute for strong power. Chapter 9 focuses on the core questions of deliberative democracy: Is government transparent? Is it trustworthy? Is it legitimate? For each of these, I use survey and experimental data to show that boards do not increase the core undergirding values of deliberative democracy. But! There is the possibility for something different. In Chapter 10, I conclude by summarizing the key patterns I have presented and then identifying policy changes that could prompt improvement in transparency, trustworthiness, and legitimacy.

I

APPOINTED BOARDS AND THE POLITICAL DEVELOPMENT OF URBAN AMERICA

Section I Introduction

In 1904, J. Pemberton Baldwin, a progressively oriented New Orleanian who proudly sat on the city's first Civil Service Commission, proclaimed that the commission was "the first attempt in this State to separate patronage from politics" (Baldwin 1904). The board had the power to change any and all internal rules and processes about the hiring, promotion, pay, and firing of public employees. Its architecture reflected key pressures of early board creation: the demands to create policy in a uniform fashion,[1] the need to get permission from the state in order for the city to create the commission, and political battles over who would control the appointments to the commission. Mr. Baldwin similarly represented the average appointed board member during this time: wealthy, white, educated, and male. A lawyer by training, Mr. Baldwin was deeply involved in New Orleans civic culture and was "proud" to serve without compensation on the city's first Civil Service Commission (Louisiana State Bar Association 1922).

Although Mr. Baldwin had lofty goals for the commission, his efforts proved unsuccessful: the Regular Democratic Organization (RDO, also called the Choctaw Club) would gain enough power to ensure that all seats on the Civil Service Commission were sympathetic to the needs of New Orleans's corrupt political machine. Despite Mr. Balwin's high hopes, public employment in New Orleans would largely be governed through a spoils system (sanctioned by the Civil Service Commission) for the next 40 years.

Today, the New Orleans Civil Service Commission still governs the internal rules over which public employees can be hired, fired, promoted, or sanctioned; the commission's size is the same as the original in 1904 and the commission's powers have not changed in more than 50 years (Vedlitz 2010; Louisiana Constitution of 1974, Article X). And while the commission's role is to shield public employees from political influence, the politics of the city still affect the commission. In 2020, for example, New Orleans's mayor, LaToya Cantrell, worked behind the scenes to replace the chair of the commission because of concerns about "an overrepresentation of union interests on the commission" (Stein 2020). The removal of the pro-union chair happened immediately before the city of New Orleans began to furlough employees and reduce the workforce because of COVID-19–related budget shortfalls. The mayor's quiet lobbying, combined with potential violations of open records laws by the city council and the commission's convoluted rules about membership[2] all obfuscated how this commission works and how elected officials might influence the outcomes of deliberation. The reality is that the commission operates largely to carry out the work and policy ends of elected officials, but in a way that skirts accountability. When the commission or its members acts in a way that differs from the mayor's interests, members are removed from the commission.

At the beginning of the twentieth century, the United States was quickly becoming an urban nation, with over 40 percent of the population living in urban areas (U.S. Census Bureau 2012). Compared to the period prior to the American Civil War, when fewer than one in ten Americans lived in a city, the increased urban population represented a durable shift both in the power and politics of cities and in the policy challenges that cities faced. After the turn of the century, city governments attempted to respond to these new demands from their citizens, managed and reinforced racist patterns of segregation, and created new governing institutions.

This section of the book examines how, as we move from the 1800s to the 1900s to the 2000s, cities have created, staffed, edited, and dissolved boards at key political junctures. The political development process of board creation meant that cities gave some boards long-lasting and deeply embedded power—for example, those boards that handled planning, land use, and financial decisions, including economic development. Cities created other sets of boards, including those that address minority incorporation, poverty reduction, and affordable housing, to pacify Black, low-income, and women residents. Cities design these boards with little power so that these groups cannot use boards to change local policy.

As James Baldwin (1966) noted, "History does not merely refer to the past. . . . History is literally present in all we do." The original divergent institutional designs of weak and strong boards have had a remarkable stickiness that persists in current urban politics: cities continue to grant planning, development, and finance boards extensive power, while limiting the power of minority interest and redistributional boards. Here, I provide an overview of the broad patterns of cities creating weak and strong boards across time.

Case Studies and Political Development

In this section of the book, I use a political development approach to argue that U.S. cities create and alter appointed boards because of policy demands, from "democratic impulses" (that were often quite undemocratic in focus or consequence) that represented major shifts in who had power in American local government, and to limit efforts of Black and low-income residents' efforts to acquire power. In short, cities use boards as tools to secure, reinforce, and exercise political institutional orders, particularly racial institutional orders (D. S. King and Smith 2005).

This section of the book develops three case studies of Richmond, Los Angeles, and New Orleans in order to understand when and why cities create boards. To understand the role of boards in the political development of each city, I engaged in archival work of primary and secondary sources in each city. I reviewed board meeting transcripts and minutes (Barari and Simko 2023), official mayoral and city council correspondence about boards, and newspaper archives, including an extensive review of Black newspapers from each city. I reviewed and used material from the *Richmond Planet*, which became the *Richmond Afro-American*, and the *Southern Workman*; the *Los Angeles Tribune* and *Soul*; and New Orleans's *Tribune*, *Weekly Louisianian*, and *Weekly Pelican*. I also drew on government reports, city charters, city ordinances, and secondary sources to understand the process of board creation, appointment, and maintenance. Together, these data allow me to provide a rich account of how the cities create and use boards during periods of historical change, political conflict, and racial unrest. While each city has a unique political history in the United States, the patterns in Richmond, Los Angeles, and New Orleans illuminate how these experiences can also apply to other places.

I selected these cities because of their simultaneously parallel and divergent experiences at key junctures in APD. All three cities created boards in an ad hoc manner early in their history. All cities experienced political competition between political machines and reformers, one of the essential conflicts in urban political development (Trounstine 2008). All three cities have a significant history with racism, racial violence, and the use of boards to enforce racist practices of white wealth accumulation. All three cities experienced direct conflict and violence over this racism. They also endured similar conflicts over power between the mayor, the city council, and the state government. Private actors (particularly white businesses) stoked this conflict for personal gain in all three cities. They all elected Black mayors and Black city council members in the 1970s and created a series of economic develop-

TABLE I.1. CASE STUDY CITIES AND KEY POINTS OF CHANGE			
	Los Angeles	New Orleans	Richmond
Machine politics	1890s–1910s	1890s–1946	No period of local power[1]
Progressive and reform politics	Powerful: 1910s–1920s	Competitive: 1946–1961	Limited: 1900–1910
Charter reform with extensive board creation or power	1925	1904, 1954, 1974	1948
Redevelopment agency	Los Angeles Redevelopment Authority (1948)	New Orleans Redevelopment Authority (1968)	Richmond Redevelopment and Housing Authority (1940)
Racial uprisings	Extensive nonviolent protest, Watts riots violence	Extensive nonviolent protest, limited violence	Limited nonviolent protest, limited violent protest
Citizen advisory committees to access federal funds	Very extensive participation	Extensive participation	Limited participation
Black political incorporation	Gil Lindsay, first Black city councilmember (1962)[2] Tom Bradley, first Black mayor (1973)	A. L. Davis, first Black city councilmember (1975) "Dutch" Morial, first Black mayor (1979)	Oliver White Hill, first Black city councilmember since Reconstruction (1948) Harry Marsh, first Black mayor (1977)
Economic development board(s)	Various boards created in 1995	Downtown Development District (1974)[3]	Richmond Economic Development Authority (1976)
Police oversight board(s)	Los Angeles Police Commission (1995)	N/A[4]	N/A[5]

[1] The Byrd Organization operated successfully as a political machine at the state level from 1890 to 1965, but concentrated its efforts on Virginia's white rural population.
[2] First appointed in 1962 and elected to his seat later that year, Lindsay went on to serve as a city councilmember for more than 27 years.
[3] The "first assessment-based business improvement district" in the United States.
[4] New Orleans has an "independent police monitor," but this is staffed by professionals and does not include an appointed oversight board.
[5] Richmond has a "Community Criminal Justice Board" that is tasked with serving as a "planning and advisory body to the City of Richmond for developing, monitoring, and evaluating community corrections programs that will provide the judicial system with sentencing alternatives," but it does not serve as a police oversight body.

ment authorities in the 1980s. And all three created new boards in the last decade in attempts to increase racial equality and social equity. Table I.1 provides an overview of key critical junctures for each city.

Yet, under the surface, each city navigates the terrain of governance in separate ways. Each has a unique history regarding how boards were created and used: Los Angeles saw a robust set of powerful boards created by the Progressive movement and women's activism during the 1910s and 1920s. New Orleans's board creation initially was internally driven, then was imposed by the state, and finally persisted as the product of an active group of white, wealthy citizens who worked to reform the city's charter, creating the framework for an extensive set of boards that were almost entirely under mayoral control in the early 1950s. Richmond generated a limited set of boards in the late 1800s and then used them to implement Jim Crow policies. It is not until charter revisions in the 1960s and 1970s (coinciding with the Civil Rights Movement) that the city created a wider set of boards.

Racism plays an important in the creation and use of boards in each city. Los Angeles was the site of both the Watts riots and the Rodney King uprising, as well as home to one of the largest Model Cities projects and urban renewal efforts. These factors demonstrate the push and pull of racism on board creation, the importance of top-down forces in the creation of local boards, and the failures of boards to change racial disparities. New Orleans, the location of the largest market of trafficking enslaved people in North America, exemplifies the use of boards to solidify control of politics in white, racist hands and also exemplifies the way that board membership served as a central point of contention by Black activists in the 1960s. Richmond, the state capital of Virginia, "continues to bear the label and the burden of the 'Capital of the Confederacy'" (Howard and Williamson 2016, 33). Richmond represents an opportunity to consider the deep roots of slavery and segregation and the role that locally appointed boards played in generating, enforcing, and recreating racial segregation in the context of ideologically and economically complex local Black politics. Taken together, these three cities tell us much about how moments of conflict and change in cities resulted in the creation of boards, how cities created boards as a tool for managing conflict and pacifying marginalized groups that were seeking power, and how these institutions persisted over time.

The Push and Pull of Board Creation over Time

Demographic, political, and economic shifts in urban America shape the creation and use of boards. The growth of urban America in the 1800s and early 1900s, immigrant populations and evolving immigration policies at the state and national levels, the first and second Great Migrations, the Great Depression, the New Deal, and two world wars all changed what cities did, who was involved in their decisions, and which groups benefited from policies. Boards served as a key institutional mechanism available to political leaders who were seeking an opportunity to control policies and bypass electoral accountability.

By 1900, important legal shifts also pushed cities to institutionalize boards. Legally, cities became creatures of the state. Rulings from state and federal courts had codified that cities exist because state governments say they can exist, and cities can be controlled by state governments in a myriad of ways (Dilworth 2010; Ethington and Levitus 2009). The ability of cities to create boards and grant them specific powers certainly abided by this rule: cities could create boards because states allowed them to do so. City charters during this time (and later revisions to charters) reflected the policy preferences of powerful individuals in cities and the political realities of what powers and responsibilities states gave to cities.

Parallel political changes also shaped the creation of boards. Demographic shifts and the policy crises of urban America in the late 1800s—filth, failing infrastructures, disease, and populations demanding government support—gave rise to political machines, or party organizations that recruited voter support by supplying material incentives like jobs, access to government policies, or government contracts. In response to the corruption and increased taxation and spending by political machines, the Progressive movement engaged in efforts to control local politics in the United States. Both forces saw boards as a tool in the 1800s and early 1900s to accomplish political ends: the ability to nominate supporters to board vacancies, to control resources, and to limit the power of political opponents.

White leaders in cities increasingly turned to boards as vehicles for segregation and racism as cities saw an increasing share of Black urban residents (Grant 2019). As the population of African Americans in cities grew from the 1920s through the 1940s (Grant 2019; Trotter 1995; Sernett 1997), racist white residents looked for local policy tools to create segregationist patterns (Trounstine 2018; Massey and Denton 1988; Guinier 1991; Stone 1980). Boards and commissions offered white residents a variety of opportunities to engage in racist forms of regulation, from institutionalizing planning boards that implemented redlining to segregating public services like parks (Kruse 2005; Retzlaff 2019) to making decisions about the investment in public works that concentrated upgrades and services to white areas (Trounstine 2018, 98) to disenfranchising Black voters in cities (Haas 1988).

As Black residents gained political rights through the efforts of the civil rights movement and the work of activists and groups in these communities, they targeted the integration of boards. While the civil rights era offered an opportunity for cities to fully integrate their existing appointed boards, most cities opted to design new boards. New boards aimed at issues of race and racism were functionally weak, without policymaking or implementation power. The growing number of boards in cities is also the result of outside intervention by state and federal governments. Resources flowing from the federal government to cities increased dramatically in the 1950s,

1960s, and 1970s. But with these resources also came costs: the federal government required cities to use boards and required that those boards be representative of the broader community. Omnibus pieces of federal legislation, from Model Cities to the Clean Drinking Water Act (also called the Safe Drinking Water Act) to Enterprise Zones, all required the use of civilian oversight committees or required that cities appoint volunteers from specific groups in the community to their boards. Cities reacted by integrating their existing boards very slowly and attempting to bypass true change in a variety of ways (Bachrach and Baratz 1970; Arnstein 1969).

The late 1970s and 1980s saw the retraction of federal funding for local policies and parallel local- and state-level tax revolts. Facing federal disinvestment, reduced intergovernmental transfers, restrictions on local property taxes, and another wave of whites fleeing school desegregation in urban areas, cities again turned to boards as a political tool. Here, limits on resources, trickle-down economics, and neoliberal economic policies all pushed cities to create boards focused on economic development, downtown development, and tax regulation. Unlike the redistribution and equity boards created in the prior decades, these new economic development boards were empowered to make real policy decisions with real resources.

In the next three chapters of the book, I take a political development approach, examining boards at critical junctures in the development of cities. Each major era of change in urban politics in the United States has led to the creation of appointed boards and shifts in those their use in cities. This is true in early Anglo American urban development through the Progressive movement. The creation and staffing of boards represent key changes in cities as racism and segregation shape local policy. During the civil rights movement and post–racial insurgency efforts at urban renewal, boards represent a key point of conflict and compromise. During the neoliberal economic development efforts (starting in the tax revolts of the 1970s and continuing today), boards became a mechanism for those with economic resources to control more political power. Finally, with urban residents today pressuring cities to address issues around affordable housing, police violence, and racial inequality, boards offer cities the opportunity to look like they are engaging in direct action without actually investing resources in change.

Moving forward in this section of the book, I use a chronological approach[3] to examine the motivating forces behind the creation of different forms of boards in cities across three key time periods: machine politics and the Progressive movement in Chapter 2; the civil rights movement and the politics of race and racism in cities in Chapter 3, and neoliberalism and modern board creation in Chapter 4. Each of these represents major points of change and cohesion in cities, and for the creation of boards specifically. At the end of the historical section of the book, I then move to a discussion of the realities of modern boards, showing that their institutional design and power are constructed carefully to maintain the status quo, that their membership reflects power differentials between groups in society, and that the implementation of a wide set of boards has little to no effect on policy or on outcomes.

2

Machines, Progressives, and the Development of City Policy through Boards

I n 1897, the city of New Orleans established an independent Board of Commissioners for the Port of New Orleans. The "Dock Board," as it would come to be called in the city, would be responsible for making decisions about investments in the Port of New Orleans, including fees for boats to dock, maintenance of the facility, and future improvements. The Dock Board's creation was produced in part from the policy demand of the increasing number of ships and trains coming into the city. But it also emerged from a political fight between New Orleans's political machine (the RDO, or Regular Democratic Organization) and reformers; these groups would fight over appointments to boards in New Orleans for the next half century (Haas 1998). The Dock Board also represented the racial politics of the time; founded after the end of Reconstruction, the board's membership was entirely white for decades, even as the workers on the dock were overwhelmingly Black or from immigrant groups (Rosenberg 1988; Arnesen 1994). Such are common efforts in cities at this time: policy demands push cities to create boards, fights between political machines and reformers shape which boards are created and who is appointed to those boards, and white supremacy keeps the power created for these boards in the hands of white residents.

Board creation in cities in the young United States followed a fairly predictable pattern: new cities relied on a wide set of ad hoc boards to create policy in response to temporal demands, but eventually city departments took over much of this work as cities developed institutional structures. As their populations increased, cities created a smaller set of more permanent boards with distinct policy power. This initial set of boards often focused on the urgent policy demands of the time: health, infrastructure, parks, and policing. By 1900, larger cities reliably had a set of boards, and those seeking power or seeking to change institutional arrangements often used boards as a key policy tool. The National Municipal League created Model City Charter plans; these pushed cities to create civil service boards and planning boards, both with independent policy powers, in order to reduce corruption and improve efficiency (National Municipal League 1916). Over the next 30 years, cities across the country would adopt a variety of boards to carry out essential components of urban policymaking. How did these boards come to be? What were the political and public policy drivers of the creation of boards? And how did boards represent early efforts at bypassing local democratic accountability?

The latter part of the 1800s saw rapid increases in the size of cities due to immigration, shifts in the economy, and a growing U.S. population; these increases elevated demand for city policies to address a wide set of social ills (Dilworth 2010). Cities struggled to provide clean water and sewage control, especially as both proved essential to control the spread of diseases like cholera and yellow fever (Melosi 2008; Duffy 1992; Capers 1938). Infrastructure demands such as the need to construct roads, bridges, and canals (Oestreicher 1989) required both funding and a set of individuals to make decisions about the policy implementation. These policy demands often overwhelmed local government. In many cities, political machines emerged in response to the space created by a growing urban population and the accompanying policy challenges (Trounstine 2008). Concurrent with the rise of machines, policy challenges also led cities to create appointed boards to address these concerns.

In this chapter, I trace the evolution of board creation as a political tool used from the nation's founding through the early 1900s. The rise of the Progressive movement in the late 1800s and early 1900s further pushed cities to create appointed boards. In the lead-up to and during this era, progressive activists "sought to prevent durable shifts in governing authority by biasing political institutions in their favor" (Trounstine 2009). Learning from political machines, which had harnessed the power of institutions to accomplish their goals, Progressives engaged in efforts to restructure local politics via institutional changes (including reforms to the forms of government and city charters), an increasing reliance on bureaucratic efficiency and power, and a focus on volunteerism. Each of these avenues of reform ended up with cities creating boards as an attempt to limit the power of their political enemies.

Early Boards in America

Few accountings[1] exist of permanent appointed boards in the colonies and early American local government. In colonial America, the landed, white, male elite eschewed urban areas, preferring a mostly rural and agrarian lifestyle (Ethington and Levitus 2009). The small urban population, direct democracy among white propertied men as the primary decision-making structure, and a disdain for urban areas among those with resources and power (Dilworth 2010) all contributed to a limited set of governing institutions in cities. The urban population of the United States remained low prior to the Civil War, with fewer than 20 percent of Americans living in an urban area. Consequently, during the period from colonial rule to the Civil War, local governments rarely used permanent appointed boards. Those boards that did exist were mostly in cities large enough to have stable policy needs. For example, New Orleans created a permanent Board of Health in 1841, right after the city's population topped 100,000, and Boston created the Overseers of the Poor in the early 1800s to handle the care of orphans and small children (Nellis and Decker Cecere 2006).

After the Civil War, with a slow and steady growth of urban areas and the creation of new cities across the country, appointed boards emerged as a tool used in ad hoc efforts to address specific policy demands. These early boards operated as de facto government departments in cities that were too small, too green, or too weak to develop their own governance infrastructure. Boards focused on the key policy issues of the time: public health concerns (including things like addressing water-borne illnesses), sanitary reforms (including sewage or garbage), the creation and care of public parks, policing and fire response, and educational governance (Jon A. Peterson 1979; Reps 1965; Rosen 2003). Urban crises like the great fires in Boston, Chicago, and Baltimore pushed cities to transform ill-functioning boards and to make ad hoc boards permanent (Rosen 2003). As cities increasingly provided or mandated the provision of education, they formed standing committees and then permanent committees to oversee schools—the earliest of school boards.

Early evidence of the transformation of boards from ad hoc to permanent tools to address pressing policy concerns is clear in Los Angeles, New Orleans, and Richmond. In Los Angeles, early efforts to solve problems with minimal resources and government resulted in the early growth of ad hoc boards (see Figure 2.1). These boards ranged from an appointed public market committee to three "investigative committees" that were tasked with evaluating smallpox, issues with water-borne diseases, and "medical claims made by Dr. Alpheus P. Hodges," who was the city's first mayor and coroner.[2] Some appointed boards switched to elected boards, and vice versa; for example,

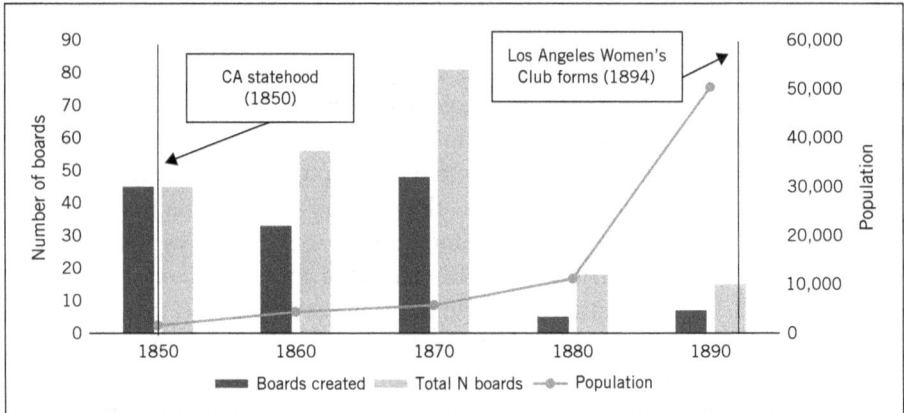

Figure 2.1 Los Angeles Appointed Boards and Commissions, 1850–1900. *Note: Black bars indicate the total number of boards created in that decade, while gray bars indicate the total number of boards overall, reflecting board terminations and boards still in existence from the previous decade. Population (dark gray line) from the U.S. Census.*

Los Angeles began electing (rather than appointing) their school board during this period and the health board went from appointed to elected and then back to appointed. This is not unique to Los Angeles: In New Orleans, an elected commission managed the police from 1803 to 1813 and off and on throughout the 1800s, until the city created a permanent appointed board by ordinance in 1873. In this earlier period, with a population under 10,000 residents, the number of boards in Los Angeles was very high: by 1870, Los Angeles had more than 80 boards in total, or almost one board per every ten people. As Steven Erie notes, politics in Los Angeles "had an ad hoc and episodic quality" (1990, 521).

During this time, board members were almost entirely local political elites, and the overlap between appointed board members and elected officials was quite high. In Los Angeles, nearly four (38%) of every ten board members also held an elected office at some point prior to 1890. Board membership was often the first step for the political ambition of this group of men (and they were entirely men, and almost entirely white). Similarly, in New Orleans, many of the first mayors also held board appointments either before or after their time in elected office. Boards represented local governance more generally: ad hoc, variable, concentrated among a small group of elites, and created in response to local crises or demands.

Institutionalization of Boards

As cities institutionalized governing mechanisms, including hiring staff and forming city departments, the need for ad hoc boards withered and the number of (permanent) boards stabilized. Instead of creating additional temporary governing institutions, cities began to craft more sustainable and permanent policymaking bodies. By the time Los Angeles passed the 10,000-population mark in 1879, the policy demands on boards accelerated and the usefulness of ad hoc policymaking bodies plummeted.[3] As a result, cities began paring down the number of boards, while imbuing them with more power and responsibilities.

The late 1800s produced increased institutionalization and power of boards in Los Angeles, New Orleans, and Richmond. As Los Angeles moved into the later decades of the 1800s, the total number of boards declined, but the ones in existence became more stable and powerful. The late 1800s saw the creation of boards that are still in operation in Los Angeles today, such as the Parks Board (1871), the Planning Commission (1980), the Public Works Board (1871),[4] and the Board of the Public Library (1890).[5] Los Angeles also created boards to address the location of cemeteries and the restructuring of the public pension program, which was fast becoming a concern for cities (Holman 2019; Jacoby 2014; McConnell and Picker 1993; Anzia and Trounstine 2024). Richmond's 1885 charter established a police board "who shall consist of the mayor and six citizens" to oversee the city's police force.[6] The health board (staffed by three physicians) similarly had their duties set forth in the Richmond charter, investing the board with "policy authority in the performance of their duties," which included inspecting wards for health and disease, a power established in the city's effort to avoid outbreaks of yellow fever and cholera. In New Orleans, the city created boards to oversee the management and upkeep of several of the city's major parks during this time period; for example, the city created a board of commissioners for "Upper City Park," which would be renamed Audubon Park in 1886.[7] The Audubon Commission remains one of the most prestigious and sought-after board appointments in New Orleans today; for example, Gayle Benson, the owner of the New Orleans Saints football team, sits on the Audubon Commission (Audubon Nature Institute 2024).

Electoral rules, political powers, and the relationship between cities and state governments also influence the creation and stability of boards. For example, throughout the late 1800s, New Orleans had an unwieldy "mayor-council-board type of government" where elected leaders shared power with appointed board members across a variety of policy areas. As cities sought to create more permanent governing structures, including boards as policy creation bodies and as implementation bodies, states exerted more control over city decisions. Soon, elected leaders in cities pushed for more clarity about their powers overall, which included who could create these boards, who was responsible for appointments, and which powers would be allocated to appointed offices versus elected offices.

City charters, or legal documents that govern the powers and responsibilities that cities have, as creatures of the state, began to formalize specific sets of local powers for boards in the late 1800s and early 1900s (McBain 1917). Throughout the late 1800s and early 1900s, boards increasingly appeared in city charters, with details of which boards cities could create, who appointed board members, and the responsibilities of the boards. When Los Angeles revised its charter in the 1920s, the existence, form, and function of boards in that charter were the subject of great debate among political leaders in the city. Eventually, the new charter granted the planning, playground, and parks boards a wide set of autonomous powers, including the ability to set their own budget, control staff, and make policy decisions independent of elected leaders.

Political Machines

Political machines, or political parties that exist to control resources and exchange material resources for voter loyalty, emerged in U.S. cities in the mid and late 1800s (Trounstine 2008). In cities where political machines survived in the long term, boards represented a key opportunity to reward followers with patronage and to consolidate power in the hands of political friends and allies (Stone 1996).[8] Political machines, which operated under the guise of democratic government but were corrupt organizations that traded votes for direct and indirect incentives, looked for opportunities both to provide incentives to their voters and followers and to control power (Trounstine 2008). Boards provided opportunities to meet all of these goals: appointments to plum positions could be offered to powerful supporters as a reward, boards spent money on services and goods and that money could be funneled to supporters' businesses or to provide jobs for followers, and control of the boards allowed the machine to further regulate the full operation of the city. Schools were often run by appointed ward committees, which would use patronage to choose teachers and vendors for schools and to pay supporters to build school buildings. In 1896 one superintendent wrote, "The unscrupulous politician is the greatest enemy that we now have to contend with in public education" (L. H. Jones 1896). One response was to move school governance away from neighborhood-appointed boards to a city-wide elected board.

In New Orleans, members of the RDO political machine "served in various capacities on all municipal boards" (Haas 1988, 82). The Regular Democrats were a direct descendent of the White League, a white supremacist organization formed to suppress Black residents of the city and to "counteract the severity of the Reconstruction government with methods which went beyond the normally accepted limit of political behavior in a democratic system" (Parker 1998, 24), including an "extralegal militia" (Powell 1999, 127). In short, the White League used racist violence to obtain control of the city. Later, the RDO "were in the vanguard of those who advocated disenfranchising black voters" (Haas 1988, 28).

The RDO ensured that machine members held the majority of seats on the powerful New Orleans Board of Civil Service Commissioners, which was responsible for hiring and firing municipal employees, on the New Orleans Dock Board, and on the Board of Liquidation, which oversaw New Orleans's public debt (Haas 1988; Williams 1961). Eventually, the RDO evolved into the Choctaw Club as the private steering organization of the political machine (Haas 1988, 1998). The Choctaw Club would come to dominate board memberships, including at one point comprising the entire membership of the Board of Assessors. And when progressive reformers pushed for the creation of a new series of boards for reform via a referendum in the 1920s and 1930s, the RDO simply made sure that the membership of every board was friendly to the political machine (P. Tyler 2009). These are common themes of board creation under political machines: the machine used existing boards as mechanisms for the distribution of incentives and policy control. When pressured, machines would create new boards and attempt to staff them with loyal cogs, but machines did not generally pursue a strategy of board creation as a central tool of policymaking.

Progressives and Board Creation

In comparison to political machines, the Progressive movement was deeply interested in the creation of boards. Primarily interested in limiting the power of political machines, the businessmen, intellectuals, and middle-class members of the progressives focused their attention on several key reforms, including shifting the election of aldermen from wards to at-large seats, pushing for nonpartisan local elections, and increasing the power of city managers and other appointed bureaucratic officials (Rice 2014). They also focused attention on creating new forms of government that would act as checks against the power of political machines. It is in these reforms that structural frameworks emerged that allowed the practice of appointed boards to flourish in U.S. cities.

Progressives were interested in two seemingly at-odds goals: to move the machinations of government as far away as possible from ordinary voters so as to limit the power of political machines,[9] while at the same time opening up new avenues for public engagement in policymaking (albeit to a more select group of participants) (Buenker 1973). These contradictory goals led progressive reformers to pursue institutional reforms that would facilitate the dilution of the power of political machines and immigrant voters, while

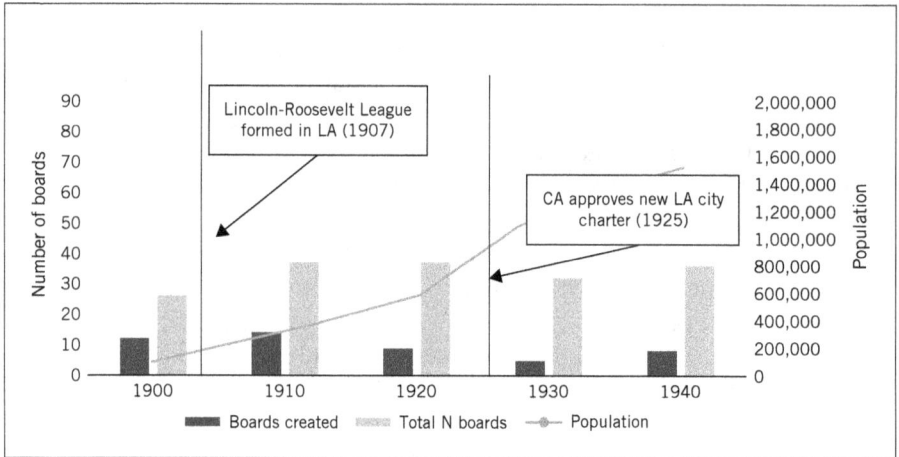

Figure 2.2 Los Angeles Board Creation, 1900–1950. *Note: Black bars indicate the total number of boards created in that decade, while gray bars indicate the total number of boards overall, reflecting board terminations and boards still in existence from the previous decade. Population from the U.S. Census.*

also providing citizen input into policymaking (Pincetl 2003; Buenker 1973). Local boards provided an ideal mechanism for both goals, as seen in both Los Angeles and New Orleans during their progressive heydays.

The progressive shifts in appointed boards were evident in Los Angeles, where progressive impulses led to the creation of a wide set of boards, including Civil Service (1902), Housing (1904), and Efficiency (1913), as shown in Figure 2.2. Progressive reformers in the city were able to successfully lobby for a full-scale revision of the city's charter by the state of California in 1925. The new charter created new boards and greatly expanded the power of specific boards that the progressives saw as important.[10] For example, the Los Angeles Housing Commission (formally named such in 1906) had a membership that "typified the multifaceted nature of Progressive reform" with businessmen, settlement workers, religious leaders, and professionals such as architects and lawyers (Lewthwaite 2009).

Institutional Reforms

Progressive Era efforts to create boards occurred via several mechanisms: passing wholesale institutional reforms, increasing the power of bureaucrats and their ability to use boards, rewriting city charters, and creating specific boards to regulate finance, health, police, firefighters, and housing. The most extreme version of institutional reforms could be found in the commission style of reform put in place in Galveston, Texas, and Des Moines, Iowa—

essentially, governing by boards. Under this model, cities elected no mayor or council, just a board of representatives, each of whom served as the chief executive of a city policy area like a streets department, water department, or civil service department. By the early 1900s, reformers saw the commission plan as offering an opportunity to create structural changes that would "do more than tinker with charters or elect short-lived reform administrations" (Rice 2014, xvi). In 1911, Woodrow Wilson noted, "No single movement of reform in our governmental methods has been more significant than the rapid adoption of the so-called commission form of government in the cities of the country."[11] Despite the enthusiasm for them, true commission governments rarely survived (Hays 1964). Instead, the commission government evolved into a council-manager form of government, with trained and appointed bureaucrats making policy decisions (Rice 2014). Yet, as path dependency dictates (Orren and Skowronek 2004), the "old bones" of the commission government did not simply disappear. Instead, in many places, boards arose to replace these oddly elected commissioners and to serve as a mechanism for overseeing bureaucrats.

Bureaucrats and Efforts to Control City Policy

Bureaucrats began using appointed boards as a tool for oversight and corruption reduction during the Progressive Era, particularly in attempts to corral and control elected officials. In 1914, investigations by New York City's Commissioner of Accounts revealed widespread corruption and incompetence by both the coroner and the elected sheriff (Farris and Holman 2024)[12]; in response, progressive activists urged the creation of appointed boards of qualified citizens to control or replace the offices (Schiesl 1980, 167, note 59). The creation of appointed boards as tools for bureaucrats to control and limit the power of elected officials was not always successful; in many places, fights over the power and composition of these boards resulted in boards that today have members appointed by a combination of the mayor, the city council, and city bureaucrats.[13]

Types of Boards Created during the Progressive Era

Financial Boards

Financial boards were among the first successful oversight efforts from progressive reformers in many cities (Schiesl 1980). The middle class and small-business owners, increasingly irritated by increases in taxes and investment in "undeserving" immigrants and the poor, wanted checks on local government's budgets and taxes. The way slowly became clear: require, by state law or citizen initiative, a tax or budget oversight board that would have to sign off on any local fiscal changes, serving as a potential veto point for efforts by machines[14] to further line their pockets with public tax dollars (Schiesl 1980, 92). For example, in the 1880s in New York City, progressives managed to force the creation of a board of estimation and appropriation (composed of the mayor, the comptroller, and representatives from corporations), which was charged with generating the budget for the city. In 1898, Baltimore adapted a similar system, with many other large cities to soon follow. With their new city charter in 1925, Los Angeles created a board of "Budget And Efficiency." These boards created and sustained the power of the city comptroller, an appointed and trained municipal employee.

In other cities, where reformers were less successful in implementing the commission form of government, the institutionalization of appointed boards into city charters provided an opportunity to nudge the city toward a less centralized (and thus less machinelike) form of government. In Los Angeles, the city's charter was codified in 1925 after more than two decades of work by Angelenos (Erie 1992; Fogelson 1993). The city's charter specifically referenced a wide variety of boards and empowered those boards with rights and responsibilities. In many ways, this was a victory for progressive reformers in Los Angeles.

Police and Fire Boards

The Progressive movement focused specifically on the creation or revitalization of police and fire oversight boards. Police commissions drew particular attention: in many machine-controlled cities, police commissions and oversight boards served as key pieces of political patronage. Progressives saw the police commissions as a possible mechanism for "depoliticizing" the provision of policing in cities by adding a buffer of citizens between the mayor and policymaking. In Los Angeles, the Progressive mayor's attempts to produce a "real business administration" (Schiesl 1975) included the re-creation of a police commission that would have "the freedom in the administration of public affairs from the dictation of political bosses and influence of political considerations" (Pacific Outlook 1909).

In most cities, these efforts were short-lived and did not result in independent oversight over the police. In many places, these boards were quickly filled with members of the police department and their friends and families, or the boards were stripped of oversight power and remained empty hulls for years. Theodore Roosevelt reported frustration with his membership on the Lexow Committee, which oversaw complaints of police brutality in New York but was essentially powerless (S. Walker 1977). In other places, the boards became a tool of political patronage (Reynolds 1936, 421). In 1888, Louisiana passed an act that placed the New Orleans police under a supervisory board. The New Orleans mayor at the time, Joseph Shakespeare, ignored this dictate and arranged his own oversight of the police, but it was repelled by a court order. A contemporary noted, "The fact that the mayor seriously believed himself a better guardian of police efficiency and morals than a board did not impress many prominent businessmen" (Schiesl 1980, 57). Later, the political machine was able "to place the boards under the mayor's control by giving him appointive and removal power over board members" (Parker 1998, 39). In short, progressives were never able to make police commissions into the robust oversight organizations that they wanted. Later iterations of police boards (discussed in the next chapter) suggest that citizen oversight over policing is rarely (if ever) an effective mechanism for restraining police actions.

Land Use Boards

Progressives quickly became "preoccupied with the question of land use" (Pincetl 2003, 26) as a tool to control cities and retain power. Progressives saw a reform of the physical space as essential to produce the social outcomes they wanted: "The urban environment, the physical embodiment of the new social order presented to these men of taste a material form they could mold for the protection of the social whole" (Boyer 1986, 6). One of the central mechanisms became the creation of planning boards.[15] While efforts emerged from professional societies to create some form of national planning policy, planning generally "emerged and matured as a manifestation of the dominant political interests and exerted a notable impact on city development" (Silver 1984, 9).

State and federal mandates, initiated by the Progressive movement and carried forth by elected officials, accelerated the use of boards by requiring that cities appoint a board focused on making decisions about planning and zoning. The Standard City Planning Enabling Act, commissioned in 1928 by Herbert Hoover, further solidified the use of local planning boards by outlining a model approach to city planning, including instituting the appointment of a planning board.[16] Later, the Roosevelt administration advocated for cities receiving New Deal housing and infrastructure monies to use planning boards in making decisions about how to spend the funds (Scott 1971). The goal was for cities to institutionalize their planning processes and to use (ideally, educated and trained) community members as resources for making decisions (Warken 1969; Scott 1971). This pressure worked: cities created boards or beefed up their existing boards to receive funds from the federal government.

Aggressive annexation[17] and pressures from the business community drove early efforts at instituting planning boards in cities. Concerns around the protection of business districts (particularly white business districts) produced the first business improvement districts and commerce boards. For example, in New Orleans, "The Association of Commerce" provided the initial funds for city planning and pressured the city to create a planning commission, of which 13 of the 20 members "should be appointed primarily from the city's commercial and civic organizations"[18] (Brownell 1975, 350–51). Seven representatives, "including three women," would be of the mayor's choosing.

Cities tasked planning boards that were created during this time with a wide range of responsibilities. Richmond's Planning Board, created in 1918 in a charter reform, was initially empowered only to study other cities and draft a planning document. Later, the city authorized the board to reform planning rules in the city and to establish standards moving forward. Similarly, the New Orleans planning commission as authorized in 1923 had limited power, but was reorganized in 1927 into a more powerful board, the Crescent City Planning Committee (Brownell 1975).

Public Goods Boards

As demand for roads, clean water, sewerage, and other public works increased, cities often reacted by creating and institutionalizing boards that would oversee or manage the construction, maintenance, and improvement of infrastructure. In New Orleans, the Sewerage and Water Board emerged from an "ambitious Progressive Era public works project to improve drainage in the 1890s" (Colten 2002, 237; see also Behrman 1914). Today, staffed by the mayor, members of the city council, members of other boards, and citizens, the Sewerage and Water Board represents one of the most important and divisive political entities in New Orleans.

Cities also created or institutionalized parks and recreation boards during the early 1900s. These boards would eventually play an essential role in the allocation of public goods in both white and nonwhite neighborhoods. While many neighborhoods had been responsible for the maintenance of their own private or semiprivate parks (à la London), an interest in centralizing park oversight, maintaining a tree canopy, and creating safe parks eventually led to commissions to oversee parks and recreation, shade trees, and sports facilities across the United States (Turnbull 2009). Many commissions were granted broad powers. When the state of California issued a new charter for Los Angeles in 1925, the Board of Playground and Recreation Commissioners was granted "full control over all playground and recreation sites," including acquisition of new land or any attempts to devote playground land "to other purposes" (Statutes of California 1925, 1090). In short, the board could decide to use park property for any purpose, without any form of accountability. The board chose to close these facilities to any nonwhite resident of the city until 1925, and it segregated park facilities well into the 1950s.[19]

Women's Organizing and Appointed Boards

Much of the demand for boards to create and manage public goods emerged from women's early activism in urban politics, especially women's early work around social welfare, education, and public works. For nearly the whole first century of U.S. history, women were relegated to their homes while men controlled the public political and economic spheres (Sapiro 1983). Eventually, women's widespread engagement around a variety of issues led to a decline in the separation between the public and private spheres (McCammon 2003; Teele 2018, 2024). As a result, well before women could formally access politics in most places, they participated in a variety of informal activities, largely in the local political arena. These "voluntary, locally based moral and social reform efforts" represented the majority of women's early political activism (P. Baker 1984, 634–35).

Women's early activism, which was rooted in a more general interest in the population in order to solve urban problems through civic volunteerism, resulted in the creation of a variety of local boards. White women's early local political activism in the urban U.S. largely emerged out of dual interests in acquiring political rights and reforming government to better solve problems (Wolbrecht 2000). The late 1800s and early 1900s saw women's efforts concentrated on these areas, with substantial shifts in local outcomes. Indeed, women's nascent political activism was one of volunteerism, focused on the "canons of domesticity" (P. Baker 1984, 625). Women's activism via "voluntary, locally based moral and social reform efforts" created a variety of private boards to address specific local ills (P. Baker 1984). This is perhaps best exemplified by the women's club movement, which began as self-improvement efforts by rich women in the post–Civil War period, modeled after French salons. These would become a central source of women's political and economic activism. Many boards of women's clubs eventually evolved into local appointed boards, produced local appointed boards with reserved seats for representatives from the local women's club, or successfully lobbied for local boards to oversee policy areas of interest to the women's clubs.

Those working on women's interests[20] soon fused with social efforts from the women's club movement, finding a sympathetic audience in women interested in "secur[ing] better conditions in life" (Croly 1898). Women's clubs successfully lobbied at local and state levels for policy to handle issues from welfare to art to education to public health, with these policy initiatives often being overseen by appointed boards or expanding the services of existing boards. In New Orleans, prominent clubwomen sat on the public board of Charity Hospital and encouraged the broadening of services offered, including the formation of nursing schools (Fortier 2014). Women's efforts to create sustained public policy around issues of concern resulted in increased power and funding for the Boston Overseers of the Poor[21] and the Joint Board of Metropolitan Improvements for example.

The women's club movement in Los Angeles exemplified both the power of these clubs and the challenges that women faced entering into politics. In Los Angeles, the Friday Morning Club was the premier women's club,[22] boasting more the 3,000 members at its peak in the early 1920s (Davis 2002). Advocates focused their attention on children's issues, fought for the institutionalization of a parks board, and led efforts to create a local bill of rights for women and children (D. Moore 1906). These efforts by women's clubs resulted in institutional power: there were de facto reserved seats for members of women's clubs on a variety of local boards in Los Angeles.[23] The Playground and Recreation Commission also noted the importance of the Friday Morning Club: when deciding a library site in the 1930s, the commission received an endorsement from the Friday Morning Club that was "ordered transmitted to the city council" as evidence of community support.[24] In other cities, activist women served on planning and education boards (Spencer-Wood 1994).

In New Orleans, women's clubs were actively involved in municipal improvement efforts. Following the 1905 yellow fever outbreak in the city, the clubs organized outreach efforts to convince residents to screen their water cisterns and pressured the city council to empower the Sewerage and Water Board with the ability to monitor household water collections (Carrigan 1988). Women in the city also organized around social service provision, parks, and clean water. The first women's representation on boards in the city was the appointment of several women to the New Orleans Fountain Commissions, which were responsible for maintaining public fountains that provided clean drinking water to the public.

Women's move more fully into public life also occurred through the municipal housekeeping movement, where women saw the city as an extension of the home (Sivulka 1999; Lewis 2011). In efforts around reforming the sanitation of cities, the municipal housekeeping movement fused political activism to women's "divinely appointed mission . . . to 'guide the house,' a new sphere of usefulness and efficiency opens with the knowledge that in sanitary matters an ounce of prevention is worth a ton of cure" (Plunkett 1885, 10).

Women's clubs and the municipal housekeeping movement quickly realized that volunteer efforts would secure only short-term gains. These women thus turned their attention to persuading local and state governments to codify services like sanitation into local government. Activists found success in cities ranging from New York to Chicago to Harrisburg, Pennsylvania (Sivulka 1999), by staging demonstrations of the utility of street sweeping (Hoy 1995) and garbage collection (Nall 2004) and the value of banning, moving, or cleaning up slaughterhouses (Rynbrandt 1999) and outhouses (Lupton and Miller 1996). These new local and state regulations included the formation of city bureaus, governed in part by appointed boards. Women's clubs and the municipal housekeeping movement fused in their interests to address concerns relating to children's welfare and public health. The creation of local boards of health and child welfare both stemmed from women's lobbying efforts (Abramovitz 2017).

Women and White Supremacy

One of the primary women's clubs emerging in this era was the United Daughters of the Confederacy (UDC), a women's white supremacist organization dedicated to memorializing the Confederacy and promoting Black suppression and segregation, particularly in the American South (Cox 2003; McRae 2018). These efforts by women were also heavily invested in maintaining white supremacy and racial segregation. As McRae (2018) notes in her study of white women's engagement with white supremacy, "For many, being a good white mother or a good white woman meant teaching and enforcing racial distance in their homes and in the larger public sphere" (4). The dominant narrative has often been that some women challenged their post-suffrage political energies into improving cities via the Progressive movement and another group of women took up racist efforts (Blee 2009; MacLean 1995; McRae 2018). McRae focuses fairly exclusively on how white women used school boards as a tool of white supremacy, showing how white women's activism introduced and reinforced school segregation patterns. These two types of activism were deeply connected, and local boards became a tool by which women both accomplished progressive ends and sought to enforce racial segregation and racism. And their intertwined nature did not end with the Progressives but extended into support for the New Deal and beyond. For example, Florence Sillers Ogden, a devoted segregationist from

Mississippi, was active in the UDC and served on the local board of supervisors for the Civil Works Administration. In this way, she was able to "harness the New Deal to bolster Jim Crow's infrastructure" (McRae 2018, 69). In Mississippi, the UDC used its influence to pressure local boards to fund monuments to the confederate dead across the state (Cox 2003).

Women's clubs also participated in the institutionalization of racism and segregation. Los Angeles's Friday Morning Club was founded by an antislavery and women's rights advocate Caroline Severance, but her interests did not persist. In 1920, members of the club voted to exclude women of color, and the club's leadership lobbied for exclusionary policies at the local and state levels (Davis 2002, 136). In the 1910s and 1920s, the Friday Morning Club's efforts increasingly focused on a campaign of Americanization, where the club trained white women to go into the home of immigrants and train immigrant wives on what it "meant to be an American" (Gullett 1995). In her history of the Friday Morning Club, Gullett notes that these efforts were focused particularly on Mexican immigrants, as they "posed the most serious challenge to the state. They were the fastest growing immigrant group, and they were perceived as coming from an especially flawed culture that hindered their ability to assimilate" (Gullett 1995, 82). In Richmond, the local Camp Advisory Board rejected a proposal to build an integrated local camping site. Frannie Crenshaw, a local white supremacist, was one of the key voices in opposition to the integration because it would be "very difficult to control the intermingling of the [white female and black male] campers during the camping season" (W. E. O'Brien 2015, 88).[25] These women's organizations thus institutionalized both the provision of local services via appointed boards and the racism and ethnocentrism of local boards.

Women of color faced a wide set of sexist and racist obstacles to political engagement in the period. Largely excluded from white women's clubs, Black, Hispanic, and Asian women formed their own clubs, including the Sojourner Truth Club and the Progressive Woman's Club. (Lerner 1974; Dickson 1987). In these "clubs, black women looked to their own groups as vehicles for advancing the entire race" (B. W. Jones 1982, 21). As an example, the white women's "Era Club" (whose name ironically stood for "Equal Rights for All") in New Orleans directly excluded Black women (Green 1997). In response, Black women founded their own clubs, including the Phyllis Wheatley Club of New Orleans, which would eventually transform into the only training hospital for Black doctors and nurses in the area (Dunnaway 2011; Kimani 2012). In other places, while Black women served as the primary activists behind the creation of education, poverty eradication, and children's issue boards, "prominent African American and white men were charged with administrative and budget decisions" because they were actually appointed to the boards where these decisions were made (Knupfer and Silk 1997).

Race and Racism in the Progressive Era

In 1890, Richmond erected a statue of Robert E. Lee, starting a string of dedications along Monument Avenue, a neighborhood developed exclusively for white residents. White leaders in Richmond, the former capital of the Confederacy, featured the monuments in an overt act to "do the work of justifying segregation and relegate African Americans to second-class status" (K. M. Levin 2020). These "efforts to sustain white hegemony in social and political relations . . . guided planning concerns throughout the twentieth century" (Silver 1984, 11). White residents used appointed boards, particularly the planning and zoning boards, to reaffirm, reinforce, and expand on racial segregation.

Local governments during post-Reconstruction South and Jim Crow looked for avenues that would allow them to enforce social and environmental inequality and segregation in many forms. Local boards emerged as a tool for imposing these unfair conditions onto African Americans. These efforts often occurred in parallel with or in tandem with Progressive Era reforms, particularly the "development of systematic urban services, particularly sewer and water" (Colten 2002). An essential conflict emerged between Progressive interests in efficiency and racist interests in reinforcing racial inequalities; eventually, funded services would spread across cities, including to Black neighborhoods, but not without significant impediments from local white elites (Colten 2002, 2006; Trounstine 2018).

Local racists turned to planning and land use boards to promote and ensure segregation and to institutionalize racist land use policies as other mechanisms became unavailable. Starting in the early 1900s, white residents weaponized zoning, including permitting construction of housing and the razing (and nonreplacement) of slums, the placement of roads and infrastructure, and the uneven disbursement of services like sewers and garbage pickup to separate white neighborhoods from everyone else (Nightingale 2006; Silver 1984). In 1910, Baltimore became the first city where white citizens attempted to explicitly zone segregation, dictating in city plans which blocks were for white homeowners and which were for Blacks. Richmond followed quickly, passing a zoning law in 1911 stipulating that "a block is White where a majority of the residents are White and colored where a majority are colored." When Baltimore's zoning law was struck down by the U.S. Supreme Court in *Buchanan v. Warley* (1917), white residents lost this formal tool for racial segregation.[26] Despite this action by the Supreme Court, cities continued to pass discriminatory laws; for example, in 1924 New Orleans passed Ordinance 8037, which "prohibits white persons from establishing a home residence in a negro community and prohibits negroes from establishing a home residence in a white community" (Colten 2002). This was again struck down by the Supreme Court. But white urban residents were not dissuaded; they crafted racist tools such as homeowner associations, electoral manipulations that barred or discounted the votes of nonwhite residents, and redlining, and used threats of violence and death to intimidate Black community members (Kruse 2013; L. N. Moore 2010; Trounstine 2018).

White residents looked to local land use as a potential tool for racial segregation.[27] If the zoning laws could not be segregationist de jure, could they perhaps be segregationist de facto? Local planning boards emerged from these other segregationist mechanisms and proved to be an ideal solution to white residents' zoning problems. Here, white residents could articulate a segregationist zoning policy without needing to write actual racial separation into local laws and resolutions. In Chicago, real estate boards were founded both to ensure that only white buyers could purchase homes in white neighborhoods (Massey and Denton 1988) and to create cartel-like protections for real estate agents (Turnbull 2009); these organizations drafted Chicago's original planning document (see Gotham 2002 for a similar discussion of Kansas City). From Miami (Mohl 2001) to Columbus, Ohio (Stach 1989), to Baltimore (home of the original segregationist zoning plan), early planning boards dominated by white men made racist decisions about the location of multifamily housing, housing density, and whether development could occur at all.

Property ownership in the United States has always been concentrated in the hands of white men (Du Bois 1935; Lassiter 2013; Kruse 2005). Progressives, largely composed of middle-class whites (Wyman 1974) were particularly well-positioned to leverage property ownership into both political power and racial segregation. The intense focus on land use policy and reform meant that Progressives were able to participate in the creation and design of many early planning and zoning boards, often designing the board membership to be limited to property owners in the city or requiring the representation of certain types of developers and business owners. These rules persist today, with most planning, zoning, and land use boards requiring membership of business owners and developers.

The distribution of Black residents in Richmond during this time demonstrates the power of these local boards to engage in segregationist enforcement. In 1930, the *Virginia Municipal Review* noted concerns with "a gradual and natural encroachment of the colored population into white neighborhoods" in Richmond as "a problem of increasing significance . . . whose solution deserves the thought and discussion of leaders of both races." Later, city-level local boards were also responsible for the nascent creation of "racialized" urban spaces (Gotham 2000). In 1910, Kansas City created its Board of Public Welfare, which was the first public welfare agency in the United States (Katz 1986, 154). The board published several reports, including in 1913 a

Social Prospectus that noted Black neighborhoods were "steeped in crime, with lost virtue, and without purpose and without hope" (Gotham 2002, 37).

Conclusions

Members of these early commissions saw their work as important. In the first meeting of the Los Angeles' Planning Commission, the board's first president, Mr. William Henry Pierce, articulated his grand vision for the role of the commission: "We are the ones who should 'Dream dreams and see Visions'—visions of the better City to be; for 'Where there is no Vision, the People Perish.'"[28] Mr. Pierce had come west seeking gold and had settled in Los Angeles in 1885, eventually running for and serving two terms on the city council. While on the council, he had become convinced of the importance of more systematic planning in Los Angeles as the city grew, and he pressured other leaders to create a formal planning board rather than rely on the City Planning Association, which was an ad hoc arrangement of more than 50 individuals working loosely to address issues associated with housing demand and infrastructure. He served as the president of the new planning board for two terms. After resigning from this position, "he retired, also from public life to devote his energies to his undertaking establishments" (Wallace 1934, 9), with his mortuary growing to the second largest in the United States before his death. Mr. Pierce represented those active in board creation and service during this time: he was a white man with political connections who was deeply involved in Los Angeles civic life, including starting the organization that would become the Los Angeles Chamber of Commerce and serving in several fraternal organizations. He saw the inclusion of a permanent planning board as essential for the future of the city: "[The board's] goal is to be just ahead, and as we approach it, it will always recede. That is as it should be: our ideals should ever be just ahead of our accomplishments."[29]

During the Progressive Era, reformers and activists strategically created boards as mechanisms to move power away from voters to mainstream experts, and to reinforce racism and nativism. Yet, even as the Progressive Era ended and reformers lost battles or turned to other causes, these boards remained, often with the powers and consequences originally intended intact. One of the enduring ways that the Progressive Era shaped urban politics is via the racism institutionalized into these boards. Over the next decades, cities used these boards as a tool to subjugate Black residents and empower white residents via land use, planning, zoning, and infrastructure decisions. Planning boards enforced racial segregation, zoning boards broke up successful Black commercial districts, and public works boards facilitated the construction of roads, highways, and freeways through historic Black neighborhoods while keeping white neighborhoods protected (Faber 2020; Winling and Michney 2021). In the next chapter, I detail the changes brought to the construction of boards from the agitation for board membership by Black residents of cities, urban unrest in the 1960s, and the civil rights movement.

3

RACISM AND LOCAL BOARDS

I n the early 1920s, Los Angeles's public park facilities were not legally segregated by race. This would quickly change. In 1925, the Los Angeles Playground Commission received letters complaining about Black residents
using the swimming pool. H. J. Long of Los Angeles wrote, "I do not know
positively, but I am pretty certain that in no other city or town in the United States are negroes permitted to bathe in the same pool with white persons. . . . Negroes are permitted to use the pools at any and all times, min-
gling as they please with the white bathers. It certainly is disgusting, and I
am not a Southerner either. The equality of the blacks is all very well, as long
as it doesn't go too far. But I'll wager you wouldn't take your wife and children for a swim in a pool thickly populated with negroes. Why do you expect other white people to do so?"[1] A variety of local associations[2] wrote in
"undivided opinion that there should be a segregation of the races,"[3] that
"the commingling of races incompatible with the best interests of both races and destined to produce a serious race friction."[4]

The Parks and Playground Commission proved a sympathetic audience
for these racist appeals. Upon receipt and evaluation of missives from "concerned white citizens," the Playground and Recreation Committee changed
the pool policy "by colored groups" so that they had access to some pools
only on some days,[5] noting that "the Playground Commission must of ne-
cessity take into account our whole citizenship and make rules for the use
of all municipal properties under our care that will cause such properties to
serve the greatest good of the greatest number."[6] Vignes Pool, the oldest of

the city's pools, became the "Negro Pool," limited to Black Angelenos every day. Reports on bacteriological results from a month later show that the Vignes Pool had a rate of bacterial matter three times higher than the Exposition Park pools.[7] Over the next few years, the commission voted to invest more than $140,000 (or $2 million in 2020 dollars) in heating, rehabbing, and covering pools in Los Angeles; Vignes Pool received far below the expected funds for improvement. The Playground and Parks Commission justified the underinvestment in the one pool open to Black Angelenos by repeatedly expressing concern that the Black population in Los Angeles was not taking full advantage of the commission's generosity[8] and noting the "loss of receipts on days set apart for negro groups."[9]

Demographic shifts in urban America also shaped the creation and use of boards. The first and second Great Migrations, the Great Depression, changing immigration policies, and two world wars all resulted in growing populations in cities in the Northeast and the Midwest and on the West Coast. One key shift was an increasing share of Black urban residents (Grant 2019). As the population of African Americans in cities grew from the 1920s through the 1940s (Grant 2019; Trotter 1995; Sernett 1997), racist white residents looked for local policy tools to create segregationist patterns (Trounstine 2018; Massey and Denton 1988; Guinier 1991; Stone 1980). Boards and commissions offered white residents a variety of opportunities to engage in racist forms of regulation, from institutionalizing planning boards that implemented redlining to segregating public services like parks (Kruse 2005; Retzlaff 2019) to making decisions about the investment in public works that concentrated upgrades and services in white areas (Trounstine 2018, 98) to disenfranchising Black voters in cities (Haas 1988).

By the time Robert Dahl evaluated his community's politics by examining New Haven in the 1950s, local boards were commonplace in cities big and small across the United States. And not just in cities: Commuters who lived elsewhere and worked in New Haven, he writes, spent their time serving the "innumerable boards and committees characteristic of Connecticut town government" (Dahl 1961, 77).[10] The boards that existed by 1950 were largely policymaking bodies with real power: very few advisory committees existed, nor had cities begun creating weak boards in response to demands by marginalized groups.

Later, as legal and political gains for African Americans during the civil rights movement forced cities to desegregate their public policies, boards again became a tool used to resist desegregation for as long as possible, particularly given that boards were protected against electoral threats. After legal segregation attempts repeatedly lost legal challenges, boards served as an avenue by which cities could funnel resources to private facilities rather than investing those resources fully in public desegregated facilities. As I detail in this chapter, Los Angeles's attempts to segregate its public pools represents an early case of how appointed boards, made up of white residents deeply attached to racist policies, acted more slowly and with more deliberate racist intent than did elected representatives. Indeed, civil rights activists (successfully) pressured elected officials to desegregate public facilities, but boards and commissions, which were relatively impervious to electoral pressures, acted more slowly in response to public pressure to desegregate.

But the increased number of boards in cities was also the result of outside intervention from state and federal governments. Resources flowing from the federal government to cities increased dramatically in the 1950s, 1960s, and 1970s, particularly with the Great Society programs and the Civil Rights Act of 1964 and accompanying policies (Martinez-Ebers and Calfano 2020). But with these resources also came costs: the federal government required cities to use boards and also required those boards to be representative of the broader community. Omnibus pieces of federal legislation, from Model Cities to the Clean Drinking Water Act to Enterprise Zones, all required the use of civilian oversight committees or for cities to appoint volunteers from specific groups in the community to their boards. Cities reacted by very slowly integrating their existing boards, but they attempted to bypass true change in a variety of ways (Bachrach and Baratz 1970; Arnstein 1969).

Much of the racial backlash in cities in the 1960s related to racist, violent, and often deadly interactions between Black residents and police departments. As such, creating police oversight boards and citizen review committees became a clear goal for those interested in increasing citizen participation and improving local race relations. In cities where minority efforts successfully exerted enough pressure to force the creation of organs like police oversight boards, cities hamstrung these tools of minority power with limp oversight capacity, limited budgets, or no ability to punish members of law enforcement who acted badly. Even in places like Detroit, where public initiatives created a powerful civilian oversight board, the implementation stalled. Those boards required cooperation from the local elected government and police leadership, and the boards did not receive this cooperation.

Boards addressing poverty often suffered a similar fate. Cities across the United States created boards aimed at poverty eradication in response to the racial conflict of the 1960s. Later, the Reagan Reconstruction devolved social policy to the local level, again prompting the creation of local social service provision boards. And yet, in creating these boards, cities thwarted poverty eradication efforts by crafting top-heavy institutions with limited resources and limited policymaking power. Cities designed these boards with three features that limited their power: esoteric or overly restrictive rules, dependence on state or federal resources without local investment, and/or a systematic lack of independent policymaking power—for example, making them "rubberstamp" advisory committees. This chapter explores the creation of these boards in response to federal and local demands, and the chapter documents the ways that cities created and staffed these boards to limit their power. Taken together, strong boards' efforts to uphold and support segregation, and weak boards acting as a veneer of democratic accountability, means that appointed boards and commissions played a central role in upholding white supremacy and racism in cities.

Race, Racism, and the Provision of Public Goods

By the time the Los Angeles Playground Commission was considering segregating park facilities in 1925, more than half of Americans lived in urban areas, with increased demand for provision of services (Cutler and Miller 2005). By this time, most large cities in the United States had several appointed boards to address issues of infrastructure (streets and water boards were both common), finances (particularly relating to pensions and as cities began to take on debt), and social services like education and health. These local boards would play a central role in the ability of white residents to limit the political power and resources of Black, Hispanic, and Asian residents. As Molotch (1972, 4) notes, "Racial segregation rests, in many ways, upon residential segregation, which generates separation of races within schools, recreation and social centers, places of work, and retail shopping facilities." Boards offered a wide set of options for white residents seeking ways to institutionalize their racism.

Boards in Los Angeles were deeply involved in the institutionalization and maintenance of racism and segregationist patterns in cities. The Playground Commission's choices to adopt segregationist policies because of appeals from racist white residents was a pattern replicated to other boards in Los Angeles and in city boards across the United States. Some of these actions foretold efforts by cities to engage in segregation for the next century (Trounstine 2018). For example, in 1922, the Los Angeles Planning Commission authorized the expansion of Crenshaw Boulevard, an entirely residential street, from 60 feet wide to 100 feet wide, with a resulting increase in car and truck traffic on the road. When the Black residents of the neighborhood tried to change the zoning of the street from residential to mixed use or commercial, which fit better with the traffic patterns, the planning commission denied these requests, even when the zoning changes enjoyed the widespread support of the neighborhood. A primary reason: commercial or mixed-use zoning would require better plumbing and electric infrastructure than they had installed under the new street, even as the commission had required better infrastructure in white neighborhoods.[11]

Efforts by white residents to find legal, formal, and informal means to segregate intensified as the population of cities became more diverse. These efforts operated in parallel with mounting pressure in cities to allow Black residents to own property—and to own property in white neighborhoods. The end of the second Great Migration, the return of Black veterans from integrated experiences in World War I, a strengthened economy, and a baby boom all pushed cities to come up with new solutions for housing.[12] The existing solutions of segregating Black residents to a few neighborhoods with a poor, old, or dwindling housing supply via steering and formal racial covenants began to fail as Black homeowners were increasingly able to integrate into white neighborhoods.

Local boards in cities across the United States engaged in a variety of actions to institute, reinforce, and defend racism and segregation. In Atlanta, the Westside Mutual Development Committee (created in 1952 by Mayor Hartsfield) helped maintain racial homogeneity in neighborhoods by fighting any attempts to engage in "block busting," or efforts to identify some white neighborhoods of poor quality where a transition to Black occupancy could happen, and plans for new Black development (Silver 1988). And in Baltimore, when the racist power structure was threatened by outside forces attempting to organize poor Black residents into a mobilized voting force, the mayor constructed a series of "task forces" that would study the "problems of the city's poor and develop proposals for combating the problems" (Bachrach and Baratz 1970, 71). This co-optation, where cities would create boards without power, staff them with appointees from poor and Black neighborhoods, and give them none of the promised resources, was "extremely effective" (Bachrach and Baratz 1970, 71).

Civil Rights Challenges to Boards

Black residents did not simply sit idly by as these boards, dominated by white elite members, made decisions that harmed the Black community. Civil rights organizations and Black organizers recognized the role of boards in perpetuating racism in their cities. Indeed, efforts at desegregation, community organizing, and the increased use of lawsuits to challenge local racist institutions focused in particular on boards and their segregationist efforts.

In many cities, Black community and civil rights groups used a legal strategy to challenge segregationist efforts from boards. In the mid-1920s, the NAACP sued the City of Los Angeles for the first time (of 26 times), seeking desegregation of public pools. After the NAACP lost one of the early lawsuits

(*George Cushnie v. City of Los Angeles and Playground and Recreation Commissioners*, in 1925), Claude Hudson, the president of Los Angeles's NAACP, wrote to the national NAACP president, "After a legal contest lasting more than months, and fought through two courts, a decision, drastic in nature, was rendered against [us] upholding the *right of the commission* as a unit of government under the guise of police regulation to segregate Negro citizens" (emphasis added). Throughout the late 1920s, the question of segregation of public pools continued to be reaffirmed by the commission.[13] The commission also regularly requested opinions from the city attorney about the "right of the City to designate one public swimming pool for the use of the Negro race and its right to admit other Negro groups to pools in other districts than the pools above mentioned."[14]

Convincing the city council to desegregate proved easier than shifting the decisions of the commission. The NAACP and Betty Hill, a civil rights activist, engaged directly with members of the city council on the issue. Members of the commission expressed concern about these machinations, noting "discomfort with who is talking to the City Council." The *Los Angeles Times* echoed this, noting that an "active negro politician was conferring" (probably Hudson or Hill) with members of the city council and using electoral threats to drive opposition to the appeal.

When the city attorney for Los Angeles[15] would not appeal the judgment, the commission, indignant, responded that the "purpose of the appeal is not primarily to determine the rights of various races to the use of the municipal swimming pools, but to determine the powers conferred on said Board in all its phases of management and control, as provided by the City Charter" (emphasis added).[16] As Hudson (president of the Los Angeles NAACP) recounted, "On three successive occasions, between June 16th and August 16th, the Playground Commission fought bitterly for a vote of the city council to instruct the City Attorney to take an appeal from Judge Gates' decision to the appellate court." On each occasion, Mrs. Hill worked vigorously to convince a majority of the city councilors of the rank prejudice and injustice of the commission's attitude and, in some instances, threatened indifferent councilmen with future political battles.

The process that Black Angelenos went through to access public facilities and fight segregation in Los Angeles was repeated over and over across the United States. These efforts were accelerated by a national investment in park construction during the New Deal. In Oklahoma City, the editor of the *Black Dispatch* expressed outrage that "none of the planned parks, paid for by federal tax dollars, were to be accessible to the city's 20,000 black residents" (W. E. O'Brien 2015, 49; Dunjee 1936). In the American South, where segregationist efforts extended well into the 1960s, boards played a pivotal role in protecting racist rules. Local parks boards initially responded to calls to integrate facilities in the same fashion as the Los Angeles Playground and Parks Commission: by creating segregated parks for African Americans, not by integration (W. E. O'Brien 2015, 2012; Retzlaff 2019).

Los Angeles was not the only place that the NAACP and other advocacy organizations used segregationist efforts by local boards as a mechanism for a legal challenge. In 1949 in Tyler, Texas, T. R. Register, a member of the Negro Chamber of Commerce, wrote to request admission to Tyler Park, a segregated "whites only" park. A board member wrote that it would "be impossible" because "there is always the possibility of a clash occurring between park patrons if the park is used by members of the white and negro races" (Kuhlman 1994; Frederick 1949). Register sued for access. In response, the Texas state legislature passed legislation calling for park facilities to be segregated, to protect "the interest of public welfare, safety, harmony, health, and recreation" (Vernon's Texas Statutes 1950). Later, local boards resisted a wide set of desegregation rulings from federal and state courts.

Seeking Political Incorporation

While legal remedies were the strategy of choice for some civil rights groups, other civil rights and community activism groups recognized the power of local appointed boards in creating or enforcing racist laws and sought membership on these boards. This was often a slow process. As the proportion of Black to white residents in many cities increased, boards largely remained in the power of white elites and served as the vehicles "through which whites sought to curb the political power of blacks" (Silver 1988, 11).

In New Orleans, efforts to desegregate the library system focused on appeals to the city's appointed library board via clergy[17] in the community and group testimony. These efforts were largely unsuccessful until the board's first woman member, Rosa Keller, appealed to the mayor, who advised the library board to open the entire New Orleans system to Black patrons. Black organizations in the city agreed to not publicize the desegregation to avoid white hostility: "Like other smoothly achieved victories in the 1950s, the integration of libraries was facilitated by elite collusion—by the guarantee of little or no publicity, and by the pressures applied by a strategically placed white elite" (Rogers 1993, 36).

The struggles by the Black community in New Orleans to access board appointments reveal the challenges of demanding representation. In the early 1960s, Black organizers in New Orleans mounted a concerted campaign to push the then-mayor Victor "Vic" Schiro to desegregate appointments to committees and to create new committees to examine race relations in the city, with limited initial success. The organizers faced resistance from the mayor, who had campaigned on a segregationist agenda and saw integration as a source of trouble (Haas 2014). Schiro was particularly resistant to the idea that Black residents could access boards with local power, as he reserved those seats for patronage and to cultivate support from New Orleanians with resources.

Nonetheless, Black organizers pushed the mayor for appointments. In 1962, the *Louisiana Weekly*, a Black newspaper, wrote that the mayor "has the prerogative of appointing persons to scores of positions but invariably these appointments have been white citizens." Of particular interest to Black organizers was representation on boards like the Housing Authority, "which derives the bulk of its finances from Negro tenants" and yet, as *Louisiana Weekly* pointed out, had "no Black members of the board." Direct correspondence from community activists echoed these concerns: "All of the appointees to date . . . are members of the Caucasian race in spite of the fact that the Negro population constitutes more than 37 per cent of the total population of our community."[18] When the mayor announced a broad set of new committees, including the Community Advisory Organization (CAO), Ernest Morial, the new president of the NAACP (and a future mayor of New Orleans) called the organization's attention to "the opportunity to volunteer for appointment to several committees." Despite many Black residents volunteering directly to the mayor and his CAO, "the appointments . . . were not forthcoming" (Haas 2014, 149). More than a year later, community activists wrote again to the mayor, noting that "not one of the more than 200,000 Negro citizens . . . is represented on your committee."[19]

Black organizers also advocated for the mayor to create new committees and include Black members, with particular interest in the formation of a biracial human relations commission (Haas 2014). In a letter, Arthur Chapital Jr., a Black veteran who was active in local politics, appealed to the mayor "to appoint a biracial committee for better human relations among the races so that a better image of New Orleans may be portrayed to Judeo-Christians, Americans, industry and business, commerce and tourism and last and by no means least, our world." Despite appeals from citizens, from the NAACP (including in letters from Ernest Morial), and from community organizers, Schiro refused to create the commission, noting that "the formation of a permanent committee of this type would seem to indicate an official acknowledgement of a problem we expected to have on a permanent basis."[20] Part of Schiro's reluctance to appoint a commission was his belief that "better results can be obtained by dealing with [white and Black] groups separately."[21]

Changes were forthcoming, both from the civil rights movement directly and from expanded access to voting rights. Beginning in 1963, civil rights leaders in New Orleans threatened—and then engaged in—more direct action to force the city to accelerate efforts to address racism and segregation. In an open letter to Mayor Schiro and the city council, Reverend A. L. Davis, a local Black activist, warned that the city would face racial upheaval unless they opened city facilities to Black members of the community and "appoint[ed] Negros to boards, agencies, and commissions in city government."[22] In response to concerns about civil rights actions in the city, Schiro desegregated public facilities, hired Black employees for city jobs, and started the process of hiring Black police and firefighters (Haas 2014).

Once the Civil Rights Act protected the Black right to vote, Black voters suddenly represented a key constituency in mayoral elections (Karnig 1979; Shah, Marschall, and Ruhil 2013; Button 2014). By the mid-1960s, New Orleans mayor Vic Schiro began the process of appointing one Black representative to several key boards in an effort to stave off protests by Black organizations and reward Black voters for their support in his reelection campaign (Haas 2014).[23] Black members of the committee were appointed to the Mayor's Advisory Committee on Housing Improvement, to the Housing Authority of New Orleans, to the board of Dillard University, the New Orleans Health Commission, and to several parks committees.[24] Black activists responded to these appointments with support and more pressure to appoint Black representatives to a broader set of boards, including the important and powerful Planning Commission (Haas 2014); archbishop Philip Hannan urged that he was "confident that such actions would prove helpful and even inspiring to our Negro citizens."[25]

The success of this slow strategy toward integration was met with direct and vocal outrage by racists on these committees and in the community. As George Soule, a member of the New Orleans Planning Commission, wrote, "I have not surrendered to the Negro nor have I lost all my freedom of choice; therefore I do not choose to sit as a member of any integrated commission or board"[26] Others complained about specific appointees; in the New Orleans case, the appointment of Alfred Dent, president of Dillard University (and one of New Orleans's most lauded Black intellectuals), was met with suggestions that he was a communist and affiliated with "Communist front organizations," with members of the public asking "Is this the kind of man we want on our City Planning Commission?"[27]

Although social movements aim to produce large changes in the status quo, often the result is that existing power structures work to try to co-opt the movement to produce the minimum amount of change possible (Clemens 1993). The creation of boards during the civil rights movement and the appointment of Black residents to boards take this same pattern: white leaders in cities did as little as they could to change anything about who had power via appointed boards, while ensuring that new boards were either dominated by white residents or had little independent power.

Urban Unrest and Boards

> Urban renewal has been compared to a sharp knife—it can carve a masterpiece—but it can also butcher a city. Urban renewal legislation and federal guidelines have been corrected to prevent the recurrence of many of the injustices of the past. Yet these measures are only as good as the people who administer them and their responsiveness to the people whom the program is designed to serve.
>
> —TELEGRAM FROM JESUIT PRIEST EUGENE P MCMANUS
> TO VICTOR SCHIRO, MAYOR OF NEW ORLEANS, 1968

The slow process of using the courts and petitioning white mayors directly for descriptive representation on boards continued to progress through the 1960s until racial uprisings began late in the decade. During the summers of 1967 and 1968, cities in the Northeast (most famously, Detroit) and the West (principally in Los Angeles) saw widespread racial strife, motivated by racism and police brutality (Joyce 2003). These racial revolts promoted a variety of responses from the state and federal governments. This violence had the potential to change policy: groups engaging in violence gain visibility and can "effectively compete and bargain with other interests to obtain policy changes favorable to their interests" (Fording 2001, 115; Wasow 2020).[28] In their view, the powerless group wants to "activate third parties to enter the implicit or explicit bargaining arena in ways favorable to the protestors" (Lipsky 1969, 2). If successful, the uprising can ultimately lead to the empowerment of the protesters, who can potentially gain concessions for their group, influence policy, and, if truly successful, reshape access to political resources.

What, then, would a successful reshaping of the political power structure look like following urban uprising in the 1960s? While the national narrative about the causes of the Black uprising focused on poverty, particularly the quality of housing and unemployment in Black neighborhoods (National Advisory Commission on Civil Disorders 1968), most instances of protests and riots were sparked by interactions between racist police departments and Black citizens (Fogelson 1968; Conyers 1981). Within the pluralistic demand-and-response frame (Dahl 1961), a successful government response would include the incorporation of Black voices into the policymaking process in addition to shifting welfare policy and criminal justice policy. In essence, Black residents of cities, long excluded from positions of power, would now become insiders with control over the policy agenda.

Both the creation of new boards to address concerns from Black residents and shifts in the membership of boards represented avenues for the reapportionment of political resources. After all, boards engaged in a wide set of political controls; membership on them was a resource coveted by rich and white residents of cities, and the policy arenas of these boards often directly impacted the lives of urban Black residents. A focus on citizen participation in response to the urban uprising offered an opportunity for a reorganization of who had political power in cities: "Citizen participation . . . is the redistribution of power that enables have-not citizens, presently excluded from the political and economic processes, to be deliberately included in the future" (Arnstein 1969, 216).

Citizen participation on appointed boards became a central component of the response to the urban uprising of the 1960s via requirements in two federal acts: the Economic Opportunity Act (passed by Congress in 1964) and the Demonstration Cities and Metropolitan Development Act (later renamed the Model Cities Program, passed in 1966) (Strange 1972a; Hallman 1974; National Advisory Commission on Civil Disorders 1968). The acts granted funds for community groups, nonprofits, and cities to create community advocacy organizations to address poverty, housing crises, and, to a much lesser extent, issues of racial inequality and racism in urban areas in the United States (Weber and Wallace 2012).

Both acts required "maximum feasible participation" (in the Economic Opportunity Act) and "widespread citizen participation" (in the Model Cities Program), although the phrases were "accidentally chosen and [the terms] were not subject to congressional scrutiny or challenge" (Strange 1972a, 656). Although the legislation did not define what "widespread" meant, which citizens needed to participate, or what that participation should look like, Housing and Urban Development (HUD) created directives about a citizen participation structure to "organize the unorganized." In its directives, HUD argued that "this would give citizens early, meaningful, and direct access to decision-making, so they can influence the planning and carrying out of the program. Leadership of the structure must be accepted by the residents as representing their interests. Residents must also have direct and timely access to technical help which they consider trustworthy" (U.S. Department of Housing and Urban Development 1968).

Debates ensued over the degree to which this "widespread" or "maximum" citizen participation meant that local governments and nonprofits had to include participation of residents of particular neighborhoods or of Black, Latino, or poor residents (Strange 1972a; Rosenbaum 1976). Eventually, the Office of Economic Opportunity and HUD concluded that participation by citizens of the community meant a minimum of 30 percent participation by those "directly affected" by the policies—that is, those in poor, Black, or Latino neighborhoods.

Model Cities and Board Creation

Perhaps the federal program that was most focused on the creation of boards was Model Cities, passed by Congress in 1966. In Model Cities, the federal government invested money in 150 cities to create five-year-long programs aimed at eradicating poverty. While participation by neighborhoods and communities was baked into the requirements for cities to qualify for Model Cities, the ways that this translated into on-the-ground efforts at inclusion varied, and varied in ways that are consistent with the weak board–strong board dynamic. The dictate to include "representatives of the poor" resulted in variation in which members of the community served on these boards.

One central requirement from the federal government for cities to receive money from Model Cities was the creation of Citizen Advisory Committees (CACs). Cities varied dramatically in the construction, composition, power, and responsibilities of these boards. Those cities that created boards without power or without the representation of the poor and Black residents were often forced by the federal government to change the rules around the boards to ensure compliance with the federal community engagement rules (Baratz 1970; Strange 1972b; Washnis 1973; Hallman 1974). Today, cities across the United States from San Francisco to Chicago to Palm Beach, Florida, continue to use CACs as governing and deliberative bodies.[29]

Many of the boards that would make key policy decisions about the allocation of (large amounts of) community development funds either started out as weak or quickly lost power and ground. In his early study of the Model Cities Programs and their boards, Washnis (1973, 19) found Model City boards to be plagued with "factional conflicts on the board, self-interest of a few, lack of balanced interests on the board, little authority or purpose for the board, poor facilities and inadequate citizen staff, and the immensity of problems and shortage of resources."

Where did these weaknesses come from? At least initially, Model Cities provided ample resources to the boards; these resources were often matched by funding from the state and from private sources (Strange 1972b; Hallman 1974). An intense federal oversight structure insured that boards met the requirements that the membership of these boards incorporated the poor, those who lived in poverty-stricken urban areas, and members of minority groups. Federal leaders and activists hoped that incorporating those most affected by these policies onto the boards would lead to the articulation of their needs in the policymaking process and open lines of communication, potentially influencing policy outcomes.

Contemporaries at the time vehemently disagreed about whether Model Cities found success in incorporating income, neighborhood, and racial diversity into their government membership. One evaluation of the Model Cities Program saw citizen involvement as a great success in "changing the attitudes of local officials, the ways that they make decisions, and in alerting other community groups of the need to involve themselves in government decisionmaking" (Washnis 1973, 4). Five years after the Economic Opportunity Act, one study noted public participation as among the crowning achievements of the act: "Several thousand citizen organizations have been formed in urban and rural poverty areas. New leaders, numbering in the tens of thousands, have emerged from among the poor, near-poor, and minority groups" (Hallman 1974, 11). Others disagreed; writing at the same time, professor John Strange (1972b, 59) notes, "Actually, poor board members. . . . rarely influence the program planning process within community action agencies."[30] Some of the debate about the success of the citizen engagement efforts is rooted in the huge variation of boards and committees that were created across the cities that obtained Model Cities funds.

Strong Boards, Powerful Board Members

Cities were very resistant to the inclusion of poor and Black residents on these boards. A survey of government officials revealed "an almost universal opposition to the concept of community organization and participation of the poor" (Strange 1972b, 58) and a belief that the decision-making of the board should be shifted to "the middle class and more conservative people" (quote from interview in Strange 1972b, 58).

As a result, mayors and city councils set up CACs composed of majority white and wealthy members. In New Orleans, Mayor Schiro urged the creation of a Community Improvement Agency (CIA) that would present "an entirely fresh approach" and "an opportunity for positive action."[31] The kicker: the CIA's decision-making power would be in City Hall, where the mayor and the city council would control any choices made by the CIA. Neighborhood Advisory Committees (composed of up to 40 members) would advise but have no decision-making power. As a result, "the CIA offered a cheap way to implement a vision of physical progress and racial amity. Even better for the mayor's office, the CIA provided a means for controlling the contracts for construction and feasibility consultation" (Germany 2011, 189).

Community organizations pressured the mayor to make his appointments to the seven-member CIA committee from neighborhoods that would be affected directly by the policies. The Urban League (a community organization aimed at advancing racial equality and Black interests) advised Mayor Schiro that "HUD guidelines suggest that there be one-third neighborhood representation on committees dealing with Urban Renewal and Model Cities Programs," following this recommendation with a list of "neighborhood groups which could recommend representatives from their areas."[32] In response, Mayor Schiro told the League, "I am confident you will agree that the make-up of the membership represents a broad segment of our community."[33] There is no evidence in the mayor's subsequent appointments that he sought out any members of any of these community organizations for appointment. Instead, Schiro "stacked [the board] with political insiders, rising black leaders,[34] and businessmen with heavy investments in New Orleans real estate" (Germany 2011, 190).[35] None of the members of the committee were poor and only one was a resident of an area targeted for redevelopment.

The CIA was organized in direct response to earlier failures at urban renewal in New Orleans. In 1949, New Orleans mayor deLesseps Story "Chep" Morrison had attempted to reform housing in the blighted area of Tulane Avenue, with the city submitting an application for federal renewal funds (Forman 1969). Property owners in the area, who would have been compensated via these renewal efforts, responded with an angry protest. Organized and prompted by white political leaders[36] (including the area's assessor), the protest led to Mayor Morrison discontinuing the project in favor of an approach that involved rehabilitation and investment in private property, as opposed to the razing and resale that was initially proposed (Crutcher 2001). As a result, Mayor Schiro knew that he needed to construct a board that would appease white developers and property owners in the city. Assessments of the CIA suggest that Mayor Morrison's approach was successful: he controlled the resources from the program, but the funds did little to change systematic inequality in New Orleans.

New Orleans is not alone. In Baltimore, the mayor initially appointed a majority white Community Action Committee and "none of the 11 appointees was either poverty-stricken or a resident of the Action Area" (Baratz 1970, 183). In Strange's (1972b, 58) study of North Carolina, the initial poor members of boards were the intimates of welfare directors or board members, including the "several poor people and blacks who were employed by board members."

Stronger boards, granted more policymaking and implementation power, largely used that power for more conservative purposes, did not pursue more revolutionary or progressive policies, and discouraged engagement by Black advocacy organizations. Instead, these boards sought cooperation from business, with the view that "private initiative and resources are necessary to fully develop the communities' potential" (Washnis 1973, 3). The boards that took this approach were often granted independent policymaking power by city councils and also were granted significant portions of the funds allocated to the cities by the federal government. Even the more successful boards, however, were hampered by "limited staff, scarce resources, little legitimacy" (Strange 1972b, 57). For example, the Model Neighborhood Board of Boston was composed of 18 members, 3 from each of six areas of the city, to "perform a policy role," but the board had "no direct program operating responsibilities" (Hallman 1974, 136). While the board eventually overcame internal conflict and a cumbersome organizational structure to exert control over policy decisions on "activities being considered for importation into the Model Cities Program" (Hallman 1974, 137), it did so largely because it was seen as a conservative body that "shuns radicals. When one black activist organization . . . attempted to win some board seats, the group lost badly 'because they scared people'" (Washnis 1973, 49).

Weak Boards, Members without Power

While cities sometimes engaged in proactive work to include poor and Black members of the community on boards, this was mostly after HUD chastised or threatened to remove funding. After pressure from the federal government and community organizations, many cities changed the structures of their CACs. In Baltimore, for example, the city council expanded the board to 14 members, including 4 representatives of the poor, and then to 21 members, 10 of whom were representatives of poor areas of the city. In North Carolina, local governments were told to identify organizations (such as churches and neighborhood associations) that could nominate individuals; in other places, members of the boards were elected from neighborhood and civic organizations (Strange 1972b).

Yet, these shifts to include a broader and more representative board were also associated with increased vetoes of proposals by the city council; for example, the Baltimore city council stopped its CAC from engaging in a voter registration drive in poor neighborhoods and ended its efforts to include "the poverty population . . . in planning and implementing" programs (Baratz 1970, 200). Other boards had no power in their original construction; for example, one ordinance noted outright that the CAC "will have no decision-making power" (Bachrach and Baratz 1970, 176).

The long-term effects of the participatory requirement on cities extended well beyond the end of the Model Cities Program. While subsequent issues with funding, local resistance to program requirements, and the Nixon administration's eventual destruction of the program ultimately limited the effects of the Model Cities, the participatory mandate generated participatory institutions across local governments, many of which persist today. In addition, the transfer of funds from the federal government to local governments to cover social service programs that began in the 1960s would last for more than a decade; as a result, cities underinvested their own funds in social services and created fundamentally weak social service boards to oversee these limited programs. The legacy of these weak organizations and the poor oversight of them continues today, with cities either maintaining weak social service, poverty, and welfare boards without autonomy or authority, or simply not engaging in participatory governance around the issues.

Policing the Police: Citizen Review Boards

Demands about public oversight over the police also emerged in the 1960s in response to urban uprisings. Police in cities had long been involved in the protection of white interests, violence and killings of Black residents, and the enforcement of segregationist policies. For example, police departments would refuse to provide Black residents with protection from white violence (Trounstine 2018; Meyer 2000).[37] In its 1961 report, the U.S. Commission on Civil Rights noted that "policy brutality is still a serious problem throughout the United States." In response to widespread distrust in the police, civil liberties violations, and the 1960s' racial uprisings, the national ACLU and NAACP called for the creation of police oversight boards.[38] The ACLU argued that an independent civilian review board "would have the power to hear complaints, investigate, and make recommendations ONLY" (Gross and Reitman 1966, 2). Acknowledging that it was "not a cure-all, which, in one stroke, would improve the quality of police recruits, remove racial prejudice from the American scene, and solve all other social ills," the ACLU recommended that "its function would be purely advisory. It would have no disciplinary powers whatsoever." While not an entirely new idea,[39] this focus by the ACLU on police violence, and violence toward Black and poor residents, was new, as was the concentration on creating boards as the vehicle for oversight.

The ACLU and the NACCP were not immediately successful in creating or institutionalizing these boards. While calls for some form of oversight emerged in many cities, few cities responded with permanent efforts at overseeing the policy. In New Orleans, the Black community, which made up more than half of the city's population, expressed widespread concerns about police violence and racism. When a 1964 study found that more than a third of the Black residents arrested reported that the police used "uncomplimentary racial epithets" (Gross and Reitman 1966), Horace Bynum, the NAACP president, advocated for a policy review board "to investigate, conduct hearings, and report its findings and recommendations to proper authorities." Unable to force New Orleans to create a board quickly, Black citizens created the Concerned Citizens on Police Matters of Police Brutality and Harassment, which would receive complaints about police brutality and relay them to the chief of police (L. N. Moore 2010).[40] This community organization without any authority served as the primary police oversight tool for more than a decade with limited success: between 1975 and 1979, New Orleans had the highest rate of police killings of civilians of any urban police force (Piliawsky 1985).

Even where community pressure and organizing were successful in the creation of civilian review boards, the implementation stymied the boards from carrying out their original purpose. In the case of Detroit, a revision to the city's charter in 1973 established a powerful civilian police oversight board to be appointed by the mayor; it just happened that Coleman Young, Detroit's first Black mayor, was elected concurrently with the charter change (Darden 2013). The city granted the commission the power to establish rules and regulations, to review and approve the police budget, to "receive and resolve . . . any complaint concerning the operations of the police department," and to "act as a final authority in imposing or reviewing discipline of employees of the department" (City of Detroit 1973; Smydra 1993).

Despite the considerable power granted to the police board on paper, critics of the board noted a variety of ways that the board simply acted as a "pro forma" disciplinary body. For example, the board differentiated between officer "instances of poor judgment and cases where malicious intent seem probable," often finding for "poor judgement" and allowing the commanding officer to discipline the officer (Locke 1967). When the board did attempt to discipline police officers in the early years of the board or investigate complaints, members of the Detroit police department routinely simply refused either to participate or to accept the board's disciplinary recommendations (Smydra 1993; Littlejohn 1981).

Incorporation and Power(lessness)

When New Orleans elected Ernest "Dutch" Morial as the city's first Black mayor in 1978, Morial pledged to eliminate discrimination "should it ever appear in this administration."[41] One of his first acts was to immediately select Black members of the community to serve on several appointed boards in the city, increasing the share of Black representatives from less than 10 percent to over 30 percent in two years. Yet, he ran up against a wide set of obstacles as he attempted to pursue descriptive political incorporation via boards.

The New Orleans Sewerage and Water Board's (NOSWB) advisory board exemplified these obstacles. While more than half of the NOSWB's employees were Black, Black workers were underrepresented among managers and the quasi-independent agency faced questions and complaints from its Black employees. When Morial attempted to intervene and force the NOSWB to adopt an affirmative action plan, the majority white board said no, asserting that the board's independence meant that it was outside the mayor's power (Hardy 2004). Eventually, Mayor Morial's legal team sued the NOSWB to force the entity to adopt a minority business set-aside plan, which required the board use at least 10 percent minority contractors. The board responded by voting to implement the plan, but several members of the board refused to participate and left prior to the vote. Given the six-year terms of the board members, Morial had to wait until deep into his second term in office to replace the members of the board who had opposed his plans (Piliawsky 1985).

These fights between a very popular mayor and a very unpopular quasi-independent agency exemplify the role that boards and their members played in establishing and protecting the white supremacist status quo in cities across the United States. Morial himself understood that these boards had the potential to reshape race relations in the city of New Orleans and sought to change the ways that the members of these boards represented the continuation of white power in a city that was now majority Black. Yet, in many circumstances, he underestimated the ability of boards to resist his efforts to promote political incorporation and change policies to assist the Black population of the city.

Morial was not alone: the first Black mayors in cities across the country faced significant obstacles when they tried to use appointment power to change local policy. In some cities, white board members refused to vacate seats on powerful boards when a Black representative replaced them. In other cities, city councils refused to confirm appointments or tried to expand the size of boards to water down the influence of Black representatives. And, state governments often intervened to prevent Black elected leaders from using appointment powers. In New Orleans, the state legislature tried to strip appointment responsibilities from Morial after his election by limiting his power to choose appointments for several of the city's most powerful boards, including the Audubon Commission, the New Orleans Aviation Board, and the New Orleans Sewerage and Water Board (Piliawsky 1985).

4

Neoliberalism and Local Boards

In 2014, the city of Richmond offered $7 million in direct grant money as part of a package to entice Stone Brewing to locate its East Coast brewery in the city. The incentive package also included $31 million in low-interest loans, the facilitation of the combination of 15 parcels of land, and extensive zoning and planning coordination. Richmond's Economic Development Authority ("the Authority") put the package together and did the work to lure the brewery with these "pricey promises," as one local newspaper called the incentives (Rolett 2014).

The city of Richmond created the Authority in 1972 as an autonomous body with a variety of independent powers. And the Authority uses those powers to try to lure companies to Richmond or to get them to stay in the city. What the Authority offered Stone Brewing in incentives was "more than three times" what other sites offered the brewer. And while the city council had to approve the final incentive package, the council was not involved in crafting the components, negotiating with Stone, or making direct decisions about the incentives. The vote was an up-or-down vote; that is, the city council could either approve or reject the entire package. In short, Stone Brewery's move to Richmond was the Authority's work.

Why does the Authority have so much independent power? After federal involvement in the creation of boards was detailed in the last chapter, this chapter picks up with the federal disinvestment in cities and a nationwide tax revolt. The late 1970s and 1980s saw the federal government's withdrawal from local politics; efforts by voters and political leaders to reduce property taxes and restrict the powers of local government to expand their authority accompanied the federal government's reduction in funding.

As a result, cities across the country grappled with plummeting revenues, changing demographics, and a variety of accompanying political challenges. A concurrent move toward neoliberal policies at the national (and global) level pushed cities to seek private answers to public problems, including the creation of independent and powerful economic development boards. These boards saw a significant transfer of authority and resources from elected officials to appointed officials across the country, reducing electoral accountability for the smaller pool of voters who remained in cities.

Following the modern re-urbanization of the American population in the 2000s and 2010s, cities today again face pressure to create boards that address liberal interests, from rent control to racial equality to women's rights. Yet, even in these new forms and in liberal cities with elected leaders who are motivated to create change, path dependency is strong. The institutional design of the newly created boards mimics older weak boards: large, unwieldy, and without power. Examples of these boards include attempts to reform criminal justice (including a new wave of police oversight commissions) and policies to engage in antipoverty work.

Federal Interventions and Retreats

How did the Richmond Economic Development Authority, a group of appointed leaders, get so much power over such large financial decisions? The roots of the Authority's power rest in neoliberal changes in cities in the United States (Weaver 2016), starting in the 1970s. The 1970s and 1980s saw significant reductions in local budgets, stemming from three sources: dramatic shifts in federal spending priorities, state-level "tax revolts," and the resuburbanization of the United States via the construction of outer-ring suburbs that provided for (mostly white) middle- and upper-class families to remove their tax dollars from cities. These changes—long-term trends of underinvestment in public housing, infrastructure, and social services and increased mobility of businesses—all pushed cities toward a new world: one where cities competed by using incentive packages of tax credits, infrastructure, and more to attract or retain businesses for jobs or future taxes.

Prior to this point, the federal-urban relationship had been characterized by financial generosity, especially for pet projects and specific programs that often changed, appeared, and disappeared (Weber and Wallace 2012; Arnstein 1969). From the 1950s to the late 1970s, federal aid to cities increased almost tenfold, funding 492 separate programs by 1978. While early federal programs focused primarily on capital programs like highways and housing, by the middle of the Carter administration the federal government provided funds for "the most intimate traditional functions of local government, such as fire protection, education, personnel administration, and parks" (Eisinger 1988, 67). As I discuss in Chapter 3, large federal programs in the 1960s and 1970s forced cities to create boards and commissions as a requirement for receipt of these funds.

The pattern of federal transfers to cities shifted (abruptly) in 1978, when Congress, reacting to rising deficits, international events, and an increased distaste among the public for taxes, applied a sharp break to the growth in federal transfers. Of particular importance for the creation of local boards was the concern in Congress about local and state "tax revolts" and the degree that these represented a national distaste for government spending via taxation (Sears and Citrin 1982).

Additional efforts by citizens to limit the spending and taxation powers of government (especially local government) accompanied the decline in federal transfers. Tax reforms in states from California to Colorado to Massachusetts aimed specifically at reforming who could tax (with a focus on local governments), how much the government could tax or increase taxes in a year (often capping property taxes or sales taxes, two primary sources of local revenue), and requiring citizen approval (often majority or supermajority approval) for tax increases (Joyce and Mullins 1991). California's Proposition 13, or the People's Initiative to Limit Property Taxation, amended the Constitution of California via a popular vote in the initiative process in 1978. The key restriction in "Prop 13" was the limitation of any property tax to 1 percent of the 1976 value of that property; assessed values of property could not rise more than 2 percent per year unless the owners resold or rebuilt the property. The proposition also required a two-thirds vote in both houses of the state legislature to change the amendment. Because of Prop 13, Californians who bought their property prior to 1976 pay extraordinarily low taxes on that property today. Homeowners can also transfer these benefits via inheritance, so many people in the state today benefit from their parent's (or grandparent's) property purchases. A new property owner might pay three or four times the taxes, because the government can only update the assessment to reflect the actual value of the property at the time of sale.

The effort in California was accompanied by initiatives in 17 other states in 1978 alone, with most states considering some form of tax reduction, including sweeping policies like Massachusetts's Proposition 2 ½ (passed in 1980), Colorado's Taxpayer Bill of Rights (TABOR, passed in 1992) and Oregon's Measures 47 and 50 (passed in 1997) (Lowery and Sigelman 1981; Buchanan 1979). These policies reduced local per capita tax revenue by up to 40 percent (Preston and Ichniowski 1991). In response, cities and state governments increased fees, transferred funding sources, and bypassed these caps through a variety of mechanisms (King-Meadows and Schaller 2007). One key mechanism by which local governments side-stepped these funding restrictions was via the privatization of service provision, with governance done by local boards.

The financial strain on local governments increased in the 1980s with Reagan's election as U.S. president. The "Reagan Reconstruction" focused on devolving authority away from the federal government to states and cities, reducing spending (with a particular emphasis on reductions in social service spending), and shrinking the size of the federal bureaucracy (Clark and Clark 1992). The Reagan Reconstruction was, at its core, anti-Black (Bostdorff and Goldzwig 2005) and anti-urban (Weaver 2016).

The financial consequences of these national and state changes were devastating for cities. Intergovernmental revenue as a percent of own-revenue fell from 26 percent in 1978 to 12 percent in 1986 (Advisory Commission on Intergovernmental Relations 1989). Local governments' need to find alternative sources for funds accelerated throughout the 1980s. These patterns are clear in Los Angles, New Orleans, and Richmond: all three cities saw the per capita funds received from the federal government fall in the period from 1977 to 1995 (see Figure 4.1). As a result, cities had to identify potential sources for local revenue "to compensate for the loss of federal aid" (Cole, Taebel, and Hissong 1990, 345).

Demographic changes also impacted local politics during this time. The 1970s and 1980s saw another wave of white flight from cities, particularly conservative, racist whites who fled urban areas as there neighborhoods became more racially diverse (Galster 1990; Crowder 2000; Kruse 2013).

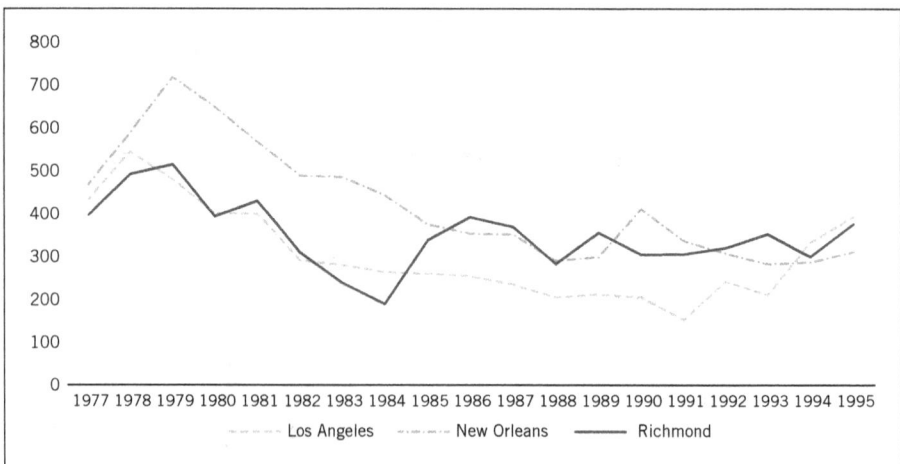

Figure 4.1 Federal Transfers, 1977–1995. *Note: Y-axis is federal transfers in millions of dollars. Data from the Lincoln Institute of Land Use Policy (2020).*

Scholars often point to the effect of policies in the 1950s and 1960s, particularly federal housing policy, as benefiting specific groups over others. Historian Kevin Kruse notes that "tax policies . . . benefited homeowners instead of renters" and "federal loan policies . . . favored the construction of new housing over the renovation of old" (2013, 244), both of which reshaped what housing stock looked like in the United States and facilitated the transfer of resources from renters to homeowners and from Blacks to whites.

Federal transportation policies that focused in the 1940s and 1950s on automobiles, road and highway construction, and investment in a car-centered America (and not on mass transit) made it easier for whites to flee cities. Roads, highways, and freeways allowed for white families to move to the suburbs and commute into the city for work. These roads were also built directly through Black communities, disrupting local economies and neighborhoods and bringing pollution and noise to previous residential areas (N. King 2021). Local boards participated fully in these transportation decisions; for example, the federal bureaucrats empowered with implementing the Federal-Aid Highway Act of 1956 regularly consulted local planning, zoning, infrastructure, and public works boards to select routes through cities for federal highways (Turner 1972; Beckman 1970; Ellis 2001). As a result, throughout the 1960s, 1970s, and 1980s a new generation of white Americans benefited from these racist structures, fleeing desegregated city neighborhoods, and constructing homes in newer middle- and outer-ring suburbs (Hanlon 2009).

New Orleans exemplifies these trends: while the city experienced more than 150 years of population growth throughout the 1800s and the first half of the 1900s, the city's population began to decline starting in 1970 as white families, fleeing school desegregation, moved to the suburbs. New Orleans transformed from nearly 70 percent white residents of the first half of the 1900s to a Black majority by 1980 (Fussell 2007; Campanella 2006). By 1980, the city's white population has dropped to just over 45 percent of the city's residents—just as the city elected its first Black mayor. These demographic patterns would continue until Hurricane Katrina in 2005, which decimated many of the historically Black neighborhoods in the city, transforming politics again in the city (Burns and Thomas 2015; Holman and Lay 2021; Lay 2022). Richmond and Los Angeles exemplified different patterns in demographic change (see Figure 4.2): Richmond's population remained relatively stable through the middle of the twentieth century, but the composition of that population changed sharply as the city moved from 77 percent white in 1950 to less than 40 percent white in 2000 (Hayter 2017; IPUMS 1970). Similarly, Los Angeles doubled in population from 1950 to 2020, while the white population in the city declined from more than 70 percent to 30 percent across that same time (Mordechay 2014).

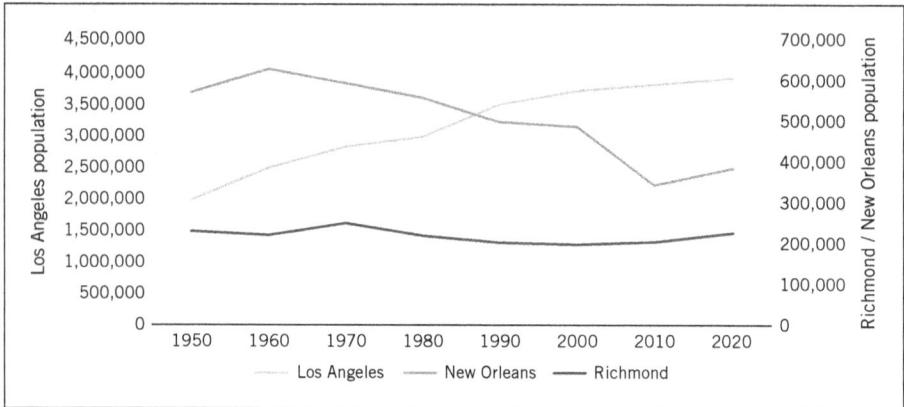

Figure 4.2 Population Change in Los Angeles, New Orleans, and Richmond.

Cities struggled to respond to these changing demographics. Facing a combination of federal disinvestment in social services, reduced intergovernmental transfers, the tax revolts, continued emptying out of urban centers (particularly by white residents), an increased concentration of poverty in urban centers, rising crime, failing property values, and a general interest in trickle-down economics and neoliberal economic policies, cities began to consider alternative sources for jobs and taxes. At the same time, neoliberal ideas of privatization, limited government, and self-sufficiency pushed cities to look for "market solutions" to their economic problems (Weaver 2016, 2021). As a result, cities turned to economic development incentives and a wide set of economic development oversight boards, corporations, and special districts, all with appointed members, to oversee these incentives.

Economic Development Boards

The rise of neoliberal economic development efforts in local politics in the United States (Weaver 2021) provided a new avenue for the creation of powerful local boards and commissions. Local governments had long been in formal and informal coalitions with the private sector, particularly real estate development (Stone 1989; Molotch 1976; Logan and Molotch 1987). For example, my earlier discussion of housing and planning boards notes the importance of the involvement of local developers in constructing and reinforcing a particular approach to land use policies. Yet, the turn in the 1980s toward public-private partnership was different, particularly in its implications for local boards and commissions. In response to the financial constraints addressed earlier, cities, states, and the federal government all sought new pathways to pursue economic development with the realities of "new localism." While tax-based incentives existed prior to the 1980s in theory, they "seldom figured prominently" as a tool to boost the economies of local governments (Eisinger 1988, 69). By 1985, Mayors at the United States Conference of Mayors meeting raised alarms about President Reagan's budget and about the need to create a new strategy of coalitions with the private sector (Herbers 1985).

The federal government also provided avenues for the creation of boards, commissions, and corporations that would aid public-private partnerships. For example, aided by the Small Business Administration's (SBA) Certified Development Company (CDC) 504 loan program (enacted in 1980), cities could organize nonprofit corporations to raise lending capital for development in a specific geographic area. By 1985, the CDC was the fastest growing program administered by the SBA (Eisinger 1988). Of particular importance for the development of boards, "by law a CDC board of directors must include representatives not only from the business and lending communities . . . but also from the appropriate levels of government" (Eisinger 1988, 99). More than 250 CDCs operate under the SBA in the United States (U.S. Small Business Administration 2020).

Cities across the United States responded to the "new localism" by creating their own economic development boards. In New Orleans, the Industrial Development Board was empowered to issue tax-exempt industrial revenue bonds, to exempt companies from a variety of local taxes, and to provide infrastructure investments at a company's request (Piliawsky 1985). Similarly, Richmond created the Economic Development Authority in 1972.[1] The board was created with a variety of independent powers and was considered by the city to be an autonomous body. Today, this is still true. Beyond controlling its own budget, the Economic Development Authority is not required to gain approval for most decisions from the city council or the mayor. The board authorizes economic development incentives to businesses, both for their relocation to the city and to retain and support existing businesses. These activities range from loaning or facilitating the transfer of amounts ranging from $5,000 to millions of dollars to businesses, offering tax breaks, coordinating infrastructure changes or extensions, waiving permitting fees or expediting permitting, creating a start-up incubator, luring the Washington Redskins' (now Commanders) practice facility,[2] and offering businesses a variety of tax incentives to move to Richmond. The board meets regularly; even through the COVID pandemic, the Economic Development Authority met via Zoom every month in 2020.

Cities created a wide set of boards and commissions during the 1980s to offer economic development incentives, to facilitate the transfer of resources from the public to private interests, and to bypass accountability for these decisions. The creation of these boards took economic development decisions out of the public eye and moved them to these appointed boards, diminishing the ability of voters to hold elected representatives accountable for transferring wealth to businesses. As Pincetl (2003, 30) notes about the creation of economic development boards in California, "Members of boards and commissions could not be recalled since they were not elected, and the nature of the boards and commissions put financially interested people in charge of policing themselves."

Cities and business elites also created Business Improvement Districts, or BIDs, as a vehicle for economic development policy in the 1980s and 1990s. The governing boards of BIDs, "composed mostly of property or business owners in the area," have nearly complete autonomy in decision-making for the BID (Mitchell 2001, 118). As one evaluation of BIDs noted, "Local government plays a limited role in the actual operation of a BID" (Mitchell 2001, 118). In Los Angeles, 38 property-based BIDs (i.e., based on where a business is located) and 5 merchant-based BIDs (i.e., based on the type of business) created in the 1980s and 1990s collect more than $60 million annually through assessments and have near complete independence in how they allocate those funds.

Weak Boards Emerge from Neoliberalism

Cities also created a wide set of boards to address pressures to supplement or replace federal social service programs during the 1970s and 1980s. But unlike the boards created for economic and business development, these boards were institutionally weak, underfunded, and without support staff—and they accomplished little. For example, Richmond created the nine-member Social Services Advisory Board in 1983 to "interest itself in all matters pertaining to the social services of the people of the City of Richmond," including monitoring social service programs, meeting with city staff members, making recommendations, and "submit[ting] to Council from time to time any other report concerning social services that the advisory board deems appropriate to bring to the attention of Council."

Like many other social services boards created during this time, the Social Services Advisory Board is purely advisory, as it has no independent policymaking powers. According to the minutes and agendas from the board, the board's activity involves receiving reports from the Richmond Department of Social Services (RDSS). Even though the ordinance creating the board requires that the body produce an annual report, the board does not produce one. I could find records of a report only in 2008, 2013, and 2017. The board meets irregularly, and it did not meet at all during the first 18 months of COVID. Roundtable discussions, which are a part of each board meeting, focus on topics like "What RDSS could do to prevent what happened in Henrico County[3] from happening in Richmond" and "All members were challenged to bring a friend/community people to the [next Board] meeting."[4]

Enterprise Zones, Rodney King, and Economic Development

The evolution of urban neoliberal policy and reactions to the Reagan Reconstruction also produced a proliferation of a new set of policies: Enterprise Zones (EZs), or public-private partnerships that would "help bring the entrepreneurial spirit to the nation's most distressed neighborhoods" (Wolf 1990, 3). EZs offered businesses a variety of tax incentives, financing, and bypasses for regulatory structures if the business would invest in certain specified ZIP codes or areas. Ronald Reagan featured EZs in his 1980 campaign, but the policies never quite fit into a set of legislation during the Reagan administration. State governments filled in the gaps: by 1983, more than 20 states had enacted a version of EZs, and by the end of the Reagan administration, two-thirds of states had some form of EZs in their business-relations portfolio (Wolf 1990).[5]

After the Rodney King uprising in 1992, the federal government leaned harder into neoliberal solutions to the problems of systemic racism, underinvestment, white flight, and declining infrastructure issues. Central to these responses was Congress's passage of the 1993 Empowerment Zone Act, which created the Empowerment Zone and Enterprise Communities Program with a focus on the "empowerment" of the economies of urban areas (Riposa 1996). These programs were neoliberal in their focus, allocating tax credits and funds for economic development in communities that met a variety of criteria (Weaver 2018; Mele 2013). Initial evaluations of the EZ programs lauded the focus on community participation, as one early evaluation noted:

> It is argued that people living in distressed communities will not be empowered simply by jobs; they need knowledge of a heretofore distant and often unintelligible political process, practice in accessing it, and experience in making it work for them in a tangible way, enhancing the community's quality of life. Empowerment zones have been structured to elicit this type of involvement—and directly account for social justice interests—to enhance one's community life chances long after this ten-year program has ended. (Andronovich and Riposa 1996)

Despite the explicit focus on community capacity and community decision-making in the Enterprise Zones Program (Gittell et al. 1998), patterns from the 1960s and 1970s continued in who sat on these boards and who had power. While EZs lead to moderate economic gains, qualitative evaluations of community participation suggest deep challenges in recruiting and sustaining community involvement in the decision-making processes (Busso, Gregory, and Kline 2013).

Part of the limited capacity for EZs was related to the design of the programs; as in the 1960s, cities managed to develop elaborate, complicated, and opaque systems for the creation and evaluation of EZs. Cities could choose how programs were implemented, including whether the program would be managed by existing city agencies or by new nonprofit organizations (Rich and Stoker 2010).[6] Some cities choose two- or three-tier structures of the community engagement in the EZ processes, while other cities created as many as 30 neighborhood-level boards to serve as the initial community organizations that would provide consultations about the needs of the area. Managing these programs provided a challenge: as one evaluation of Enterprise Zones noted, "Although community participation was required . . . neither the federal government nor most of the city governments provided any financial resources" to facilitate that participation (Gittell et al. 1998, 535). As a result, evaluations of the programs found that community participation varied wildly across EZ cities (Hebert et al. 2001).

Even when community participation was high in the EZ process, this "participation did not always translate into influence" (Rich and Stoker 2010, 779). As with the design of other boards, cities controlled the institutional designs of the community involvement in the EZs, including the number of boards, the board members, and the resources directly controlled by the boards; rarely did cities empower these boards with real resources and influence. Rich and Stoker's (2010) evaluation of Atlanta, Baltimore, Chicago, Detroit, New York, and Philadelphia found that even as citizen involvement in the process was active, it was not influential. As a result, they conclude, "None of the local EZ programs brought about a fundamental transformation of distressed urban neighborhoods" (Rich and Stoker 2010, 791) even as there were slight gains on the economic status of these areas. Subsequent programs like the Opportunity Zones program contained in the Tax Cuts and Jobs Act of 2017 similarly concluded that the "legislation fails to incentive community engagement" (Jordan 2020).

The Resurgence of Police Oversight

In August 2017, in response to efforts to remove Confederate monuments, white supremacists organized a rally in Charlottesville, Virginia. Clashes between the white supremacists and the counterprotesters turned violent, with one white supremacist ramming a crowd with his car, killing Heather Hayer and injuring 35 other counterprotesters. In response to this, Molly Conger,[7] a self-described "socialist dog mom," now attends every city council meeting, board, and commission meeting,[8] and many "court hearings & trials related to our ongoing nazi problem," that occurs in Charlottesville.[9] One ongoing set of these meetings revolves around the city's efforts to establish a civilian review board. While Ms. Conger initially felt positive about the creation of the board, her observation of the creation process soon soured her on it. She tweeted, "i remain utterly uninspired by the police civilian review board, but i must do my duty."[10] Why, if civilian oversight boards were the topic of the ACLU's efforts in the 1960s, is a modern-day Lois Lane reporting on the progress of creating one in 2021 in Charlottesville, Virginia? Why, as I outline at the very beginning of the book, was AOC encouraging people to pressure their local governments to create oversight commissions?

While cities sporadically created police oversight boards from the 1940s forward, few large cities adopted civilian oversight boards until the 1990s (Saltzstein 1989). Starting in the early 1990s, national events have pushed surges in their creation. National attention on police brutality and racism increased following the dismissal of charges against the police officers who beat Rodney King (Bobb 2003), the police killings of Sean Bell and Oscar Grant (Roychoudhury 2023), the shooting of Michael Brown in Ferguson, Missouri (Cooper and Fullilove 2016; Ofer 2015), the choking deaths of Eric Garner in New York and George Floyd in Minneapolis (Marcus 2016; Harden 2016; Wu et al. 2023), and countless other instances of police violence. Each time protests and media attention focus on police killings, there have been calls to engage in criminal justice reform at the local level (Olzak 2021). Like in the 1960s and 1970s, calls for criminal justice reform suggest the creation of civilian oversight boards.

But the institutional design of these boards regularly challenges their effectiveness. As one assessment of these boards notes, "The purpose of these boards is to give every civilian the opportunity to correct any perceived injustice" (K. King 2015, 93) or, as the National Association for Civilian Oversight of Law Enforcement outlines: "MEANINGFUL" civilian oversight includes boards that are proactive, independent, community-driven, and empowered (NACOLE 2023). Central to meaningful oversight is that these boards should have the power to engage in investigation and adjudication on their own, including "subpoena power . . . allowing them to investigate, gather, analyze, and review information" (NACOLE 2023).[11]

By the fall of 2023, Charlottesville's Police Oversight Board, created in 2018, had yet to hear a single case relating to police misconduct. The board can review only those investigations that have been first completed by the Charlottesville Police Department's Internal Affairs Division, and as of 2024 that division has yet to refer a case to the board (Evans 2022; Carrier 2024).

Despite the efforts of a wide set of activists, community members, and observers, police oversight boards largely lack power. Most big cities in my dataset (87%) have police oversight boards, with most cities creating their oversight board since 1992. But the powers of these boards rarely meet NACOLE's standards: 40 percent of police oversight boards nationally have advisory powers and another 35 percent have review capacity, meaning that they can evaluate cases that the police department sends to them, but they have no powers to investigate on their own. The remaining 25 percent of boards do have independent investigative power, but of those, all but one require that current or former police officers sit on these boards. My analysis aligns with work by political scientist Arvind Krishnamurthy (2023), who finds that 96 percent of boards in large cities are unable to discipline or sanction officers. As a result, while research shows that police misconduct (particularly killings) leads to the creation of oversight boards (Olzak 2021), the boards that are created rarely shape any kind of police behavior or outcomes (Krishnamurthy 2023; Green and Aldebron 2019), perhaps because these oversight mechanisms are themselves racially biased and lead to the intensification of police violence against Black residents (Kraft and Newman 2023; Faber and Kalbfeld 2019).

Police violence against civilians, particularly Black residents of cities, is widespread in the United States (Sharara et al. 2021; Schwartz and Jahn 2020). High-profile instances of police killings and violence have forced cities to create oversight boards over the last 30 years. But these oversight boards are designed in the same style as the boards that cities created in the 1960s to address civil rights or poverty: the veneer of accountability without power or authority.

A Liberal Turn? The Creation of Boards in the 2020s

On June 18, 2020, New Orleans formally created a Street Renaming Commission to "make recommendations to rename streets, parks, and places in New Orleans that honor white supremacists" (Street Renaming Commission 2021, 2).[12] Simultaneously, the city also created a variety of Police Community Advisory Boards (PCABs), which are district-level participatory boards. Each of the eight PCABs (which have 7 members, so 56 members in total) "does not have any decision-making authority, but will meet quarterly." According to a document from the New Orleans Policy Department (NOPD), the PCAB members should "get to know your police district leadership and officers," by attending meeting and events and conducting community meetings and "understand NOPD operations so you can assess and then make realistic and practical recommendations that can be implemented in your neighborhood, and/or scaled up into other neighborhoods as well."

New Orleans was not alone: cities across the United States created a variety of commissions to evaluate the presence of statues honoring white supremacist leaders of the Confederacy after a national outcry focused on the continued structures of white supremacy. In the 2000s, 2010s, and 2020s, voters in cities across the country sought Progressive candidates (Holman and Lay 2021; de Benedictis-Kessner, Jones, and Warshaw 2022; Benjamin 2023; de Benedictis-Kessner, Einstein, and Palmer 2025; B. Levin 2020; Voelkel and Willer 2019) and pushed cities to engage in work that ranged from combating white supremacy to creating social housing to protecting renters' rights (Michener 2020). Like New Orleans, cities across the country created boards to address these concerns. And as in cities before them, these boards and commissions are weak, lack independent power, and engage in deliberation without accomplishing policy outcomes.

In New Orleans, the Street Renaming Commission has met its concrete goals: the city has renamed streets and landmarks, including removing Robert E. Lee's name from a central boulevard in the city. A detailed report, produced by the members of commission, documented the racist actions of a variety of members of the New Orleans community who had streets, parks, and other public facilities named after them. In short, the board was a success, in a very narrow and specific way.

The PCABs, in comparison, have done very little. As they were intended to do. The chair of one PCAB made headlines by criticizing the district attorney and the city council during a crime spike (Lippincott 2022). In a letter to city and state officials, the PCAB requested that the governor send "the state troopers to patrol the highways. We asked the state legislators, the state senators, the state [representatives] to fight for more lighting on highways because of the heinous crimes, and we ask that they find funding to fund the youth-based programs" as well as asking that members of the New Orleans political leadership not fight with each other (Lippincott 2022). Other PCABs organized events for neighborhoods to support their local police. While this was advertised as an opportunity for the community to shape what policing looks like in New Orleans, the City of New Orleans created the PCABs because of a suggestion from the NOPD's Consent Decree (WDSU Digital Team 2021), the agreement between the Department of Justice and the NOPD regarding necessary changes in the department after systematic problems, including civilian deaths and maltreatment, corruption, and bribery (Powell, Meitl, and Worrall 2017).[13] Again, a requirement for community participation has led to 56 individuals taking positions on boards that have no power and whose primary responsibility is to conduct meetings.

Between 1900 and 2020, America's cities went through several major points of deep change. The outcome of these policies from the past, still in effect either in fact or in practice, lingers today (Green, Strolovitch, and Wong 1998; Trounstine 2018). As political scientist Jessica Trounstine (2018) documents, early choices in land use, planning, and zoning influence levels of segregation, which then influence the policy choices that cities make and the resources each city has available to make those policy choices. Decisions made by appointed boards and commissions across the United States facilitated the cycle by which the uneven provision of public goods reinforced segregation.

The policy shifts and political shifts that produced appointed boards over the last 50 years mimic those of the prior 50 years, and the 50 years before that: cities create both weak boards and strong boards for different purposes. Cities create strong boards as tools to decide about policy, to control political resources, and to deny political opponents access to governing power. Their goal was not deliberation; it was to maintain power in the hands of white men with economic resources. These governance structures could facilitate deliberative democracy, including allowing ordinary citizens to engage in deliberation with policymakers and then report back to the community. Instead, cities create these boards to give the appearance of democratic deliberation, of choice, and of freedom (Mullin 2008), while still reinforcing the existing hierarchies and structures of power.

This section of the book has provided a broad overview of key points in the history of urban America that led to the creation of boards and commissions. At each stage, I argue that cities take advantage of moments of political strife to create strong boards that undermine political accountability. Cities jump at the opportunity to create strong boards and grant them extensive power, as a mechanism for shoring up power among political elites. In response to political challenges from marginalized groups, cities create weak boards that serve little purpose but to distract those who are agitating for change. The stories of weak and strong boards in the past are also stories of these boards today: the boards created in the 2000s, in the 1970s, in the 1950s, in the 1920s are often still present in cities today. As William Faulkner wrote in his 1951 novel *Requiem for a Nun*, "The past is never dead. It's not even the past." The path dependency of political conflicts and their outcomes in the form of boards continues to shape how cities make decisions and who has power in cities today.

II

STRONG AND WEAK BOARDS TODAY

Section II Introduction

Grants Pass, Oregon, a sleepy town located in Josephine County on Interstate 5 in the southwest corner of the state, is rarely in the news.[1] However, in 2023 and 2024, the city attracted national attention for the case of *City of Grants Pass v. Johnson*, a case recently decided by the U.S. Supreme Court. Josephine County, like many areas of the West Coast of the United States, faces a homelessness epidemic, with estimates of one of every hundred residents of the county currently experiencing homelessness (Mc-Namara 2023), a rate nearly ten times the national average (NAEH 2023).[2] While a previous circuit court decision (*Martin v. City of Boise*) held that cities could not arrest individuals for sleeping in public spaces if they had no other place to go, Grants Pass imposed civil fines, rather than criminal charges, for using sleeping bags or bedding in public parks. A class action lawsuit filed by Debra Blake, a Grants Pass resident who had experienced homelessness and racked up thousands of dollars in fines for sleeping in parks, challenged the city's resolution (Cohen 2023; Parfitt and Weekley 2023).[3] One of the lawyers for the plaintiffs described the case as follows: "The question before the Supreme Court is whether a person who is homeless and involuntarily without shelter can be punished for sleeping outside with a blanket" (Mead 2024). Ultimately, the Supreme Court ruled that Grants Pass was within its powers to fine individuals for sleeping outside, even if the city did not provide adequate shelter.

The same year that Debra Blake sued Grants Pass for its treatment of the unhoused, the city's Housing Advisory Committee presented a "One Year

Action Plan for Housing and Community Development" that outlined the city's plan to prevent homelessness. The plan included authorizing emergency payments for five households and programs for up to 150 homeless youth (yes, *five households*). Estimates put the homeless population in the county in the range of 750–900 people, and Grants Pass, which has a population of just under 40,000, has "somewhere between 50 and 600 persons" living without housing (*City of Grants Pass v. Johnson* 2024). The Housing Advisory Committee, made up of 15 members from community advocacy groups, homeowners, renters, and developers, meets monthly for at least 75 minutes. Public comments regularly focus on homelessness. But the committee itself had been silent on *City of Grants Pass v. Johnson* and on the city's policies regarding homelessness. Across three years of meetings, the committee had made three recommendations in total about homelessness. Even though there is a board that specifically addresses housing and there is a legitimate housing crisis in the city and the area, the board has done almost nothing to address the problem. Why? This is the question that Section II of this book looks to answer through an exploration of strong and weak boards today.

Cities operate in highly restricted environments stemming from a lack of autonomy in their institutions and from constraints put on them by their state and the federal government (Einstein and Glick 2017). City leaders govern with limitations on their functions and finances (Anzia 2020, 2024; Einstein and Glick 2017). That cities cannot control the movement of people, companies, or money across their boards exacerbates these problems (Hirschman 1970; Trounstine 2018; Tiebout 1956).

The restrictions on cities mean that they tailor their public policy choices to meet the demands of businesses, those with capital, higher-income residents, and white residents, as these are the groups that provide resources and can most easily leave a city when dissatisfied with local decisions. A long history of white control of local political resources institutionalized racial segregation into local policy, particularly land use policy (Trounstine 2018). That white residents "fled" desegregation, emptying out city centers and dropping the value of property within city boundaries, taught cities that they should prioritize the interests of white residents because their exit threats are viewed as more legitimate than the exit threats of people of color (Boustan 2007; Wilson 2019; Troesken and Walsh 2019).

One policy area where cities do have power is control over local land use planning. As a result, landowners and developers have a policy path through local government to increased personal wealth (Logan and Molotch 1987; Trounstine 2018; Yoder 2020). The constraints on cities lead to arrangements that fuse the "popular control of government and the private control of economic resources" (Mossberger and Stoker 2001, 813; see also Burns and Thomas 2004; Stone 1989). These regimes involve informal relationships between elected officials and local actors, with business playing a key role, as "business and the resources they control are too important for the enterprises to be left out completely" (Stone 1989, 7). I thus argue that cities have created a wide set of *strong boards* to address issues like land use, budgeting, economic development, and civil service.

In other issue areas, however, I argue that cities do not want effective boards because they do not want to have bodies that make robust policy. Cities routinely seek mechanisms that will allow them to underfund (or defund) redistribution policy (Paul E. Peterson 1981) or ignore the demands of groups who have long been excluded from power (Browning, Marshall, and Tabb 1984; Bachrach and Baratz 1970).

Scholars find consistent and systematic biases against those seeking outcomes that conflict with the goals of the regime, to expand the universe of policies offered, or to provide substantial redistribution benefits (Logan and Molotch 1987; Shefter 1977; Trounstine 2006; Holman 2015). Given the lack of access to power, marginalized groups often pressure local leadership for change, using both traditional methods (such as voting, fielding candidates, or using interest group activism) and nontraditional methods (such as boycotts, protests, and riots) (Benjamin and Miller 2019; Browning, Marshall, and Tabb 1986; Burns 2006; Wasow 2020). When these outsider and marginalized groups advocate for change, local leadership responds by creating weak boards that give the appearance of response but do not change anything (Camou 2014; Strange 1972a).

In the previous section of the book, I chronicled the fits and starts and staying power of the political development of boards. But do these differences in origins carry through to which boards exist in cities today and the powers granted to those boards? Cities could, after all, change boards in ways that level differences between weak boards and strong boards. For example, a city might engage in a charter reform and give all boards equal amounts of power, or a state legislature might dictate a broad, equitable change to how cities manage these boards.

I find no evidence to support the idea that cities have made boards more equitable in modern times. Cities today continue to grant strong boards the ability to generate and implement policy while weak boards are institutionally designed without teeth: they are less likely to have the capacity to make or enforce policies. In this chapter, I first discuss the datasets used in the second part of the book and then catalog the types of boards that exist, the policy areas that boards oversee, and the legal functions that boards play in cities. I then connect the variation in legal authority of boards to a discussion of political institutions more generally. In doing so, I consider cities to be loosely bound political institutional orders that derive authority from political institutions and derive power from both formal and informal relationships between political actors and private individuals and businesses (D. S. King and Smith 2005; Stone 1989). Throughout this section of the book, I argue that these political institutional orders delegate power to boards unevenly and that this uneven pattern serves a purpose: to benefit the existing political institutional orders.

Quantitative Methods and Data Used in This Book

To evaluate questions of which boards exist, what power they have, and why their institutional designs matter, I turn to two sets of quantitative data. As all scholars of local politics in the United States know, finding comprehensive and reliable data on what, why, and how cities do what they do—or what they actually do—is a significant challenge (Trounstine 2009; Warshaw 2019; de Benedictis et al. 2023). This project is no exception: collecting, organizing, categorizing, and analyzing data on local appointed boards and commissions is a time-consuming and often frustrating process. Given that there is not any kind of a database of boards and commissions, I gathered this data by hand.

Data Collection Process

I created the Large Cities Dataset to examine the 100 largest cities in the United States, which includes cities ranging from New York, New York (population 8.6 million), to San Bernardino, California (population 220,000). More than half the U.S. population lives in these 100 largest cities (U.S. Census Bureau 2012). These cities vary in terms of partisan versus nonpartisan elections, as well as in mayoral partisanship (although they have more Democratic than Republican mayors, reflecting urban America more generally), and in their number and use of boards and the responsibilities of appointed boards and members. Examining the behavior of these large cities is also a best-case scenario for uncovering professional and well-managed boards that serve specific functions for cities.

All of the cities in California as a group provide a different form of depth in understanding why the average American city has boards and commissions; I thus created the California Cities Dataset of all members of all boards in California as a mechanism for understanding board use by smaller cities. Because the population of the cities in my California sample ranges from 112 residents in Amador to 3,792,621 residents in Los Angeles, I can leverage these variations to understand how policy demands might shape the creation of local boards. Cities in California also vary enormously in diversity of population; in race, ethnicity, income, and industry; and in politics, from conservative areas in California's Central Valley, where Donald Trump won 72 percent of the vote in 2016, to places in the Bay Area, where 85 percent of the county voted for Clinton.

To collect the quantitative data, I developed a four-part process for myself and my research assistants to follow. I followed the same process for the Large Cities Dataset and the California Cities Dataset. I began the process by looking online for the information and developing an individual protocol for a research assistant to use in gathering data if there was information available.[4] If the information was unavailable, I then contacted either the staff member in charge of the boards[5] or the city clerk to ask for the information, following up if necessary. For the remaining cities (28 in my large city sample and 113 in California), I determined if state law required sharing information and, if so, prepared Freedom of Information Act requests.[6] This process was unsuccessful as it produced information for only two of the large cities and four California cities. Finally, I used a crowdsourcing process (Sumner, Farris, and Holman 2020) to double-check that the data were not available, asking workers online to try to find lists of boards, board members, and agendas and minutes of boards for the gaps in our dataset. I obtained no additional information from this method with regard to cities that were completely missing from the dataset, but I did fill in information on agendas and minutes that I had not previously collected.

Issue Areas of Board Authority

The 6,413 unique boards in large cities and 1,393 in California handle a wide set of issues, ranging from economic development to code regulation to women's issues to mobile home oversight. To evaluate which boards are common and what they do, I created 20 categories of board issue areas via theory-driven and organic coding. Working with a research assistant, I coded each board into one of these 20 board categories, based on the board name and description.[7] Table II.1 describes the issue areas and provides the number of cities with boards in those areas in both the Large Cities Dataset and the California Cities Dataset.[8]

TABLE II.1. ISSUE AREAS AND PRESENCE IN CITIES		
	Cities with board	
Board	Large cities (%)	California cities (%)
Animal Control, including zoos and animal shelters	39	2
Children and education, including youth councils, mentoring, and antibullying initiatives, but not including elected boards of education	88	31
Civil Rights, including minority rights; police oversight; recognition of Native American, Hispanic, and African American history; and disability rights	64	6

(continued)

Board	Cities with board	
TABLE II.1. ISSUE AREAS AND PRESENCE IN CITIES (*continued*)	Large cities (%)	California cities (%)
Civil Service, including pensions, hiring, and sanctions	95	36
Code Regulation, including code enforcement and regulation of electrical, plumbing, and building codes	100	60
Community, including neighborhood boards, community relations, and citywide engagement efforts	98	65
Culture, including arts, music, sister cities (surprisingly popular), and library	97	57
Economic Development, including tax incentives, improvement districts, tourism, and other development-oriented services	100	99
Elderly, including senior citizen services, aging, and retirement	64	22
Environment, including climate change, urban forests, nature preserves, and wetlands	86	33
Ethics, including regulation of public officials, city employees, and elections	70	6
Fire and Police, including 911, EMS, and public safety	77	28
Health, including regulation of health occupations, public health, and counseling	77	20
Infrastructure, including public works, ports, bridges, and roads	91	44
Judicial, including public defenders, criminal enforcement, and sentencing	75	16
Parks and Recreation, including parks, sports, and recreation activities	86	63
Planning, including zoning, historic preservation, and design review	96	100
Poverty and poor people's interests, including affordable housing, social services, and redistributional policies	76	64
Taxes and Budgeting, including income tax regulation, budget oversight, and municipal borrowing	88	22
Women's Issues, including status of women boards, pay equity, and violence against women	28	2
Veterans, including veteran support, military base coordination, and patriotic efforts	14	10

Weak and Strong Boards

Cities use boards as a tool to maintain inequality and status quo arrangements of local power. To do so, cities create and fill boards for two quite different purposes and with varying consequences. In some issue areas (namely financial and planning boards), cities want strong boards that generate policy and make decisions. In comparison, cities use weak boards that handle issues associated with redistribution and identity politics; they do so not to generate policy but to pacify agitation from marginalized groups and to give the appearance of democratic deliberation.

I start by categorizing boards by the issue areas that each board oversees, ranging from planning and zoning boards to those overseeing social services programs to boards that offer licensing and monitoring for types of businesses. Working from these issue areas, I identify those areas where I argue that cities want strong boards, or those boards that address property, zoning, economic development, finance, and protective services. Weak boards address identity issues, including the status of women, African Americans, Latinos, youth, disability, and other marginalized groups, along with boards that provide or examine redistribution policies, like affordable housing, welfare policies, and services for marginalized groups.

How does this categorization play out in a single city? There are 105 active boards in New Orleans, as shown in Table II.2.[9] Of those boards, I classify 57 (or 54%) as strong boards. I classify another 31 boards (29%) as weak. New Orleans's board structure both resembles other cities and represents

TABLE II.2. NEW ORLEANS BOARDS, CLASSIFIED BY ISSUE AREA AND STRENGTH

Type of board	Number of boards	Power	Examples
Children	2	Weak	Children and Youth Planning Board
Civil rights	2	Weak	Human Relations Commission Advisory Committee
Civil service	4	Strong	Board of Trustees for the Police Pension Fund, Civil Service Commission
Code	2	Strong	Board of Building Standards and Appeals
Community	20	Weak	Broadmoor Neighborhood Improvement District
Culture	6	Allocative	Arts Council of New Orleans, New Orleans Access Television Board
Development	16	Strong	Downtown Development District, New Orleans Regional Business Park, New Orleans Tourism Marketing Corporation
Environment	4	Allocative	Southeast Louisiana Flood Protection Authority—East; New Orleans Mosquito, Termite and Rodent Control Board
Ethics	1	Allocative	Ethics Review Board
Fire and police	19	Strong	Law Enforcement Management District of Orleans Parish, Orleans Parish Law Enforcement Streamline and Accountability Commission, Sanford "Sandy" Krasnoff New Orleans Criminal Justice Council, Upper Audubon Security District

(continued)

TABLE II.2. NEW ORLEANS BOARDS, CLASSIFIED BY ISSUE AREA AND STRENGTH (*continued*)

Type of board	Number of boards	Power	Examples
Health	2	Weak	Health Education Authority of Louisiana, Orleans Parish Hospital Service District—District A
Infrastructure	5	Allocative	New Orleans Aviation Board, Parking Facilities Corporation, Sewerage and Water Board of New Orleans
Library	1	Allocative	New Orleans Public Library
Parks	4	Strong	Audubon Commission, New Orleans Recreation Development Commission
Planning	8	Strong	City Planning Commission, New Orleans Historic District Landmarks Commission
Poverty	4	Weak	Edward Wisner Donation Advisory Committee, Metropolitan Human Services District, Neighborhood Housing Advisory Committee
Taxes	4	Strong	Finance Authority of New Orleans, Revenue Estimating Conference
Veterans	1	Weak	Mayor's Military Advisory Committee

the city's unique history and culture. A final set of 17 boards (16%) handles allocative issues, including culture, environment, infrastructure, and the library; these are boards where cities are interested in using the board to create policy but want to retain control over the ultimate outcome.

Institutional Design of Boards

For each board, I collected how the city describes the board's basic actions. In many cases, this information was enough to indicate the type of board. Using board descriptions and initiating ordinances from city websites and aggregating sources like Municode and LexisNexis, I hand-coded 10 percent of the initiating ordinance into any of five categories: boards that are autonomous, given quasi-legislative, administrative, or quasi-judicial power, and boards that are advisory. I then used this coding to train a semi-supervised text analysis model to classify each board, based on board descriptions and initiating ordinances, into one of those categories.

After examining the power allocated to boards, I turned to basic information about the board that might shape the board's functioning, deliberation, and decision-making: the number of members of the board (board size), whether the board makes decisions through majority rule or consensus, and what rules exist about who can be a member of the board.

TABLE II.3. MEMBERSHIP REQUIREMENTS FOR BOARDS	
Requirement	Example
General	How many seats have any requirements?
City employees	Any requirement that a city employee sit on the board, such as a member of the planning department?
Development	Any requirement for a member from a development group, like the chamber of commerce, or a member with a particular background, like a developer?
Identity	Any member with a specific identity, such as from a specific group like disabled individuals or from a racial or ethnic group?
Nonprofits	Any requirement that a member have a background in nonprofit or education work, such as a member of a disability advocacy organization?
Political leaders	Does the board require the inclusion of the mayor, city council, state legislator, or other elected individuals such a sheriff?

Cities often apply general requirements to all board members and specific requirements for the membership of some or all their boards (see Table II.3). Because board requirements are often "seat set-asides" (i.e., a seat is earmarked for a member of a particular group, such as developers or a former police officer) (Barnes 2016; Beauregard 2017), I code the information about membership requirements at the board level, including both whether there are requirements at all, and, among those that exist, what the city requires for board membership.[10]

How do these membership requirements holistically shape who is qualified to sit on a board? To assess this, I calculated a "diversity score" for every board in my dataset, using a measure developed by scholars studying diversity at the state and legislative levels (Hero and Tolbert 1996; Hero 2000; Barnes and Holman 2018, 2020b). Drawing from Sullivan's (1973) construction of a single diversity measure for any political body, geographic area, or group, the measure is a probability term for each body in question, where a single number represents the proportion of members on a board where a randomly drawn pair of individuals will differ in their membership requirements, assuming sampling with replacement (Hero 2000; Hero and Tolbert 1995; Palmer and Simon 2010). For my purposes, the diversity score is calculated as follows:

$$A_W = 1 - \left(\left(\sum_{k=1}^{p} Y_k^2 \right) / V \right)$$

Y_k = the proportion of the board membership requirements falling in a given category within each of the variables

V = number of variables
p = number of categories within all of the variables

This is then aggregated to the board level, so that each board in the dataset has a percentage of seats reserved for development (or not) or social services (or not) professions, as well as elected officials (or not), city employees (or not), and an identity group (or not). I took the sum of squares, divided that value by six (given the number of variables) and subtracted from one.

Gender and Race of Members

Who sits on these boards and commissions? In Chapter 7, I investigate the ways that gender, race, and economic power shape access to board appointments overall and whether individuals are appointed to weak or strong boards. I use several methods to examine distribution by gender and race: information directly from cities and three processes based on the board members' first and last names. Some cities provide information about appointees' gender and race, and I rely on that as true information when it has been provided. In cities where this is not provided, I use the appointees' first names in the R package gender and the gender API; each method produced a prediction (0 to 1) of probability that any appointee is a woman (Mullen, Blevins, and Schmidt 2015). I took the mean across these predictions and used internet searches to confirm gender for any member whose probability landed under 0.95 or above 0.05 or where the two packages produced a value that differed by more than 0.02. To estimate the race and ethnicity of the appointees, I start with those individuals for whom the cities provide this information. I then use the wru package (Khanna, Imai, and Jin 2017), which uses a Bayesian predictor algorithm to calculate race/ethnicity probabilities. The wru package draws on a surname list from the U.S. Census and the 2010 Decennial Census. I supplement this with a random forests estimation of race and ethnicity (de Benedictis et al. 2023; Breiman 2001). Again, I search for information on those individuals whose names produce conflicting prediction information.

Appointed and Elected Office

One of the key roles that appointed office serves for the appointees themselves is to assist in seeking elected office. To examine the degree to which appointed office is associated with elected office, I examine two data sources: all appointed board members and all those seeking local elected office in California, which facilitates a comparison between the two pools, and a survey of civically engaged women in Richmond, Virginia. In Richmond, an organizer of civic engagement in the city sent an invitation email to her network; from this email, 228 took the survey (Holman, Iyer, and Wolbrecht 2023). Among other questions, the survey inquired about the level of interest in appointed office and elected office. In Chapter 7, I compare interest across the two kinds of positions.

Looking Forward

What do these boards look like, and who serves on them? The next two chapters answer these questions. This section of the book examines the institutional rules of boards in Chapter 5, focusing on the ways that I can measure power and the ability to create policy. I use a combination of information about the specific powers granted to the board and the institutional characteristics of the board, including membership rules, size, and decision-making. In Chapter 6, I move to an examination of when and how descriptive representation varies across boards. Here I first call back to the political development of boards to discuss how women and people of color have fought for access to appointed boards. I then show patterns of when and where women and people of color serve on boards, as well as the factors associated with their higher and lower levels of participation.

5

INSTITUTIONAL RULES MATTER

It is just hard, you know. Hard to make hard decisions.
Hard to get this group to come to something we agree
about. I mean, we all agree about the big stuff . . . that
the city should spend more on welfare, that we shouldn't
have hungry kids . . . but how to actually do that. So many
different ideas. And no one is at the front of the ship. So we
just drift.

—MEMBER OF A SOCIAL SERVICE BOARD
(AUTHOR INTERVIEW, 2019)

In 1925, the Los Angeles Planning Board was in a "fight for the future of Los Angeles."[1] The board, created in 1920, was in the midst of arguing that the new city charter should expand the powers of the board and give it more autonomy to create zoning in the rapidly growing city; the board was rather self-congratulatory at the time, referring to planning as "one of the highest phases of self-government."[2] Under appropriate zoning, the "law steps in and undertakes to prevent those wrongs against general welfare which are too intangible to be classified as attacks on property or wrongs against persons, but which, nevertheless, do attack and wrong both. The enactment of a Zoning Ordinance is one of the best proofs of a community's capacity for self-government."[3]

The charter reform, advocated for by members of the Zoning Board, allocated a much larger portfolio to the board. Creation by or changes to a board's power by city charter, or to the legal agreement between the city and state that allows the city to make decisions in some policy areas but not others, is common. These changes in authority mattered: the Los Angeles Planning Commission's (Figure 5.1, dotted line, circles) powers expand dramatically via the charter reform in 1925. When the new charter went into effect in 1926, the board's members increased their activity, the number of meetings, and the scope of those meetings. In comparison, Los Angeles Parks Commission's (solid line, diamonds) powers do not shift with this charter revision (although they do shift with a later charter revision!) and the board does not see a similar increase in activities.

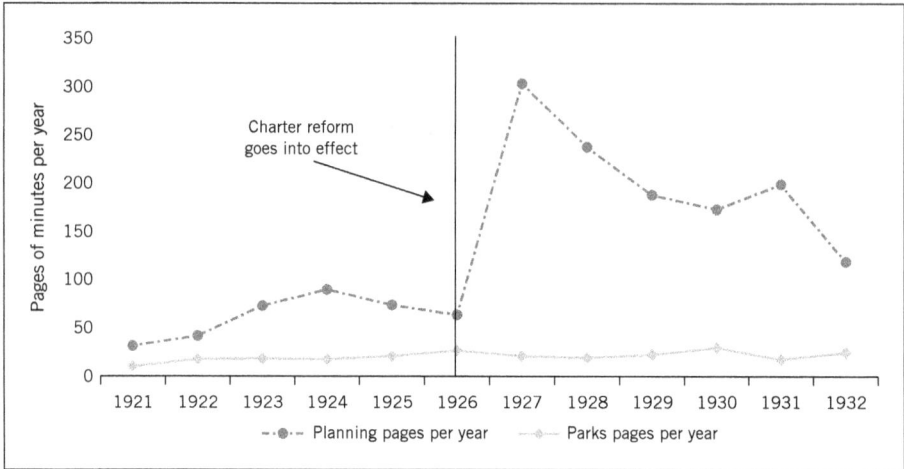

Figure 5.1 The Los Angeles Planning Board Increased Activities after a Charter Reform.

Today, the Los Angeles Planning Commission remains a powerful entity in the city. Karen Bass, the mayor at the time this book is being written, has pledged to address housing availability and affordability. However, her proposal for a new streamlined affordable housing process (City News Service 2023b) and large multifamily developments (Quintana 2023) must first pass through the planning commission to gain approval. The University of Southern California's plans for a new women's soccer and lacrosse stadium likewise require approval from the planning commission (City News Service 2023a). The planning commission also regularly refuses to make decisions on large developments and on multifamily affordable housing, often falling back on concerns about California's Environmental Quality Assessment (CEPA) (Coon 2023; Sharp 2023; Newton 2011). A recent roster of the commission's nine members included six real estate professionals, two nonprofit leaders, and a lobbyist for an association of governments.

I argue that the "rules of the regime" (Crepaz 1996, 5) affect the ability of these institutions to make decisions and shape policy. What does it mean for boards to have different levels of power? And, what is power? In this chapter, I examine how and when the institutional rules laid out when cities create boards then shape each board's ability to function as a policymaking unit. The power, responsibilities, and resources of these boards vary by the board's legal creation. If I expect strong (weak) boards to have more (less) power, then design of these boards should reflect these differences. While political science, public policy, and public administration agree on the importance of institutional design for the functions and power of political bodies, we know almost nothing about the functional design of appointed boards.

Cities are more likely to allocate policy authority to strong boards, while weak boards do not have independent power and regularly serve only advisory functions. As a result, by initial design and power, strong boards have more power to be effective decision-making bodies with a clear path to policy implementation; weak boards are less likely to have access to these powers but engage in more deliberation, by design. But the institutional differences do not end with the allocation of authority. Here, I show that differences in power also emerge from choices that cities make about how the boards will operate: board size, decision-making rules, and membership requirements all vary across weak and strong boards. These decisions mean that strong boards are better positioned to make and carry out decisions, while weak board design means frustration and stymied decisions.

In this chapter, I evaluate and validate my classification of boards into "weak" or "strong" categories to demonstrate that these boards are actually weak and strong in the power they hold: what kinds of powers are allocated to the board, what is the size of the board, what are the voting rules of the board, and what kinds of membership requirements does the board have for its members? For each of these, I rely on how cities themselves describe these boards, gleaned from places like city charters, city legislation, board descriptions from websites, and advertising materials.

What Kind of Powers Do These Boards Have?

To evaluate whether weak boards (including identity, redistribution, and community-oriented) and strong boards (i.e., planning, finance, and police/fire) hold different levels of power, I used a variety of sources to classify boards into one of five types: boards that are autonomous, given quasi-legislative, administrative, or quasi-judicial power, and boards that are advisory. Autonomous, quasi-legislative, administrative, and quasi-legislative boards are policymaking bodies: they promulgate public policies, regulations, and ordinances; they make decisions about regulatory or statutory violations; and their decisions are binding, including decisions regulating the behavior of city agencies and elected officials. Advisory boards do not make policy but instead recommend actions to elected officials or bureaucrats.

Autonomous boards are the most powerful and independent, while advisory boards are the least powerful and most dependent. Given that quasi-judicial boards engage in checks on legislative and administrative decisions (Cunningham 1975; Yang and Callahan 2007), I consider these boards to be slightly more powerful. I consider quasi-legislative and administrative boards to be equally powerful in different ways. Each type of board should be considered a Russian nesting doll of sorts, potentially also fulfilling duties outlined in the descriptions of the weaker forms of boards. For example, an independent board might also engage in quasi-legislative action or serve in an advisory capacity in some areas.

As I discussed in the introduction to this section, I classified boards by taking a random selection and consulting how the board is described in such

TABLE 5.1. TYPES OF BOARD POWER				
Type of board	Governance	Function	Allocated power and responsibility	Share of boards (%)
Autonomous	Self-governing	Independent policy-making	Report to city council or mayor, but city does not directly check their decisions	9
Quasi-judicial	Self-governing	Fact-finding and deci-sion-rendering about regulatory or statutory violations; represent city as prosecutor; make decisions bind-ing on city agencies or members of the public	Decisions are binding	9
Administrative	Independent governance in conjunction with bureaucratic staff	Carry out administra-tive functions, admin-ister funds; responsible for agency operations; make decisions bind-ing on city agencies or members of the public	Decisions are subject to bureaucratic and elected oversight; city council and/or mayor retains veto power	22
Quasi-legislative	Independent governance in conjunction with bureaucratic staff	Promulgate public policies or regulations; make decisions bind-ing on city agencies or members of the public	Make decisions about legal standards, write ordinances with city council approval; city council and/or mayor retains veto power	12
Advisory	No self-governance	Fact-finding and advisory	Advisory and fact-finding power only; board has no indepen-dent policy-making power; any decision requires council or mayoral actions	48

documents as board descriptions, city charters, legislation, and mission statements. For example, a youth board's description of "acts as an advisory board" with no reference to policy implementation, budgeting, independence, or judicial powers places this board into the advisory category. Or a design review board that "establish[es] procedures and regulations to preserve existing areas of natural beauty, cultural importance and . . . harmonious with surrounding developments" is quasi-legislative. A discussion of each type of board is included in Table 5.1.

> **Autonomous boards:** State governments, regional authorities, and cities all create autonomous boards. Examples often include authority over policy areas that require coordination across different local governments, such a regional transportation board or a mosquito control and vector board. But city-specific autonomous boards exert policymaking power in a variety of settings. For example, in Spokane, Washington, the East Sprague Business Improvement District provides a variety of services, including "clean & green, district beautification, branding & marketing, safety & security and administration," and has independent power to make decisions across those policy arenas.
>
> Autonomous boards operate as an independent administrative structure without oversight from the city council or mayor in making these decisions. Decisions from the boards are binding, including to city agencies and the public. In New Orleans, one of the most powerful boards is the Audubon Commission, which has the power to "direct the city of New Orleans to provide and appropriate funds for the maintenance, embellishment, and improvement of Audubon Park and to issue and sell bonds of the City of New Orleans."[4] While the mayor appoints members of the commission (with advice and consent of the city council), the commission operates as the governing body for an independent agency with a $25 million+ budget.
>
> **Quasi-judicial boards:** Quasi-judicial boards render decisions about the implementation of city ordinances, including making decisions about variances to ordinances.[5] This might include conducting hearings, gathering evidence, compelling testimony, and determining resolutions to issues such as zone variances, civil rights issues, and civil service. Decisions from these boards are usually binding, with appeal available only via the court system. Generally, any board that hears appeals, makes decisions about the rights and interests of the city, and renders binding judgments is considered a quasi-judicial board.

Administrative boards: Administrative boards engage in decision-making about the implementation and evaluation of city programs, including the allocation of municipal funds. Any board that engages in the allocation of city resources (by the board either making decisions itself or approving decisions made by a bureaucratic employee) via a direct byline in the city budget is a de facto administrative agency.

Quasi-legislative boards: Quasi-legislative powers are common among strong boards, including many planning and zoning boards that set independent policy in the city around land use. In Alhambra, California, the Design Review Board "has design control over all commercial, industrial and residential planned development."[6] As the board actively sets policy for the city, I consider it a quasi-legislative board. Most quasi-legislative boards act in consultation with a member of the city's bureaucracy or have a requirement for a representative from the city's bureaucracy or an elected official to sit on the board. Cities retain some form of veto power over the decisions made by legislative boards, but city approval is not always required for the board to create policy.

Advisory boards: Advisory boards engage in research and fact-finding and do not engage in self-governance. They have no independent policymaking power, but instead can make recommendations to the city council. Advisory boards can be assigned professional bureaucratic staff to assist in insuring that the board complies with open meetings and records laws, receives the information it needs to make recommendations, and provides guidance. However, unlike on quasi-legislative boards, members of the city staff are rarely members of these advisory boards themselves. I consider any board an advisory board that is described as "advisory," as one that "studies and makes recommendations." For example, Richmond describes advisory boards as those whose "purpose is to provide advice and comment to the Council, the Mayor or any City agency."[7]

To evaluate my expectations to predict the amount of power that a board will have, I examine their forms of power based solely on their issue area classification into weak boards and strong boards. I estimate a multilevel model (with clustered errors at the city level), predicting each type of board with weak and strong boards as the central controls in the model, and I present post hoc predicted probabilities in Figure 5.2. Consistent with my expectations, weak boards are far more likely to be simply advisory, with

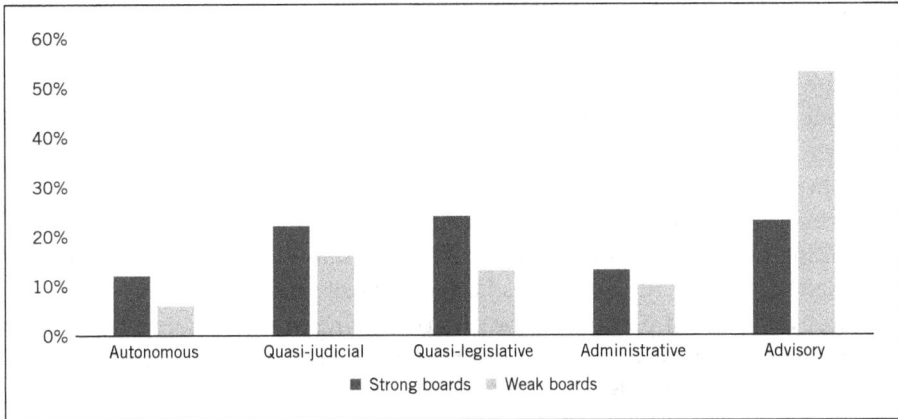

Figure 5.2 Strong and Weak Boards and Allocated Authority. *Note: Share of boards with these powers. Post hoc predicted probabilities from a model estimating the power of a board, with city-level clustered standard errors.*

more than half of weak boards holding only information-provision authority, compared to less than a quarter of strong boards ($p < .01$). And strong boards are more likely to be an autonomous board ($p < .01$) and to be quasi-judicial ($p < .05$) and quasi-legislative ($p < .05$); there is no difference in the likelihood that a board will have administrative powers.

Design for Effective Decision-Making

But the powers allocated to a board are not the entirety of determining a board's ability and capacity for policymaking. In this section, I argue that the two primary governance structures of boards (majority rule and consensus) mean that the size of the board and the membership and homogeneity of the board's members and mechanism of agenda control all directly and indirectly affect the ability of the board to make decisions. Decisions about the size, membership, and agenda control can be seemingly innocuous. What does it matter if a board has 7 members or 11 members? Why would it matter if 20 percent of one board's seats are reserved for members of the development community? And what does it matter if a city staff member is a member of the board versus assigned as a liaison. These decisions about institutional membership shape the board's ability to make decisions, thus further increasing the power of strong boards—which can quickly make decisions—and reducing the power of weak boards.

Rules matter. Rules about decision-making in political bodies are particularly important. Boards and commissions use two broad patterns of rule-making: consensus and majority rules. Consensus decision-making brings "a significant range of individuals chosen because they represent those with differing stakes in a problem" with a focus on ensuring "that the mode of discourse is one where all are heard and all concepts are taken seriously" (Gregory 1998, 461). Consensus decision-making structures emerged from the CAC and CDC mandates of the 1960s and 1970s. Over time, cities have come to rely on this as a "key element" (Salsich 2000, 715) of the decision-making process for many boards and commissions. Other boards are governed by majority rule structures.[8] Under majority rule, where decisions are met by 50 percent plus one of the group agreeing to the outcome, agenda-setting, majority size, and alignment of preferences all shape the ability to make decisions. The ability of a group to find consensus or come to a majority decision is dependent on several factors: the size of the group, the homogeneity of the group, and the presence and skill of a facilitator.

Board Size

Scholars have long argued that the size of legislative bodies represents a key decision that determines the efficacy and efficiency of the body (Olson 1965; Buchanan and Tullock 1962; Chamberlin 1974).[9] I draw on this research to argue that cities will design strong boards to be smaller with less cumbersome organizational structures, while weak boards will be larger and less agile. As Olson notes, "Unless the number of individuals in a group is quite small, or unless there is coercion or some other special device to make individuals act in their common interest," there is little to push a group "to achieve their common or group interests" (1965, 2).

Studies in decision-making show that smaller-sized groups are more likely to be able to come to both a majority decision and a consensus decision. As groups of decision-makers grow in size, the probability of conflict-free decision-making decreases and the length of time to generate a consensus decision extends (Olson 1965; Crain and Tollison 1977). While group size shapes the ability to come to a decision across both sets of decision-making structures, stricter decision-making rules (like those found under consensus requirements) will have higher "decision costs" (Crain and Tollison 1977, 240). Within the context of legislative size, the recommendation is thus to have a smaller body when adopting stricter rules, in order to reduce decision costs. Again, Olson notes the challenge of larger groups: "The larger the group, the farther it will fall short of providing an optimal supply of any collective good, and the less likely that it will act to obtain even a minimum amount of such a good. In short, the larger the group, the less it will further its common interests" (1965, 36).

Under the assumption that all institutions are designed to produce decisions at some optimal rate, smaller bodies should have stricter decision rules, while larger bodies should feature less strict rules. But if the institutional goal is not to reduce decision costs, but instead to create structures that will make the decisions of some institutions less costly while other bodies' decisions become more costly, then the incentives change. If cities are interested in creating boards (i.e., strong boards) that will be able to make decisions easily and quickly, the cities should endow those boards with smaller memberships and less strict decision rules. Other boards, created with the intent to promote deliberation while stymying decision-making (i.e., weak boards), might by designed with features that would reduce the likelihood of decisions: a larger size board with more strict decision rules.

I find evidence of these differences across weak and strong boards in cities. Strong boards' average membership size is 7.2 members (median = 7), while weak boards' average size is 12.3 (median = 15). Consensus rules are more common in weak boards: 22 percent of weak boards report using some form of consensus rule-making, compared to just 7 percent of strong boards.

But what do these differences actually mean for decision-making? Both weak boards and strong boards consider issues where there is near universal agreement and where there is strong disagreement. How might the size and decision rules shape the likelihood that the board will come to a decision? To provide examples of how size and decision rules might shape decisions about important local issues, I use the Kinder Houston Area Survey[10] to select four issues, overseen in some way by an appointed board, which vary in their level of agreement in public opinion (see Table 5.2).

As an illustration of the ways that board size and rules might affect the ability of a board to make decisions, I evaluate the probability that the group could come to a decision using a binomial distribution.[11] I examine both majority (defined at agreement of 50 percent+1 of members) and consensus (defined as an outcome where everyone supports an outcome) decision-making. I start with two issues where 9 of 10 people agree on the issue—implementing a general plan to help with issues of growth and creating a mass transit system—and calculate the odds that the group will be able to make a consensus (light gray line in Figure 5.3) or majority decision (dark gray line in Figure 5.3) across the number of people on the board. In essence, I ask this: Can a group agree, given the number of people in the group, the rules of decision-making, and the overlying distribution of preferences?

In the right pane of Figure 5.3, the probability that a group will come to a decision on an issue with very high levels of agreement is highly dependent on both the size of the group and the decision rules. For a board with seven members and majority rules (the average size of a strong board), there is

TABLE 5.2. LEVELS OF AGREEMENT ON ISSUES HANDLED BY BOARDS		
Issue	Public views	Board
Unlike some cities, Houston does not have a general or comprehensive plan for future growth. Would you strongly favor, somewhat favor, somewhat oppose, or strongly oppose creating a General Plan to guide Houston's future growth?	89.8% of the public "some-what" or "strongly" favors developing a comprehensive plan	Planning Commission (strong)
How important for the future success of the Houston area is the development of a much improved mass transit system? Would you say: very important, somewhat important, or not important?	89.0% of the public says it is "somewhat" or "very" important	Metropolitan Transit Authority (weak)
Do you think that the increasing ethnic diversity in Houston will eventually become a source of great strength for the region; or: a growing problem for the region?	68.6% of the public says it is a source of strength	Mayor's Advisory Council of New Americans (weak)
Which of these statements comes closer to your own view?—We need better land-use planning to guide development in the Houston area; or: People and businesses should be free to build wherever they want	74.2% of the public selected "better land-use planning"	Houston Industrial Development Corporation (strong)

Note: Data from the Houston Kinder Survey.

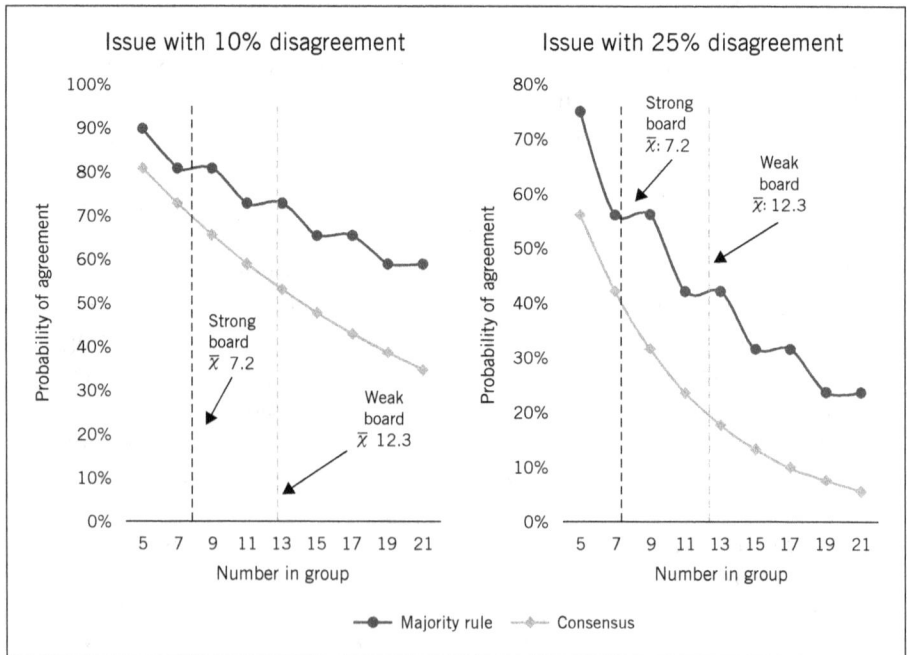

Figure 5.3 Majority and Consensus by Level of Agreement.

81 percent probability that the body could come to a decision on an issue with high levels of agreement. In comparison, a board with 12 members (the average weak board) and consensus rules has just a 55 percent possibility of coming to a decision, even as the issue has high levels of agreement, simply because of the odds on an increasing number of individuals on the board who hold a different opinion. As the level of agreement declines on the issue, the probability of coming to a decision also declines. In the left pane, an issue where only a quarter of the public disagrees (like over whether the city needs better land use planning), a board with strong board characteristics has a 56 percent chance of agreement, compared to just 20 percent likelihood for a board with 12 members and a consensus design.

The difference in sizes and voting rules for weak and strong boards is by design and is rooted in a long history of cities creating large, powerless boards when pressured to expand opportunities for Black and poor residents to serve on boards during the civil rights era. For example, when cities created boards and commissions to oversee the implementation of various aspects of the Model Cities Program in the late 1960s and early 1970s, cities often created smaller boards dominated by white residents and those with political power. Pressure from the federal government to include poor and Black residents rarely led to cities replacing white or rich board members with poor or Black representatives (Hallman 1974; Bachrach and Baratz 1970; Strange 1972b). Instead, the cities reduced the power of the board as they increased the membership.

Examples also abound of cities creating larger, powerless boards during this era. In New Orleans, the Community Improvement Agency (CIA), a powerful board dominated by real estate developers, stayed at seven members for the board's entire lifespan. But the half-dozen Neighborhood Advisory Committees, which were supposed to collect feedback for the CIA and serve as the representative bodies for poor and Black residents, ranged in size from 7 to 40 members.[12] Boston's Model Neighborhood Board featured 18 members, 3 from each of six neighborhoods.[13] The "elaborate structure" of the board resulted in a body contemporaries concluded "was not too effective" (Hallman 1974, 137).

Another common trend was that cities would simply add seats (and remove power) as pressure increased (often from the federal government) to democratize the membership of these boards. In New Orleans, the Model City Advisory Committee started at 7 members and then grew to 13 as HUD and Black New Orleanians pressured the city to include representatives from community organizations. Similarly, in Baltimore, "direct pressure from Washington" forced the city council to increase the size of the Community Action Committee board to 15 and then to form a complementary committee of 35 members. As Bachrach and Baratz note, "Whether a commission

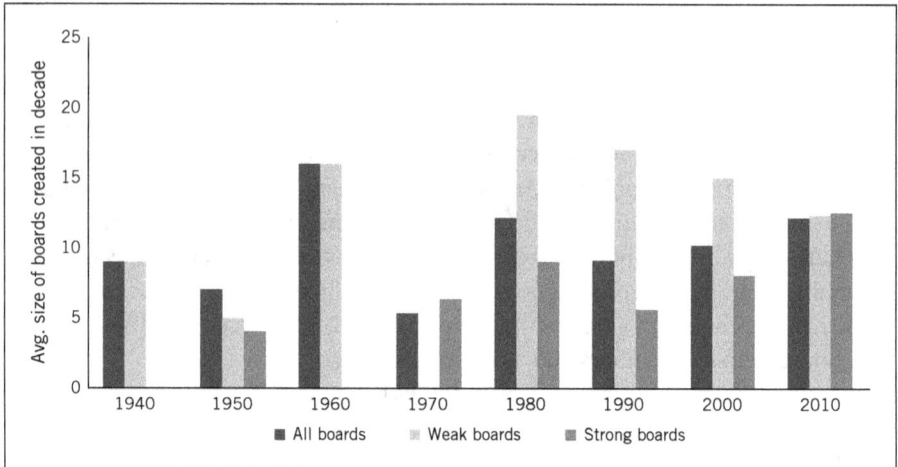

Figure 5.4 Decade of Creation and Board Size, Richmond, Virginia.

of 35 could operate effectively is open to question" (1970, 195). In Los Angeles, the Commission for Community and Family Services, which has been in operation since 1902, moved from 5 members in 1955 to 13 members by 1961. The move coincides with pressure to add poor and Black members to the board's membership. In each of these circumstances, the power of the board to set policy and spend money was removed as the size of the board increased.

One possibility is that differences in size are an artifact of the year that a board was created; earlier boards might simply have been smaller, while later boards were larger. But large weak boards continue to persist in many cities after the 1960s. Social service and identity boards created in the 2000s are large, incumbered organizations with complex decision-making rules. The Sanford "Sandy" Krasnoff[14] New Orleans Criminal Justice Council, created in 2005, has 24 "criminal justice stakeholders" with the goal of "diligent cooperation" to facilitate coordination on criminal justice issues. Similarly, the Los Angeles Mobile Home Park Task Force has 15 members. In comparison, two development-oriented boards created by Los Angeles around this time have 5 and 7 members. In Richmond,[15] the size of boards has not increased over time. Strong boards created in the last several decades have been smaller than weak boards created during that same time; for example, the average size of strong boards created in the last 30 years is 8.7 members, compared to 14.7 for weak boards (see Figure 5.4).

Membership Requirements

Beyond controlling boards through membership, cities accelerate power in strong boards and limit power in weak boards via requirements about who gets to serve. While size and rules shape the ability of a group to make decisions, the diversity of the personal and professional characteristics, experiences, and backgrounds of the members of that body also matters (Kanthak and Krause 2010; Hero 2000; Crowder-Meyer, Gadarian, and Trounstine 2015). There are many reasons to want more diversity in a body: the diversity of a group changes policy outcomes (Clayton, Josefsson, and Wang 2017; Holman 2015) and shapes the quality of decision-making (Barnes 2016); it also improves the public's trust and belief in democracy (Barnes and Saxton 2019; Dovi 2002). These core ideas formed the federal requirement discussed in Chapters 3 and 4 that "the poor sit on policy making boards with elected officials" (Washnis 1973, 14–15); the requirement was expected to produce better policies that more accurately addressed the problems of the urban poor (Lynn and Kartez 1995; Washnis 1973).

But heterogeneity also slows down the process of decision-making (Calvo and Sagarzazu 2011; Pachón and Johnson 2016), particularly when membership reflects diversity of opinions over controversial issues (Kanthak and Krause 2010). For example, when the ideological distance increases across political institutions, the speed of decision-making declines (Klüver and Sagarzazu 2013) and disparate interests can lead to "destructive levels of conflict" (Witt 1999, 62).

Interviews with weak and strong board members echo these factors: when asked about agreement and conflict on their board, a weak board member noted that "there are just so many voices in the room. It is hard to agree on anything, even if we, you know, actually do agree on a lot of stuff." Another board told me that "the other members of the board—I don't disagree with them—we just have different ideas about things like execution or funding." Strong board members, in comparison, note that their boards "are a really well functioning unit." In discussing a conflict about offering incentives for a minor league ballpark development, another board member noted the disagreement but said that "in the end, we all got on the same team. The [city name] team. We made it happen. I think everyone was happy with what we decided."[16]

Diverse bodies produce better outcomes, but they do so less quickly and are less likely to come to a decision at all, while homogenous bodies produce lower-quality outcomes but they do so more quickly and with a greater likelihood of coming to a decision. The strong and weak board structure demonstrates this trade-off, where cities design strong boards to be homogeneous and effective (and to produce lower-quality outcomes) and design weak boards to be heterogenous and ineffective (but, theoretically, to produce better outcomes). One path to ensure that strong boards are homogeneous and weak boards are heterogenous is via membership requirements. Boards vary within and across cities in their membership requirements, both in whether there are requirements at all (or not) and in the types of requirements. For example, the New Orleans Board of Trustees of the Municipal Employee's Retirement System has five members, including the city's director of finance and director of personnel, a member selected by the employees of the city, and retirees of the city. A final member is appointed by the mayor without formal requirements for the seat.

Weak boards are less likely to have requirements for seats at all. Across large cities, 19 percent of seats on weak boards have membership requirements, compared to 39 percent of seats on strong boards. When modeled in a regression, the strong board variable is significant and positive ($p < .01$). In short, strong boards have a higher share of seats with specific requirements than weak boards do. This also applies in case study cities: 26 percent of the seats on weak boards in Richmond are reserved seats, compared to 80 percent of seats on strong boards.

But it is not just general requirements: the specific characteristics required for a board seat also vary across weak and strong boards.[17] For each board with reported membership requirements, I calculate the share of seats required to be filled by city staff, members of the development community, citizens with a particular identity, members of the nonprofit community, and elected officials (see the Section II introduction for a discussion of each of these categories).[18] I estimate the probability that a board has requirements of membership in one of these categories and present these values in Table 5.3.[19]

Strong boards are significantly more likely to require members to be city employees, to have a business background, or to be elected officials, while weak boards are more likely to have identity membership requirements and are slightly more likely to have nonprofit requirements.

The ability of a political body to make decisions (and high-quality decisions) is not just a function of who sits on the board but also a function of the overall diversity of that board. I create a single probability term as a diversity measure for each board (Sullivan 1973; Barnes and Holman 2020b, 2018) that accounts for the probability that any two seats (if you randomly

TABLE 5.3. STRONG BOARDS ARE MORE LIKELY TO REQUIRE MEMBERSHIP FROM CITY EMPLOYEES, ELECTED OFFICIALS, AND PEOPLE WITH A DEVELOPMENT BACKGROUND

	City employees	Identity	Development	Nonprofit	Elected officials
Strong boards	0.01*	−0.06*	0.04*	−0.01*	0.01*
	(0.00)	(0.00)	(0.00)	(0.00)	(0.00)
Observations	23,349	23,349	23,349	23,349	23,349

Note: Ordinary least squares regression with clustered errors at the city level. The dependent variable is the share of seats on a board in a given city with a requirement. The model contains boards only from cities where the city reported seat requirements for at least one board. * = p<.05.

drew them from a board) would have different requirements. The diversity measure means that higher (lower) measures indicate more (less) diversity on each board vis-à-vis the level of diversity overall and in other boards. The overall diversity index of .32 can be interpreted as a 32 percent chance that two board seats, drawn randomly from a board's members, would have different membership requirements. Overall, strong boards have a lower level of professional diversity (median .26) than do weak boards (median .35); the difference indicates that the odds of drawing two seats from any board with different requirements are much higher when selecting from weak boards than from strong boards.

The New Orleans Tourism Marketing Corporation, which "fosters, develops, promotes and maintains the hospitality and tourism industry of the City of New Orleans," has 15 members, including the 3 city council members (20% of the board) and 11 members who are required to have some kind of development background (73%),[20] producing a diversity score of .42, or a 42 percent chance that if you randomly selected two seats on the board, they would be from different backgrounds. In comparison, the Sanford "Sandy" Krasnoff New Orleans Criminal Justice Council, which "advises the Mayor and City Council on policy matters regarding crime control and criminal justice activities and coordinates the administration of criminal and juvenile justice for the city," has 25 members. Of those seats, 16 percent are designated for elected officials, 48 percent for city employees, 16 percent have social service requirements, 4 percent for each of the development and identity categories, and 12 percent for citizens at large.[21] The diversity score for seat requirements on this board is 70 percent, meaning that if you randomly selected two seats from the board, the odds that they will be of different backgrounds are seven in ten.[22]

Given the importance of group homogeneity in shaping decision-making and given that occupational backgrounds shape policy preferences (Barnes, Beall, and Holman 2021; Barnes and Holman 2020a; O'Grady 2019), these differences in diversity of requirements could shape the ability of a board to make decisions. I again apply probability calculations, as I did with Figure 5.3, asking this: If board diversity might indicate disagreement, then how would this shape the ability of members of that board to come to a decision? Figure 5.5 shows the pure probability of agreement for a board with 16 percent, 26 percent, 28 percent, and 35 percent diversity under majority rules (each value is the average and median diversity for strong and weak boards). While boards with low levels of diversity (26%, or the median for strong boards) have a high probability of agreement at smaller levels, the agreement declines as the board size increases. Boards with high levels of diversity (35%, or the median for weak boards) produce more disagreement (never exceeding 50%), with that disagreement increasing as the size of the board grows.

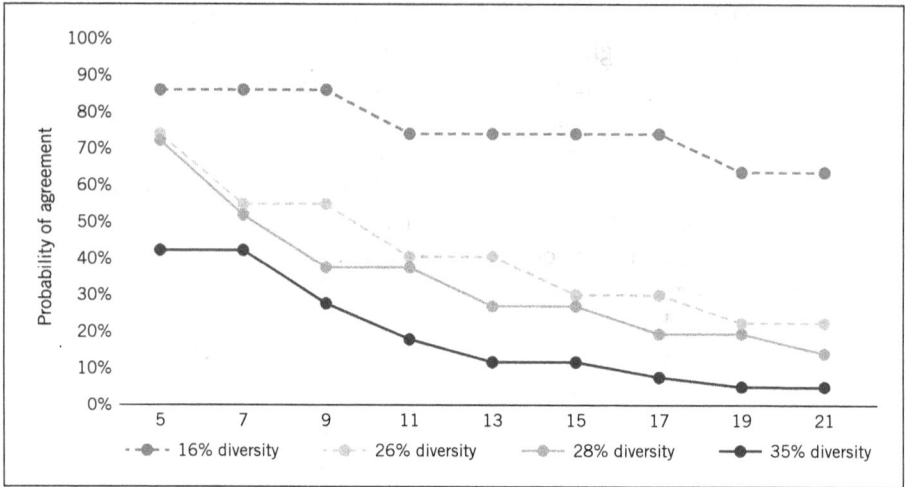

Figure 5.5 Probability of Agreement with Majority Rules by Board Diversity and Board Size.

Not all groups are equally likely to disagree with each other, which could shape the level of conflict on a board. For example, extensive research shows that elected officials pursue development projects with gusto and enthusiasm (Logan and Molotch 1987; Stone 1980, 1989; Schaffner, Rhodes, and Raja 2020; Trounstine 2008) and consider economic development the most important policy arena (Holman 2015; Einstein and Glick 2018; Einstein and Kogan 2016). Similarly, city staff assigned to a particular department often have preferences that align with that department; in essence, if you work in an economic development department, you prefer more development (Wolman and Spitzley 1996; McCabe et al. 2008). As a result, a board that is 20 percent city staff, 20 percent elected officials, and 20 percent development could be grouped together with 60 percent of the board's membership favoring development. Similarly, nonprofit leaders and those with an identity seat would often be oriented in the same direction. For example, someone who works in a disability-rights organization and someone with a disability might pursue similar outcomes.

If I collapse development, city staff, and elected officials into a single category, and nonprofit and identity requirements into another, the diversity of strong boards decreases to 0.16 and weak boards to 0.28. As shown in Figure 5.5, this dramatically increases the probability of decision-making in strong boards, across the size of the board. In comparison, the diversity of weak board membership increases slightly, but is still low and drops below 50 percent after the board size exceeds seven members.

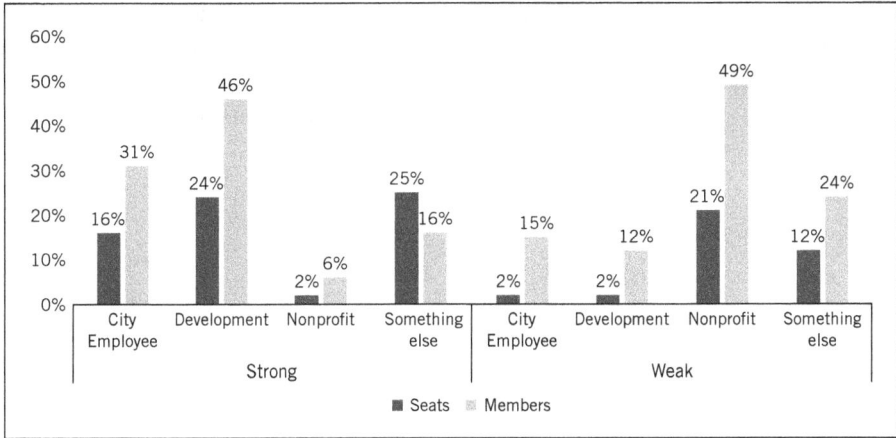

Figure 5.6 All Board Members and Their Backgrounds in Richmond, Virginia.

Membership requirements matter, and who is actually appointed to these boards exacerbates these patterns. To evaluate the backgrounds of people who actually serve on these boards, I downloaded the applications for every person that sat on a board in Richmond, Virginia, in 2018 and coded their backgrounds into four categories: the development sector (contractors, architects, engineers, business owners, and developers), city employees, social services and education, or something else.[23] Figure 5.6 compares the formal requirements ("seats," dark gray bars) and actual backgrounds of members ("members," light gray bars). Strong boards' membership requirements set aside a quarter of seats for development-related backgrounds, but the actual membership of these committees is nearly one-in-two with development backgrounds. A similar share of weak board members come from nonprofit backgrounds, even as the requirements apply to only 20 percent of seats. It is not just the membership requirements that drive who sits on boards but also reinforcing patterns of recruitment and networks.

Institutional Rules and Appointed Boards

Institutional differences and practical considerations produce very different decision-making environments for weak and strong boards. For weak boards, the overarching picture is one of benign neglect of dysfunctional organizations where deliberation among a diverse membership is prioritized over decision-making. The boards are constructed to be large, diverse bodies with little agenda control. As a result, the members of these boards often just do not attend meetings (the average attendance rate in Richmond for weak boards is 67 percent, and boards often fail to meet quorum) and the boards produce very little policy. Strong boards, in comparison, are agile decision-making organizations with homogenous memberships. As a result, strong boards regularly make a wide set of decisions, while weak boards simply . . . do not.

6

Descriptive Representation and
Board Appointments

In the middle of Uptown[1] New Orleans, Audubon Park, a 315-acre public park, provides a golf course, playgrounds, a walking and biking path, and a bird sanctuary. Audubon Park is managed by the Audubon Commission, an appointed board that acts as landlord for the organization that runs New Orleans's fanciest public park and the city's zoo and aquarium, and controls a variety of pieces of public land. The Audubon Commission's 24-person board reads like a "who's who" of New Orleans: from local business leaders to celebrities to philanthropists, an appointment to the Audubon Commission has been and still is a key tool for mayors to reward supporters and cultivate connections with the powerful in the city.

The Audubon Commission's membership represents the factors that produce varying memberships across boards: members of the community express differing demands for the types of boards that they want to sit on, and elected officials strategically use board appointments to reward followers and supporters or to cultivate relationships with those who have resources. Demands from race, gender, and race and gender groups for descriptive representation are unevenly distributed in any city or for any board; for example, women are more likely to be interested in a status-of-women board than are men, and this difference may be particularly stark in some cities where a culture of women's organizing is robust compared to other cities. As a result, weak and strong boards have uneven distributions of race and gender and economic and political resources of members.

The Audubon Commission is a board whose positions are in high demand. Mayors regularly appoint members of old New Orleans families and the newly wealthy to the Audubon Commission. Historically, mayors focused on whether an individual could make "personal gifts" to the park or support the mayor politically as a precursor to appointment. In a note in 1960 urging the mayor to appoint one John Carrier to the Audubon Commission, a state legislator noted Mr. Carrier's connection to a wealthy family with international connections and resources.[2] In his response, mayor deLesseps Story "Chep" Morrison noted that he would "consider" the candidate but said, "We ought to advance someone who will help us. Carrier has never lifted a finger for us."[3] The membership of the commission also reflects interest in the board: archival correspondence is filled with rich white people asking for appointments to the Audubon Commission, noting that they live on or near the park, that their parents have served on the board, or that they have donated money or in-kind goods.[4]

As of this writing, the commission includes individuals like Gail Benson (who owns the Saints, the Pelicans, and a host of other local businesses and is New Orleans's richest resident); lawyers, doctors, and financial analysts; as well as local philanthropists and those involved in education and environmental advocacy. More than 80 percent of the members have donated funds to one of the current mayor's political campaigns, compared to 26 percent of board members in the city and less than 1 percent of the city's overall population. Like on other boards in New Orleans, just under half (45%) of the board members are women and 36 percent are Black (in comparison, the city of New Orleans's population is 59 percent Black).

How did this board—and other boards—end up with the membership that it has? This chapter examines why some people are appointed to some boards and other people are appointed to others. Understanding heterogenous board power helps explain why some appointments work in some ways and others work in other ways. To present this argument, I offer a contemporary evaluation of who sits on boards across large cities and a deep examination of board appointments in New Orleans, considering the role that race, gender, race and gender, and political power play in shaping who sits on which boards. I then use data from New Orleans to show that political donors are overrepresented in political office, particularly donors to the mayor's campaigns, suggesting that connections to political power directly shape who can access political power via boards.

Who Sits on Boards?

In the United States, power is concentrated in the hands of elites, predominantly white men from elite backgrounds. White, rich men dominate political office (Bratton 2006; Brown 2014; Barnes, Beall, and Holman 2021; Holman 2017; Crowder-Meyer and Lauderdale 2014), corporate boardrooms (Terjesen, Sealy, and Singh 2009; Zhang 2012), and positions of social and economic power. These patterns are true in local politics as well, with women holding less than a quarter of mayoral and city council positions (Holman 2017; Warshaw 2019) and county commissioners (McBrayer and Williams 2022). More white representatives hold local elected office than their share of the urban population (Juenke and Shah 2015; Kirkland 2020; Schaffner, Rhodes, and Raja 2020).

Local board membership is a departure from these patterns; boards have higher levels of representation of women and people of color than is found in elected office in the United States. Women make up 43 percent of the board members and residents of color hold 35 percent of seats in the data I have collected. Women of color, who have been systematically denied access to power for all of the country's political history (Brown 2014; Cargile 2015; Silva and Skulley 2019), make up 16 percent of board members, which is a far higher share than women of color hold in any elected political office (Brown 2014; Brown and Gershon 2023). White men are still overrepresented on boards in comparison to their share of the population, but the number is much lower than white men's overrepresentation in elected office at any level in the United States.

But, as one might expect, the representation of board members by gender and race is not evenly distributed across weak and strong boards. Men, white people, and especially white men are more likely to sit on strong boards, while women, people of color, and women of color hold a larger share of seats on weak boards. These patterns hold, even when controlling for city characteristics and local politics.

Descriptive Representation
on Boards over Time

One of the great challenges of democracies in the twenty-first century has been designing ways to increase the diversity of those who hold political power (D. Z. O'Brien 2015; Heath, Schwindt-Bayer, and Taylor-Robinson 2005; Karpowitz, Monson, and Preece 2017). Disrupting the status quo and changing who has power has proven to be a remarkably difficult task, often requiring broad institutional changes, such as gender quotas (Barnes and Holman 2020b; Barnes 2016; Preece 2016). Board appointments are seen as a tool for training future elected leaders (Sanbonmatsu 2006; Sanbonmatsu and Dittmar 2020; Holman, Iyer, and Wolbrecht 2023), and local elections regularly feature individuals who have previously sat on appointed boards and commissions (Holman and Lay 2021; Benjamin 2023).

Across time in the United States, women and people of color have recognized that exclusion from formal means of power like board appointments means that their group is also excluded from important policy decisions. White women's activism around board membership emerged from the "voluntary, locally based moral and social reform efforts" in a broad set of cities in the early 1900s (P. Baker 1984, 634–35; Holman 2015; Wolbrecht 2000; Holman, Iyer, and Wolbrecht 2022). In many cities, activism on issues like children's services, education, hygiene, and housing led to the appointments of the women to boards, albeit at low levels and with appointments entirely constrained to these boards—women did not move from the hospital oversight committee to the planning board, nor did they then hold elected office after their time in an appointed position (Holman, Iyer, and Wolbrecht 2022).

Access to board appointments was exclusively limited to white residents until the mid-1900s. As I discuss in Chapter 2, women's activism in the early 1900s directly contributed to the creation of boards and to expansions of services by cities via policy set by boards, as well as the preservation of whiteness in board power. Throughout the first half of the 1900s, women's representation on boards grew—albeit slowly. Figure 6.1 provides the share of women and white appointees in Los Angeles from 1900 to 2020. Three events in the figure also influenced who was appointed: women's right to vote once California granted of women's suffrage in 1912; the passage of the Voting Rights Act of 1965 in Congress that codified a variety of protections for political participation for people of color, women, and women of color in the

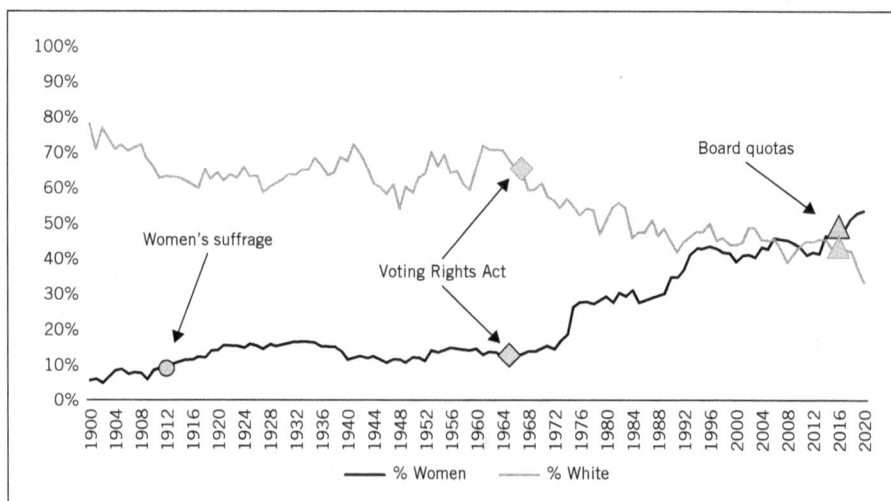

Figure 6.1 Share of Women and White Members on Boards in Los Angeles over Time.

United States; and mayor Eric Garcetti's implementation of gender, race, ethnicity, and neighborhood quotas for appointed boards in the city in 2017.

The civil rights movement "aimed to force city governments to end their massive, blatant, common, and virtually complete discrimination and exclusion" of Black residents (Browning, Marshall, and Tabb 1984, 5). Increasing access to the ballot for racial minorities represented a key win by the civil rights movement, primarily through the passage and enforcement of the Voting Rights Act of 1965. Because of increased access to suffrage, the Black electorate increased in share and power in most large cities in the United States. In New Orleans, for example, the Black electorate went from 17.5 percent in 1964 to 25.2 percent in 1966 and to over 35 percent by 1970. The increased political power of Black voters in New Orleans led directly to the appointment of Black representatives to key commissions, as I discuss in Chapter 4. Black organizations in New Orleans pressure on Mayor Schiro for the appointments in exchange for electoral mobilization led to the appointment of two Black members to the Community Investment Agency in 1968 (Germany 2011). Women's activism in the 1970s and 1980s also led to the creation of a variety of commissions on the status of women (SOW boards) and the increased appointment of women to boards and commissions (D. Stewart 1980; Flammang 1985).

Political incorporation at the elite level, through the election of Black and Latino representatives to office at the local level, "has been at the center of the struggle for political equality" for decades (Browning, Marshall, and Tabb 1984, 8). In the late 1950s, local elected representatives were exclusively white. By 1975, "more than 3500 blacks held elective office across the country, three times the number six years earlier" and a marked increase from a decade before, when no large city had a Black mayor (Cole 1976, 4). Indeed, by the late 197, Black mayors held office in large cities across the United States, from Atlanta to Cleveland to Los Angeles to New Orleans to Richmond to Washington, DC. What Browning, Marshall, and Tabb (1984, 8) call an "astonishing achievement" reshaped the landscape of who held formal power in cities.

These Black and Hispanic leaders were also often the product of efforts at political incorporation on appointed boards. The demand for boards and appointments via the 1960s federal programs led to minority leadership development and incorporation: leaders of community organizations that were started via Model Cities harnessed their community connections, and a base of Black voters eager to vote for Black candidates to gain political office. Newark's first Black mayor, Kenneth Gibson, gained political experience in a community action program, Boston's first Black city council member was first selected to represent his neighborhood on the Model Cities Board, and similar paths to office were seen among the first Blacks and Latinos elected to office in New Haven, Connecticut, Durham, North Carolina, and Oakland, California (Piven and Cloward 1971; Strange 1972a; Browning, Marshall, and Tabb 1984). In New Orleans, urban renewal "created new channels for black power" and created opportunities for several Black leaders to seek election (Germany 2011, 195).[5] Similarly, women elected as the first woman mayor in several cities had previously served as members of appointed boards and commissions (Flammang 1985; Merritt 1977; MacManus 1992, 1981; Mezey 1978).

The share of women on boards in Los Angeles also reflects broader changes in women's status in society across time: here we see a dramatic uptick in women's appointments to boards that directly corresponds with women's broader entrance into the workforce, particularly college-educated white women. In this time period, we also see the second wave of feminism engage in a concerted campaign to use legal tools (including the Voting Rights Act) to remove de jure roadblocks. By 1970, there were more than 20 chapters of the National Organization for Women, and women's engagement on boards and commissions often focused on efforts to shift or remove city policy that explicitly discriminated against women. For example, in 1973, women organized to successfully pressure the city to create the Los Angeles Commission on Assaults; this board eventually ran the city's first rape crisis hotline (Spain 2016, 63). In 1975, the city also created the LA City Commission on the Status of Women; one of the tasks assigned to this commission was to evaluate the share of women on boards, resulting in an increase in women on many boards that had not previously had a large share of women members.

In 2015, Los Angeles mayor Eric Garcetti requested that the Commission on the Status of Women create a report to guide the city's efforts to increase gender parity; one of the areas where the commission identified clear opportunities for change was gender parity on appointed boards. As a result, Mayor Garcetti issued an executive order in 2017 requiring gender, race, ethnicity, and neighborhood balance on appointed boards and commissions. By 2023, the mayor's quota had succeeded: women currently hold more than half of board seats, and race and ethnicity distributions look very similar to the city's population more generally. Yet, these measures still lead to the segregation of women, people of color, and women of color onto weak boards, even with the quota in place.

Gender, Race, and Board Membership Today

Today, women and people of color hold large numbers of positions on appointed boards, especially as compared to their representation in elected office. Women hold just over 45 percent of board positions, with Black (22%), Latino (18%), and Asian (5%) community members holding large sets of seats. But these values vary enormously both across cities and within a giv-

	Board members (%)	New Orleans population (%)	Difference (%)
TABLE 6.1. WHITE PEOPLE AND MEN ARE OVERREPRESENTED ON NEW ORLEANS BOARDS			
Women	43	53	–10
White	50	33	16
Black	37	59	–22
Latino	8	6	3
Asian	5	3	2
White men	30	17	13
Women of color	23	37	–14

Note: Negative values in the "Difference" category indicate that the group is underrepresented compared to their population share; positive values indicate that the group is overrepresented.

en city; for example, women range from holding zero to 100 percent of board positions within in a single city, and Black community members make up between 2 percent and 48 percent of boards across cities.

Some of the variation (particularly for people of color) could be due to the uneven representation of these groups in city populations; for example, in the 100 largest cities in the United States, Black people make up between 3 percent and 80 percent of residents. For a better comparison, I provide the race and gender of representatives on boards in New Orleans compared to the city's overall population. Here, the patterns of white residents' overrepresentation continue (see Table 6.1). Black people make up nearly 60 percent of the population in New Orleans, but they hold 37 percent of board appointments. And while women of color are 37 percent of the population, they make up 23 percent of board appointments. White men are particularly overrepresented, making up just 17 percent of the New Orleans population but holding 30 percent of board seats. Interestingly, Latino and Asian representation exceeds their (smaller) share of the population in the city.

Appointments to Weak and Strong Boards

The distribution of women, residents of color, and women of color across the strong and weak boards is indicative of the general distribution of power in society. But just because a group can gain some access to positions on boards does not mean they necessarily have access to powerful appointments. The concentration of minority representation on some commissions (like the human relations commissions) and the absence of minority representation on "commissions dealing with economic issues like redevelopment and ports" were clear to the early scholars examining minority incorporation (Browning, Marshall, and Tabb 1984, 158). And scholars of gender and appointments have long noted that women's access to even highly prestigious positions, such as on a presidential cabinet, is often constrained to specific areas where women are seen to have strengths (Barnes and O'Brien 2018; Krook and O'Brien 2012). While descriptive representation is not a guarantee of substantive changes (Childs 2006), if men, white people, and white men are the majority of strong board members, this provides further evidence that these boards protect the status quo in cities.

In their evaluation of the minority appointments to commissions, Browning, Marshall, and Tabb (1984, 292) note the variance in the power of the commissions: that some "may be entirely symbolic; in others, they are key steps in the extension of control over city government and associated agencies." Marshall and colleagues acknowledge that the appointment of minority representation to commissions "where some real threat to other interests was involved" would usually be lower and "negotiated to mollify both sides" (Browning, Marshall, and Tabb 1984, 157). They also note, however, that "because minority representation on commissions did not typically involve minority control over decision-making, it appears that dominant coalitions used commission appointments to provide symbolic representation to minority groups" (158).

Extensive research on women's participation in appointed and elected positions at the state and national levels suggests that women are more likely to express interest in and be selected for positions in bodies associated with women's socialized strengths and concerns, such as on health commissions or school boards (Swers 2013; Crowder-Meyer, Gadarian, and Trounstine 2015; Deckman 2007; Holman 2017). These differences also appear in highly prestigious posts, such as cabinet ministries, where women are less likely to hold positions associated with men's socialized traits (Krook and O'Brien 2012; D. Z. O'Brien 2015; Schwindt-Bayer 2010; Armstrong et al. 2022). In the 1970s and 1980s, women also made up the majority of members of boards that addressed women's issues (Shurlle 1996; Sapiro 1983). Drawing from this research would suggest that women and people of color would be overrepresented on weak boards and less represented on strong boards.

To help readers understand gender, race, and gender and race differences in appointments to weak and strong boards, I predict the share of each board that are women, white, and women of color in a model that includes the board strength, characteristics of the mayor, and the city, including factors like the city's ideology and the mayor's partisanship. In Figure 6.2 I show these results: cities appoint women at high rates to weak boards, where women make up 48 percent of weak board members but 40 percent of strong board members. I see a flip of this pattern for white residents, who hold half of weak board positions, but 58 percent of strong board positions. And women of color hold one-in-five weak board positions but 15 percent of strong board

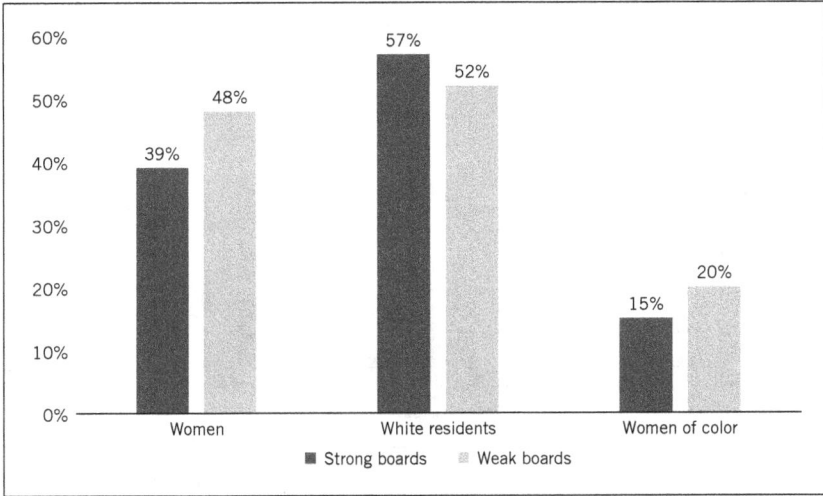

Figure 6.2 Women, White Residents, and Women of Color on Weak and Strong Boards. *Note: Results from post hoc calculations from multilevel models at the board level (N = 17,049) estimating the share of seats in each category by board strength. Controls for Large Cities Dataset versus California Cities Dataset, mayoral gender, race, partisanship, city income, population, and ideology.*

positions, consistent with expectations emerging from the literature the intersectional experiences of women of color (Brown et al. 2024).

Looking at the share of women, white people, Black people, white men, and women of color on boards in New Orleans shows similar patterns (see Figure 6.3). Women hold more than half of the weak board positions in the city; this share is equivalent to women holding positions at parity with their representation in the city's population. But women hold only 36 percent of strong board positions. These patterns continue for white residents, who hold more than half of positions on strong boards. Interestingly, I do not find large differences in strong board appointments and weak board appointments for Black residents of the city, who hold 38 percent of strong board positions and 34 percent of weak; both are below parity, as almost six of ten residents of the city are Black. Women of color, who make up 37 percent of the population, hold 28 percent of weak board positions and 19 percent of strong board positions.

Are there factors that are associated with the gender, race, and race and gender distribution of board members? The election of women and representatives of color to office has the potential to increase the diversity of board appointments. Given that weak board positions are not high-prestige positions, these positions may be the ideal circumstance where a mayor could

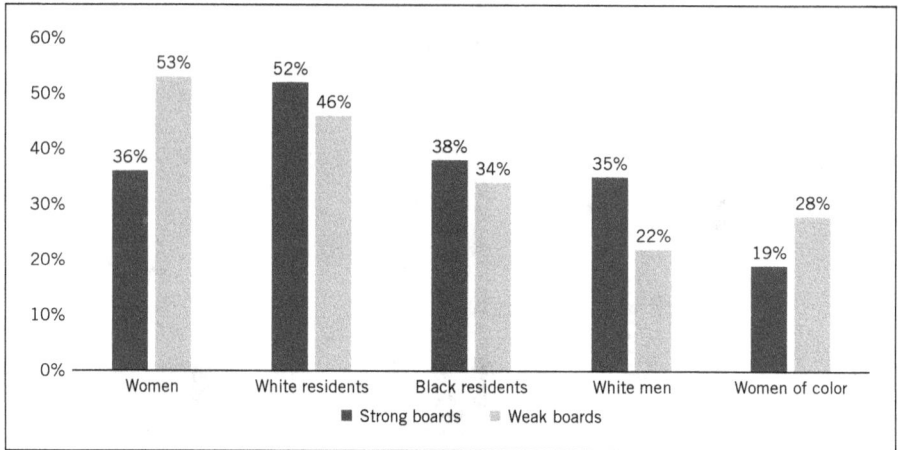

Figure 6.3 Gender, Race, and Board Representation in New Orleans.

strategically decide to appoint a more gender, racial, or ethnically diverse set of members.

The election of Black (and, to a lesser extent, Latino) mayors and city councilors in the United States in the 1970s and 1980s changed who sat on boards and commissions. Browning and colleagues found that the election of minority representations increased minority members of appointed boards with "substantial gains in minority representation on boards and commissions . . . in every city" with a Black or Latino mayor (1984, 157–58). In Richmond, Eleanor Sheppard, the city's first Black woman to serve on the city council (and the first Black representative on the council in the post–civil rights era), focused on appointments as a key tool for change in the city. When her fellow councilmembers elected her vice mayor and then mayor in the 1960s, she worked to appoint a majority of Black representatives to every commission in the city (Lacey 2017; Randolph and Tate 2003). She also promoted urban renewal through the creation of Richmond's Citizen Association, an organization focused on participatory democracy on neighborhood boards in the city.

During an interview with a woman mayor in North Carolina, I asked her about what did not get enough attention in her city. She immediately responded: "Appointments! Who serves on these commissions? They actually make all the important decisions." When I later asked her to describe one of her accomplishments during her time in office, she pointed to the policy change that boards now had to report the gender and race of all their members. "It is easy to ignore that we [women of color] don't have power if you don't have the numbers. But numbers—they give you leverage. You can say, um, nope, when some man comes to you and says they deserve to be on the economic development commission. Sorry, we already have a lot of you." Tracking board appointments in this city before and after the mayor's election revealed that she was successful: women's appointments increased from 32 percent to 48 percent and Black residents, who made up more than half of the city's population, went from 37 percent of appointments to 55 percent of board members.

The mayor's comments align with some scholarship on the impact of electing women to political positions; generally, scholars find that women in local office increase women's representation in the bureaucracy (Meier and Funk 2016; Saltzstein 1986) and women party leaders are more likely to recruit women to run for local office (Crowder-Meyer 2013). At the state and national levels, some scholars find that women's leadership is associated with higher levels of women's appointments (Jacob, Scherpereel, and Adams 2014), while others find little to no effect (Krook and O'Brien 2012; Barnes and O'Brien 2018; Armstrong et al. 2022). At the same time, the research that finds few effects effectively argues that the high prestige of these positions makes these appointments highly strategic, limiting women's ability to appoint more women.

Mayoral partisanship could also shape the descriptive representation on boards. The partisanship of mayors and city council members shapes a variety of policy outcomes, including the budgets of cities and counties (de Benedictis-Kessner and Warshaw 2016, 2020), but little work directly examines how partisanship in local office influences appointments. Partisanship at other levels of office shapes the diversity of appointees, with more women and people of color receiving judicial appointments from Democratic political officials (Solowiej, Martinek, and Brunell 2005). In Figure 6.4, I examine whether the race, gender, and partisanship of the mayor influence the gender, race, and gender and race of board members with controls for the city's population, income, race, and ideology. In this coefficient plot, a negative value indicates that that mayoral characteristic is associated with a decreased share of the group on the board, while a positive value indicates a positive effect; if the whiskers on the dots cross the dotted line at zero, the effect is not statistically significant.

White mayors appoint a higher share of white people to boards, but only to strong boards; these mayors are also less likely to appoint women of color to strong boards. In fact, the mayoral characteristics are mostly associated with changes in the composition of strong boards. Democratic mayors appoint fewer white people, more women, and more women of color to strong boards. I find little evidence that the gender of the mayor shapes the composition of the board membership. That mayoral characteristics do not seem to change the characteristics of weak board members suggests that mayors may not consider these kinds of appointments worth focusing on in questions of representation.

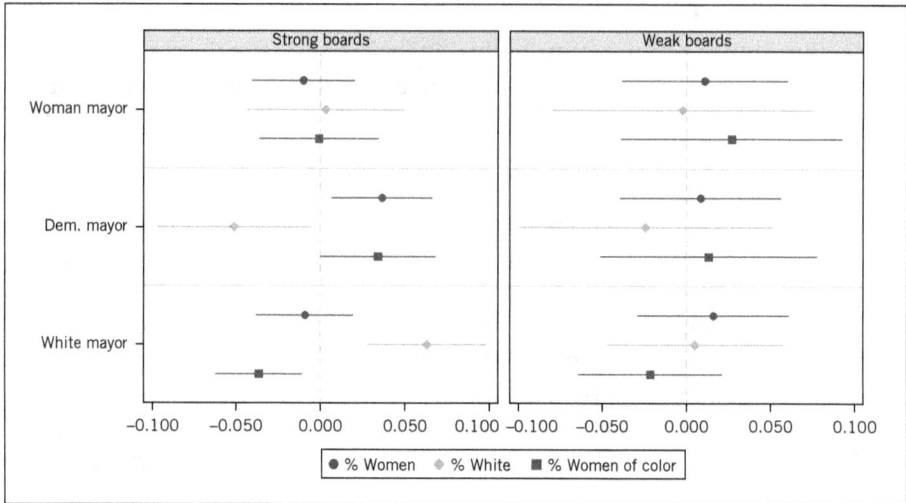

Figure 6.4 Share of Women, White People, and Women of Color on Strong and Weak Boards. *Note: Results from post hoc calculations from multilevel models at the board level (N = 17,049) estimating the share of any board that are women, white, or women of color. Controls for Large Cities Dataset versus California Cities Dataset, city income, population, and ideology.*

Money Rules Everything around Us

In 2021, mayor LaToya Cantrell appointed Jeffrey Vappie, a police officer and a member of her private security detail, to the Housing Authority of New Orleans (HANO) board. Vappie's appointment came under greater scrutiny when a series of news articles detailed how Vappie and the mayor regularly spent long hours together at a city-owned apartment in the French Quarter (Zurik and Sauer 2022). A later investigation revealed that Vappie had been paid by the city for the time he spent in board meetings, as he considered such attendance part of his duties as the mayor's private security: "It's no different than any other part of my duties as it relates to executive protection. The only difference is that it was on the board for HANO" (WGNO 2023; Myers 2023b). Vappie eventually resigned from his position on the board amid this controversy.[6]

Patronage is the ability of political actors to use their discretion to appoint individuals to positions (Panizza, Peters, and Ramos Larraburu 2019, 148).[7] Qualitative data points to elected leaders using board appointments in this way. In his notes about appointments in the early 1960s, deLesseps Story "Chep" Morrison, the "reformer mayor" in New Orleans, notes, "I feel obligated to Mr. Aaron Mintz for his assistance in the campaign. I have a lot of obligations from the campaign that I am trying to discharge through these prestige appointments."[8] Considering another appointment, a local political leader wrote to Morrison, "Boyd has been a loyal and faithful supporter of yours in all your previous campaigns, he has the time to devote to civic endeavors, and a keen interest and desire to serve. . . . If you would consider Boyd for an appointment, I would consider it a favor to me."[9] The mayor appointed both Mintz and Boyd to boards following these discussions.

Today, board appointments are rarely so explicitly related to patronage, but these tools of political connection allow individuals to access positions of power (Colonnelli, Prem, and Teso 2020). There are, of course, exceptions: Mayor Cantrell's appointment of her security guard Jeffrey Vappie to a board represents one. Such actions suggest that while direct patronage might not be the dominant force in appointments, it may continue to play a role in small ways.

But board appointments do provide an opportunity for political leaders to reward followers, and those who support political campaigns are the ideal pool of individuals to reward. To examine whether political leaders award board positions to those who support them politically, I classified whether every current board member in New Orleans had donated money to Mayor Cantrell's two mayoral campaigns; because of the nature of campaign finance information and to make sure that I was identifying the right individuals, I searched for each board appointee and individually verified whether they had donated money to the mayor.

Overall, donors are tremendously overrepresented among board members, as compared to the general population (see Table 6.2). Less than 1 percent of New Orleanians donated to the mayor's two political campaigns, but donors make up just over a quarter (26%) of board appointees. Given the insular nature of politics in New Orleans (Burns 2003; Burns and Thomas 2015; Rast 2001, 2009; McNitt 2011), this is perhaps not surprising. I also examine whether the board members donated to any other political candidates[10] or to the mayor's opponents[11] over the prior six years. After all, political donations are highly correlated with broader political activism (Grumbach and Sahn 2020; Grumbach, Sahn, and Staszak 2020), donation activities are highly influential in local politics (Anzia 2022; Reckhow 2009; Benjamin 2022; Benjamin and Miller 2019), and board appointments might simply reflect these patterns.

TABLE 6.2. POLITICAL DONORS ARE OVERREPRESENTED ON BOARDS, PARTICULARLY STRONG BOARDS

	Mayor's donors (%)	All political donors (%)	Donors to opponents (%)
Overall	26	36	18
Strong board members	34	32	13
Weak board members	19	38	21

Note: Donation records from Mayor Cantrell's two mayoral campaigns. Opponents include the top three finishers in each round of her mayoral campaigns.

Political donors are overrepresented among board members (second column from left in Table 6.1): 36 percent of board members have donated to any political campaign, compared to the 2 percent of the population of New Orleans who are political donors across this time. But when I specifically look at donations to the mayor's political opponents, that number drops to 18 percent, suggesting patterns not just in political activism but also in political alignment with the incumbent political administration. Weak and strong board appointments during this time also suggest the importance of not just political activism but political connections: while the majority of the mayor's donors are appointed to strong boards, political donors more generally are more likely to be on weak boards and donors to opponents are much more likely to be appointed to weak boards.

These patterns of privilege associated with campaign donations provide an alternative explanation for the race and gender differences in appointments discussed earlier in this chapter. After all, women, people of color, and women of color are underrepresented in donor pools (Tolley, Besco, and Sevi 2022; Besco and Tolley 2022; Barber, Butler, and Preece 2016; Tam Cho 2003), and political donations provide a tool for reinforcing white supremacy in urban contexts (Krell 2016). To understand the relationship between donations, race, gender, and appointments, I first examine the patterns of donations to the mayor and then look at the likelihood that a donor sits on a strong board versus a weak board.

Women donors are overrepresented among appointees, as are women of color, especially as compared to white donors, Black donors, and white men who were donors (see Table 6.3). And these donations appear to "pay off" for women and women of color: women donors hold more seats on strong boards. It is possible that Mayor Cantrell's status as the first Black woman elected to the mayoral office in New Orleans or the issues that she focused on in her campaigns (Holman and Lay 2021) elicited support from a particular set of women in the community, which led to these patterns in appointments.

TABLE 6.3. POLITICAL DONORS WHO ARE WOMEN, ESPECIALLY WOMEN OF COLOR, ARE OVERREPRESENTED ON BOARDS

	Share of appointees who are donors (%)	Donors on strong boards minus weak boards (%)
Women	43	29
White donors	25	18
Black donors	21	14
Women of color	30	24
White men	23	10

Note: Donation records from Mayor Cantrell's two mayoral campaigns. Opponents include the top three finishers in each round of her mayoral campaigns.

A Pathway to Power? Board Appointments and Political Ambition

Serving on appointed boards is often the first step in seeking elected office, linking appointees to important political elites that facilitate connections and links to political donors (Adams 2004), and providing evidence to voters and elites that these individuals have the necessary experience and capacity to lead (Sanbonmatsu 2006). While scholars have pointed to appointed boards as a pathway to political office (Caroll and Sanbonmatsu 2013), particularly local office, this research has largely focused on backward evaluations of the backgrounds of people who hold political office; in a way, this is selecting on the dependent variable as it does not tell us about the individuals who hold appointed office but do not seek political office.

Here, I investigate the link between appointed office and elected office through two approaches that remedy this problem: First, I look across the full set of appointees in California and match this to all of the candidates for local office. Next, I use a survey of politically engaged women in Richmond, Virginia, to show that only 5 percent of those interested in board appointments also express political ambition.

Is there overlap in who serves on boards and who runs for office? In California, more than 20 percent of these pools overlap, with a higher share among men, those from business or development backgrounds, and those on strong boards. Generally, a very small share of Americans ever run for office: the Pew Research Center estimates place this at 2 percent of the public. I find that over one in five board members have also run for political office at the local level in California. But, as Table 6.4 shows, this overall rate disguises quite a bit of subgroup variation: men who sit on appointed boards are much more likely to run for office than are women. Strong board members are more likely than weak board members. And, because candidates in California put their

TABLE 6.4. APPOINTEES WHO ARE MEN, WITH DEVELOPMENT BACKGROUNDS, OR ON STRONG BOARDS ARE MORE LIKELY TO RUN FOR ELECTED OFFICE

	Probability of running for office (%)
All board members	18
Women on boards	11
Men on boards	22
Board members with development background	23
Weak board members	7
Strong board members	21

Note: Data from California; board membership measured in 2018, political candidacy measured across 2012–2022. Post hoc predicted values from models with logistic regression models with city fixed effects.

occupations on the ballot (Anzia and Bernhard 2022; Bernhard and Holman 2025), I also find that people associated with development (including real estate agents and owners of development agencies or construction companies) are much more likely to run for office, a finding that mirrors Kirkland's (2022) evaluation of business owners running for local office. As I have detailed at other places in this book, the overlap between those groups, such as that men and those with development backgrounds are more likely to sit on strong boards, means that a particular group of appointees is the ones with political ambition.

Some board appointees considered their appointment a step in the process of running for office or demonstrating their capacity to voters. In my discussions with board members, running for political office came up organically at several points, particularly from men who sat on strong boards. One member told me that "being here, understanding how the sausage is made, it is really helpful. Not just for me professionally, but if I wanted to run for city council." Others mentioned the connections they made sitting on a board: "You know that saying 'It's not what you know, it's who you know'? Well, that's the thing in cities our size—you gotta know everyone to do things like run for mayor. Now I do."

But serving on an appointed board might also decrease political ambition. Some members told me that board membership soured them on elected office. One woman, an appointee to a criminal justice reform board, recounted a controversy on the affordable housing board: "It just made me realize: Oh, I'm on the losing end of this little thing. I am going to be on the losing end of every policy in local government. I do think we should build housing, we should build affordable housing, we should spend city beautification money on it. That's what I would do as mayor. But now they won't ever elect me to that position." Overall, an appointment to a board is associated with political ambition, but specifically among men, developers, and those who sit on strong boards.

As a deeper dive into how ambition for appointed office and elected office relate to each other, I also draw on a survey of civically engaged women in Richmond.[12] Here, I asked whether people had no, some, or quite a bit of interest in either serving on an appointed board (board ambition) or seeking local political office (elected ambition). Generally, women express more disinterest in elected office (65 percent saying no interest) than appointed office (41 percent with no interest). Looking at the overlap, I found that more than one in five women said they had no interest in elected office, but quite a bit of interest in appointed office, but only 1 percent indicated low appointed ambition but high elected ambition. And only 6 percent had high levels of ambition for both elected office and appointed office. These survey results suggest that, even among those women who are highly engaged, ambition for appointed office does not necessarily correspond to ambition for elected office.

Boards and Descriptive Representation

Who has access to the "hidden" power of appointed boards and commissions in cities? The distribution of women, residents of color, and women of color across the strong and weak boards is indicative of the general distribution of power in society. While descriptive representation is not a guarantee of substantive changes (Childs 2006), the fact that men, white people, and white men are the majority of strong board members provides further evidence that these boards protect the status quo in cities.

The high levels (but uneven distribution) of representation by women and residents of color and women of color across boards point to issues with assuming that descriptive representation will lead to changes in the power and resources of a group. Indeed, the descriptive representation of women, residents of color, and women of color is more consistent with Dovi's (2012, 12) contention that "those in power can appoint, nominate, and support . . . descriptive representatives in order to make it seem as though they respect democratic norms, while actually weakening and undermining democratic commitments." Work on descriptive representation at the federal level suggests that it can obscure objections to policies or issues with undemocratic processes (Clayton, O'Brien, and Piscopo 2019).

In many ways, a local government with both elected officials and bureaucrats and appointed boards and commissions represents an ideal polycentric government: "a social system of many decision centers having limited and autonomous prerogatives and operating under an overarching set of rules" (V. Ostrom 1953; Aligica and Tarko 2012, 327). These governance structures could facilitate deliberative democracy, including allowing ordinary citizens to engage in deliberation with policymakers and then reporting back to the community.

Does any of this representation matter? One possibility is that descriptive representation is simply enough and the uneven distribution of women, people of color, and political donors across weak and strong boards does not matter, as the purpose of representation is just to have voices in any room. But another possibility is that the uneven distribution of descriptive representation across boards has consequences for policy and for views of democracy. I address these questions in the next section.

III

DO BOARDS MATTER?

SECTION III INTRODUCTION

A mid a crime surge in 2022, a rash of car burglaries scared the residents of Lakeview, one of New Orleans's more wealthy and white neighborhoods. Brian Andrews, the president of the Lakeview Crime Prevention District, told a reporter, "Residents are scared. They are scared in their homes. Scared to go to the grocery store, scared to pump gas." In response, the neighborhood increased its funding for the Crime Prevention District: "If the city can't do it, we will do it" (O'Connor 2022). News stories from the next year regularly detailed car break-ins, including a break-in to a city councilmember's car (D. Jones 2022). In 2023, residents of the neighborhood again expressed frustration, this time regarding communication between the city's 911 system and the off-duty officers who worked for the Crime Prevention District; one resident saw a car burglary occurring, called 911, and then fell asleep waiting for the off-duty officers patrolling the neighborhood to come by to check on the scene (D. Jones 2023).[1]

The Lakeview Crime Prevention District represents the challenge of investigating when and how boards might matter in influence policy or quality of life. New Orleans' weak and strong boards are similar overall to those of other similarly sized cities, but it has far more police- and fire-related boards than most cities. The average number of police- or fire-related boards in a large city is 3.4, compared to 19 in New Orleans. At the root of the large number of boards in New Orleans? The 13 "crime prevention" districts in New Orleans, which are each managed by an appointed board with an elected president. The Lakeview Crime Prevention District (established in 1998) was the first of these in New Orleans. Each district levies an annual flat tax (usually between $100 and $600) on properties in a geographic area. Those funds go toward paying overtime to NOPD officers to patrol the geographic area in NOPD-marked cars. For example, the Audubon Area Security District, which covers a residential area of Uptown New Orleans (average home sale price of $760,000 in 2022), charges each property owner $525 per year.[2] In 2015, the Audubon Area Security District spent $170,000 for officer patrols; 98.8 percent of the tasks that these off-duty NOPD officers completed involved checks on homes while the owners are on vacation, resident escorts, and confirmation of a message received (radio checks). The appointed boards for these security districts are majority white and male.

Each of these security district boards, which were created via a state legislative mandate, theoretically provides an additional layer of police protection in these neighborhoods. These neighborhoods do not differ from the rest of New Orleans in just their security zones: more of their residents are white, they are wealthier, and they have more valuable property. And, perhaps most importantly, security districts are largely ineffective: in his study of them one scholar notes, "Security districts reinforce inequality, are ineffective against violent crime, and sidestep desperately needed debates around public safety and criminal justice reform" (Malone 2018, 2019). Malone's findings echo evaluations of security districts in Texas, which have no effect on crime rates or closure rates (Tao and Collins 2024). But residents of these areas expect that these security districts will keep them safe; as a result, "the feel-good story about taking a stand within each neighborhood masks a reality that is more complex and problematic" (Malone 2018, 2019).

So far, in the first section, this book has focused on the ways that cities create two different classes of boards: strong boards, which have the power to create policy, and weak boards, which do not. In the second section, I show that weak and strong boards operate in very different ways, with different voices on those different boards. In this third section, I ask this: Does it matter whether a specific board exists in a city? And does the membership of those boards matter, both for policy outcomes and for views of local government?

Advocates of deliberative democracy argue that deliberative structures can help shift and improve the policy agenda by democratizing the voices that are included in the process. Beierle (1999) argues that public participation can improve policy outcomes by increasing the substantive quality of decisions, while others point to public meetings setting the policy agenda and informing elected officials of the public's (nuanced) views (Adams 2004). Others suggest that citizen participation can provide active residents with information about policymaking (including lessons about the complicated nature of policymaking) (Luskin, Fishkin, and Jowell 2002; Irvin and Stansbury 2004).

But do these boards shape the outcome of local policy? Why and how? Do they change how individuals view government? In Chapter 7, I look at whether the presence or absence of specific boards in a city shapes that city's policies and practices and whether the membership of boards influences what kinds of policies those boards produce. At the core of this chapter is an effort to answer a question that is fundamental to democracy: "In what ways does participation make a difference in the decisions and policy outcomes of government, and what kind of difference?" (Checkoway and Van Til 1978, 35). In Chapter 8, I then use a combination of experimental and survey data to consider the ways that boards might influence what individuals think about their governments, including trust in government and government legitimacy.

Assessing the Effect of Boards

How does one evaluate whether the presence of a board matters? Three specific challenges emerge: cities do not create boards randomly, cities do not fill boards randomly, and boards may just be an extension of the preferences of elected leaders.

Cities do not create boards randomly: cities may create boards to address specific policies because they are already making policy in those areas and the creation of the board is simply one vehicle of that policymaking effort. In this circumstance, the effect of a board on an outcome may actually be capturing the effect of a broad set of policies from the city, not the effect of the board at all. For example, cities created police oversight commissions in the 1990s and 2000s in response to local organized pressure from activists; these activists were often motivated by acts of violence and misconduct by police (Francis 2021).

Cities do not fill boards randomly. As I have detailed in the previous chapters, cities do not fill boards by lottery or through random placement. As a result, a motivated elected official might find the right advocate or policy entrepreneur to sit on a board where the official wants to make policy . . . or may place the advocate on a weak board when the official does not care about the issues that the advocate wants to see addressed. Qualitative evidence of this abounds: mayors in New Orleans routinely discuss placing individuals with whom they agree politically or from whom they need political help on strong boards; on the nomination of one individual, Mayor Schiro wrote, "As much as I would like to go along with your view point, it so happens that Frank Gillio is the current president of the union, and, in effect, if we failed to confirm his appointment we would be going to the 'teeth' of the desires of the union members as expressed in a democratic way."[3] But the alternative also happens: when a local economics professor cornered Mayor Schiro at social events and then sent him letters over and over in the 1960s asking for an appointment, the mayor placed the professor on the Welfare Board, which had little to no power in the city.[4] About another potential board member, the mayor's secretary wrote, "I did a little checking on [board member] and the persons I spoke to did not feel that he would really add anything to the Board," but then later nominated the individual to a weak board.[5]

Boards are not distinct from elected officials: One challenge of assessing the effect of a board on policy is that the board's membership might directly reflect the interests and desires of elected officials in the city. Examples abound from both historical assessments and boards today. In his foundational study of urban politics, Robert Dahl examined the activities of the Citizen Action Commission (CAC) in New Haven, Connecticut. This board oversaw redevelopment activities, but as Dahl notes in his discussion of the CAC, the board "never directly initiated, opposed, vetoed, or altered any proposal brought before them" (Dahl 1961, 131). Other studies of boards in the 1960s found that the mayor staffed the board "primarily [with] representatives of the economic elite" (Bachrach and Baratz 1970, 14).

Scholars today also echo these concerns: "Citizen involvement sometimes is considered shallow—it occurs after the issues have been framed or the decisions have been made" (Yang and Pandey 2011, 880). Today, boards' membership often reflects the interests of the elected leaders who appoint these individuals. In New Orleans, one reporter following a story about the abrupt departure of the 911 center's director tweeted, "Nearly the entire [911] board is made up of city officials who report directly to the mayor. One of the exceptions is Brobson Lutz's seat. And Lutz has long been the sole source of dissent on the board." It is thus possible that boards simply do what the mayor wants because the membership reflects the mayor's interests. As a result, the board's preferences may not change anything, because they are the same as if the elected officials made the decisions.

Because of these difficulties, I examine scenarios for 'most likely' policy change: agenda-setting during focusing events (Kingdon 1984; Birkland 1998), representation at points of "uncrystallized interests" (Mansbridge 1999), and a role for policy entrepreneurs (Kingdon 1984). I contrast this with theories of representation to argue that the presence of specific weak boards is less important for policy change than who sits on strong boards.

Contemporary Policy Debates
and Appointed Boards

To understand the effect of boards on policy, in Chapter 7 I look at issues relating to gender and racial equity, policing, housing, and reactions to

COVID-19. I selected these policy areas both for importance and for convenience: these issues represent key struggles and challenges in cities today, and they also offer an opportunity for testing the power of boards in a variety of ways.

Gender Equity

To examine the effect of boards and representation on policy outcomes, I look at two forms of gender equity policy and one outcome. As the first policy, I examine whether a city signed on to the Cities for the Convention on the Elimination of All Forms of Discrimination Against Women (CEDAW) campaign (Och 2018). Initially adopted by the United Nations in 1979, CEDAW is a widely ratified international human rights treaty that countries sign as a pledge to engage in specific actions to increase gender equity (Forester et al. 2022). Member states of the UN that adopt CEDAW are required to address discrimination against women and put policies into place that will help achieve gender equality; ratification is associated with increased human rights for women, including abortion access (Englehart and Miller 2014; Hunt and Gruszczynski 2019). The United States (alongside Iran, Somalia, and the Sudan) is one of just six countries that have not ratified CEDAW. As a result, activists have turned to subnational efforts to convince states and cities to incorporate parts of the treaty into policy. The Cities for CEDAW campaign lobbies cities to adopt ordinances or resolutions that address gender equality (Runyan and Sanders 2021; Boyd 2023). I examine whether the presence of an SOW board is associated with an increased probability that a city ratifies a Cities for CEDAW resolution.

Policies around sexual misconduct are the second issue that I examine. The role of the government in addressing sexual harassment and sexual assault rose in prominence in the mid- to late 2010s. During the 2016 presidential election, Hillary Clinton's status as the first woman in U.S. history to win the nomination of a major political party's ticket, along with her focus on the "first woman" status and on feminine issues, increased attention to women's issues (Wilz 2016; Conroy 2018; Heldman, Conroy, and Ackerman 2018). Donald Trump's actions also focused attention on gendered issues: his use of "hyper" masculinity (Conroy 2018) and gendered attacks (Cassese and Holman 2019; Heldman, Conroy, and Ackerman 2018), allegations of sexual misconduct (Barbaro and Twohey 2016), and derision of the #MeToo movement (Holman and Kalmoe 2021a; Archer and Kam 2020; Klar and McCoy 2021), among others. A release of a 2005 Access Hollywood video where Trump bragged about sexually assaulting a woman and used derogatory language (Benoit 2017; Farenthold 2018) raised the salience of sexual misconduct even more.

Events following the 2016 election further increased the salience of sexual misconduct as a public policy problem. Abuse allegations against filmmaker Harvey Weinstein led to a viral acceleration of the use of the hashtag #MeToo (Farrow 2017; Lee and Murdie 2020), a movement founded in 2006 by Tarana Burke to provide Black girls and women who had survived sexual violence with access to resources (Burke 2019). The #MeToo movement spilled over to politics, with sexual assault accusations being leveled against members of Congress, state legislators, and local government officials (Gessen 2017; Dil 2023; Sorensen 2020). In response, several states and a wide set of cities passed legislation to strengthen workplace protections (Rampell 2018). I examine whether an SOW board is associated with an increased probability that a city adopted one of three common workplace policies during this period: adopting antiharassment protections for city employees (22% of cities[6]), banning automatic arbitration and NDAs for sexual misconduct (24% of cities), and creating policies that protect employees from misconduct by elected officials (12% of cities). Some cities adopted all three of these policies, while others adopted single policies and others none at all.

Ban the Box

In 2004, a series of summits of formerly incarcerated individuals identified job discrimination and housing discrimination as key barriers to success after jail or prison. Organizers formed the All of Us or None campaign, which began pressuring governments, businesses, and nonprofits to revise job, services, and housing applications to remove the box that applicants were expected to check off if they had previously been convicted of a crime. Following the campaign, a majority of states and over 150 cities and counties adopted Ban the Box (BTB) policies, limiting the ability of employers (including the city as an employer) to eliminate candidates simply because of a conviction or an arrest record. The effectiveness of the BTB policies has been widely debated in the scholarly community (Doleac and Hansen 2017, 2020). I draw on Owens and Gunderson's (2023) work on assessing when a city adopts a BTB policy, and I examine whether cities that have minority empowerment boards or criminal justice reform–oriented boards are more likely to adopt a BTB policy.

Police (De)Funding and Oversight

Following the murder of George Floyd by a police officer in Minneapolis and the subsequent national unrest and policy demands from Black Lives Matter, debates emerged in many cities about the degree to which police budgets should be changed in light of public attitudes about police violence and racism (Cohen et al. 2019; Sances 2023; Cobbina-Dungy, Soma Chaudhuri, and DeJong 2022; Harris, Walker, and Eckhouse 2020; Hoang and Benjamin 2023).

Most cities did not actually defund the police (if any did at all) following calls by activists and the public in 2020 (Hoang and Benjamin 2023), even when public leaders publicly supported the calls. But the rhetoric was certainly part of the public conversation, and such policy discussions might influence how people view the legitimacy of government. I thus use police defunding and oversight as a means for understanding public attitudes about decisions made by boards versus elected officials.

COVID-19 Policy

The COVID-19 crisis began, continued, and persisted in the face of federal government inaction. As the federal government refused to act and states engaged in a variety of actions and nonactions, local governments scrambled to address the urgent crises created by the pandemic (Farris, Holman, and Sullivan 2022; Holman, Farris, and Sumner 2020). In response to the policy vacuum at the federal level and the uneven spread of infection across space in the country, local governments created a jigsaw of policies, like stay-at-home orders, social distancing requirements, business closures, and eviction moratoria (Farris and Silber Mohamed 2022; Holman, Farris, and Sumner 2020; Rocco, Béland, and Waddan 2020). These actions were unevenly dispersed; that is, some cities engaged in early and broad action to implement these COVID policies, while other cities adopted some or none of the policies. Later in the COVID crisis, the "second pandemic," or the economic consequences of the economic shutdowns, prompted an additional set of city policies. As people were unable to pay rent and evictions loomed as an economic, social, and public health disaster, some cities passed a variety of eviction moratoria to protect renters. I use the presence of a health or housing board as a mechanism for understanding whether boards matter in times of policy urgency. As about half of cities have these boards, this provides an opportunity to examine whether their presence is associated with more robust COVID and COVID-related policymaking.

Following localized outbreaks and widespread disfunctions at the state and federal levels, some local leaders drafted and implemented public health policy responses to the progression of the virus. These policies included states of emergency and restrictions to slow the spread of the virus, such as social distancing restrictions, business and public space closures, and masking requirements. Some cities reacted very quickly to the spread of the virus: San Francisco ordered schools closed with only 12 detected cases, while New York's mayor closed schools after 329 cases. I examine if any particular city in my board's dataset adopted any of these three policies: capping the size of social gatherings; closing some businesses, such as bars or music venues; and mandating shelter-in-place. As with my previous work on how local governments responded to COVID (Holman, Farris, and Sumner 2020), I counted whether a city adopted any of these policies in the first month of active response to COVID-19 (March 1, 2020, to April 1, 2020).

Housing and Evictions

Housing availability and affordability is a central issue in cities across the United States, with more than 90 million households (or close to three-quarters of all U.S. households) priced out of the home ownership market. Housing affordability influences a wide set of individual and community outcomes, ranging from physical and mental health to child welfare and development to the economic viability of cities (Ramphal et al. 2023; Sills and Rich 2021; Anthony 2023). Affordable housing is also personally impactful for individuals: in a 2023 poll, 37 percent of those surveyed said that they personally had difficulty finding affordable housing (CNN 2023).

Evictions and the COVID-19 Pandemic

The eviction crisis predated the COVID-19 pandemic in the United States, but the compounding economic crisis that accompanied the pandemic left many individuals and families without the means to pay their rent, thus risking eviction (Einstein et al. 2020; Ong 2020; Desmond 2012; Leung et al. 2023). Beyond concerns about the experiences of individuals going through the process, there were also concerns that evictions had the potential to increase exposure to COVID-19 (Benfer et al. 2021). While the Centers for Disease Control and Prevention eventually issued a temporary nationwide eviction moratorium (Walensky 2021), the federal action came very late for many who were faced eviction early in the pandemic. But again, the COVID crisis produced an uneven patchwork of policies, as some people lived in places where their local government acted more quickly. In response to pressures from housing advocates and renters, a wide set of cities issued local eviction moratoria as a public health measure to provide protection for renters and to reduce the spread of COVID-19 (Farris, Holman, and Sullivan 2022; Sills and Rich 2021; Leifheit et al. 2021; Callison, Finger, and Smith 2022; Ali and Wehby 2022). These moratoria varied in their characteristics, but generally they limited the ability of landlords to use the legal system to remove a tenant from a property for nonpayment of rent. Even in places where states acted, local governments largely acted before their states or acted in concert with state governments.

Do Boards Matter for Public Perceptions of Government?

Because all cities have boards, knowledge about these boards can be difficult to measure. You cannot simply ask: Does your city use appointed boards and commissions to make policy? The answer does not vary. But cities do differ in the presence of specific boards and the powers invested in those boards. For example, while many cities have police oversight commissions, many cities also do not. And those commissions that do exist vary tremendously in their powers and responsibilities. In Chapter 8, I examine the public perceptions of a variety of government actions through four studies.

Survey Study: Who Makes the Decision, Elected Leaders or Appointed Leaders?

To measure public awareness of boards, I surveyed 789 people who lived in cities with 100,000+ population. I asked them, "Without searching for anything on the internet, do you know if your city has a police oversight board?" Response options were yes, no, and don't know. If a respondent answered yes, their city had a board, I asked whether the respondent was aware of the board's powers and I listed ten powers identified by the National Association for Civilian Oversight of Law Enforcement (NACOLE), including monitoring, auditing, and investigations, and what the membership rules were for the board. I compared their responses to whether the city had a police oversight board of any kind and to the actual structure and power of the board. I fielded the survey through the LUCID platform in the fall of 2021, restricting the survey to respondents who lived in ZIP codes in large cities.

Experimental Studies

To understand the effect of boards on attitudes toward government legitimacy and trust in local government, I rely on a series of experiments in which I describe a policy decision as handled by a city council or by an appointed board and compare responses to the same decision. These experiments vary in the substance of the policy at hand, the characteristics of the decision-making process, and those making the decision.

Experimental Study 1: Who Makes the Decision, Elected or Appointed Leaders?

In the fall of 2020, participants accessed Amazon's Mechanical Turk ($N =$ 325) website where they read a newspaper article and answered a series of questions. The content of the newspaper article was randomly assigned: some participants received a control condition article that featured a story about a rescued dog that was reunited with its owner. Those in the "board" treatments received an article that focused either on housing or on regulating the police; for example, the housing article discussed how a local planning board had decided to tear down a condemned historic home to build multifamily housing, while the policing article described a decision by a civilian oversight board to move funds from police training to training unarmed mental health professionals as an alternative response to emergency calls about individuals in crisis. The articles described the appointed board as having members "drawn from the local community." Other groups read an article with these same policy discussions, but the decision to tear down the building or shift funding was attributed to an elected city council.

Experimental Study 2: When You Disagree with Government Decisions

In Experimental Study 2, I examine how confronting a political decision that someone does not agree with might shape someone's views of trust and legitimacy, and how this might vary by appointed or elected board. In the this experiment, done in the spring of 2021, participants on the LUCID platform ($N = 849$) were first asked their position on two controversial local issues: (1) reducing funding for the police and (2) changing zoning codes to allow multifamily housing to be built in neighborhoods that had single-family homes.

For both issues, I asked respondents to indicate their support for or opposition to a policy proposal: "reducing the budget dedicated to the police to spend more on other local services" (55% opposed) and "eliminating zoning rules to increase the supply of multifamily housing" (35% opposed); these policy questions were asked randomly within a longer battery of questions about the respondent's support for a wide set of local policies. Later in the survey, I asked the respondents to read a short newspaper article about a local policy decision. As in Experimental Study 1, the newspaper article described the decision as being made by an appointed board or by an elected city council. The newspaper article's content again randomly varied on whether it was about housing or about defunding the police, but every respondent was told about a decision that was counter to the respondent's choice. For example, if the respondent said that they supported defunding the police, the newspaper article described how the city council or the appointed board had decided to continue funding police training (instead of funding the training of mental health professionals). Similarly, if someone opposed eliminating zoning rules, they read an article about how the council or board had decided not to enforce zoning rules, thus allowing multifamily housing. The control condition in this experiment is a story about a neighborhood garden that became a fairy garden during COVID because of donations from neighbors.[7]

Experimental Study 3: Failure to Launch and The Absence of Policy Action

In the third Experimental Study, conducted in the fall of 2021, I ask: If the city decides not to act on an important issue, does that nonaction by appointed boards or elected leaders influence trust in government or views of government legitimacy? I again turn to policing and housing as the two issues of examination and use a LUCID sample ($N = 853$). In this study, participants read a newspaper article about how the city decided to not sanction a police officer who had beat a subject or had not intervened when a developer who had promised to build affordable housing had instead built market rate condos. Again, there is a control condition (a story about a local teen winning a poetry contest) for comparison. After participants read about the nonaction (i.e., they were not assigned to the control condition), they were randomly assigned to read about how the board or the elected council made the decision: whether there was "robust debate and deliberation" or "a marked lack of debate and deliberation" on the issue in the board and the city council.

Experimental Study 4: Descriptive Representation and Who Makes an Unpopular Decision

In the fourth Experimental Study, in the spring of 2022, I ask, Does it matter who makes an unpopular decision? Here again, I turn to police brutality and housing as the two issues of examination and I use a LUCID sample ($N = 2379$); this sample was constructed to oversample Black respondents ($N = 784$). In this study, as in Experimental Study 2, I assigned participants to read about a decision that was the opposite of their policy preference. But here, I also varied the descriptive representation of the board or the city council making the decision, with one set of articles describing the board or the council as having members "drawn from the local community" and another having a "majority Black" membership. Again, there is a control condition (a story about a local juggling competition for charity) for comparison. In this study, I compare the control group to the treatment groups and the treatment groups to each other. I then examine how Black respondents evaluated their local government after the board or the council was described as majority Black or not.

Outcome Measures for Experimental Studies

In all four studies, I asked participants about their trust in government: "How much trust and confidence do you have in your [level] government to handle [level] problems? A great deal, a fair amount, not very much, or none at all." The "[level]" included local, state, and national governments.[8] To measure legitimacy, I asked five questions that probe beliefs about government legitimacy, drawn from the literature on judicial legitimacy (Robinson 2012; Nielsen, Robinson, and Smyth 2020; Badas 2019; Badas and Stauffer 2018). I asked for agreement with these statements:

> Government should be made less powerful if they make decisions most people disagree with.
> I believe the people making decisions here are competent in their jobs.
> I believe the people making decisions are in tune with the needs of people like me.
> I believe the people making decisions are in tune with the needs of those most affected by the decision.
> I believe the people making decisions are in tune with the needs of the city as a whole.

Responses on all measures were scaled from 0 to 1, with "1" representing more trust and legitimacy. Because these are experimental conditions with randomization, I simply compare the levels of trust and government legitimacy across the conditions using Analysis of Variance (ANOVA) tests and difference of means tests, where appropriate. Experimental Study 4 includes an additional analysis where I look at how the race of the survey-takers influenced their response to the treatments; here, I use ordinary least squares (OLS) regression to estimate the effect of the treatments overall and on Black respondents specifically. The results of these studies are detailed in Chapter 8.

The following chapters focus on questions about whether boards matter, in terms of policy or public attitudes. In Chapter 7, I look at the policy effects of boards, starting with COVID-related policies and outcomes and proceeding to gender equality, #MeToo–related policies, and Ban the Box policies. Chapter 7 compares the policy and outcome effects of descriptive representation on boards overall, on weak and strong boards, and on boards in elected office. In Chapter 8, I turn to the question of whether boards change how people view their governments. Using police oversight and housing at the two central issues, I examine the level of knowledge about boards and reactions to policy decisions when those decisions are made by boards or by elected officials. Chapter 9 serves as a conclusion, where first I identify some of the core issues associated with how cities use boards, then present parallels to other forms of governance, and finally suggest policy changes.

7

THE POLICY CONSEQUENCES
OF UNEVEN POWER

In the fall of 2023, Tyler Morris, the director of the Orleans Parish Communication District—which oversees New Orleans's 911 operations; communications for the city's police, fire, and emergency medical services; and 311 service calls—resigned from his position, saying he would "spend some time with my family and friends who have felt my absence and are often deeply impacted by this 24/7 job." While Morris claimed that he had "decided to pursue a doctoral degree," his resignation actually followed a series of events where he first crashed a government vehicle[1] and then possibly (probably) altered a department policy to avoid scrutiny over the fact that he did not go through drug or alcohol screenings after his crash (Perlstein 2023).[2]

Morris tenured that resignation to the Orleans Parish Communication District Board (OPCD), which is "made up of city officials who report directly to the mayor" (Maldonado 2023). The board, which includes New Orleans's director of public health, New Orleans's chief accounting officer, and the city's police superintendent, sets policy for the OPCD and for emergency services more generally in the city. Each of these individuals serves as long as they hold their current jobs. Morris's tenure had been marked by a variety of controversies, including 911 operators misreporting details of calls, resulting in slow responses from fire and police; issues with translations of calls from non-English speakers; and several deaths resulting from emergency responders never showing up or going to the wrong address (Perlstein 2023). Despite these controversies, the OPCD generally approved of all requests from the director, and meeting minutes suggest very little pushback against any policy decisions made prior to the director's car crash.

Advocates of deliberative democracy argue that structures focused on producing dialogue between members of a community can help shift and improve the policy agenda by democratizing the voices included in the process. Beierle (1999) argues that public participation can improve policy outcomes by increasing the substantive quality of decisions, while others point to public meetings setting the policy agenda and informing elected officials of the public's (nuanced) views (Adams 2004). Others suggest that citizen participation can provide active residents with information about policymaking, including lessons about the complicated nature of policymaking (Luskin, Fishkin, and Jowell 2002; Irvin and Stansbury 2004). But do these boards shape the outcome of local policy? Why and how? To examine this question, I look at whether the presence or absence of specific boards in a city impact that city's policies and practices and whether the membership of boards (including the race, gender, and occupational backgrounds) influences what kinds of policies those boards produce. At the core of this chapter is an effort to answer a question fundamental to democracy: "In what ways does participation make a difference in the decisions and policy outcomes of government, and what kind of difference?" (Checkoway and Van Til 1978, 35).

Agenda-setting is the process by which political bodies consider specific issues, problems, solutions, and alternatives. The ability to control "the definition of the alternatives" is the "supreme instrument of power" (Schattschneider 1975, 66) because this can expand or limit the frontier of the types of problems that a political body considers solving. The decision agenda involves deciding both what a body will discuss (a collection of problems and solutions) and the order in which the body will discuss those items.[3] If they matter, appointed boards help set agendas for their city in general, and specifically around issues that relate the portfolio of the board.

I examine three "best-case" scenarios for boards to matter in local democracy and policymaking: Do boards help guide policy direction in times of crisis? Do boards provide a mechanism to encourage cities to act on low-salience issues? And do boards lead to substantive action on newly salient policies? In each of these circumstances, I find little evidence that boards influence policy, raise the profile of low-salience issues, or challenge the status quo.

Does this mean that boards do not matter at all? I next examine whether the membership of boards matters. Here I find effects, but only for strong boards: the representation of women and people of color on strong boards is associated with the adoption of specific policies of interest, including the provision of parental leave, sexual harassment policies, and the Ban the Box policy, where cities remove requests for criminal justice records at the initial hiring screening. In comparison, the share of women and people of color on weak boards does not change policies, in part because weak boards do not change policy. I conclude the chapter by examining why it is that representation matters on strong boards but not on weak boards, proposing two paths to power: the interactions between the board and city staff, and the existing relationships between strong board members and elected leaders that could serve as a conduit of information and influence between elected and appointed bodies. Here, I show that weak boards can influence policy but only in conjunction with shared representation in positions of power. Weak boards alone are ineffective at changing policy.

Windows of Opportunity and COVID-19

Do cities with weak boards that focus on a particular policy area make better policy, more quickly, in a time of crisis? Kingdon's (1984) framework for understanding policymaking argues that times of crisis can open up an opportunity for policy entrepreneurs to set the policy agenda and drive policy. The COVID-19 pandemic was a "quintessential focusing event" (Béland et al. 2021), in that it was a sudden, rare occurrence that was large in scale and all members of the policymaking community (and the public) found out about the problem in a simultaneous fashion (Birkland 1998, 2006).

The COVID-19 pandemic, the economic consequences of it, and the patchwork of responses to it allow me to examine the ways that appointed boards do—and do not—matter in shaping local policy. I look at specific outcomes that are directly dependent on political decisions by cities: Were cities with public health boards more likely to act at all to produce COVID-related policies early in the crisis? In the case of public health boards, the involvement of the public in decision-making during a crisis can serve not just to increase access to a broader set of views but also to incorporate expertise into these discussions, given that many public health boards are staffed by people with medical or public health backgrounds. Research on the COVID-19 response specifically has identified the importance of people with a medical or public health background participating in policymaking (Hodges et al. 2022; Cairney and Wellstead 2021).

Were cities with boards that specifically address affordable and the public provision of housing more likely to put eviction moratoria into place? And did the presence of public health boards or affordable housing boards translate into lower levels of COVID deaths and evictions in those places? In the case of housing policy, research on state and national housing policy has found that the incorporation of housing policy advocates and those experiencing housing crisis into the policy process was associated with a higher likelihood of implementing a COVID-19 eviction moratorium and a more robust policy (Benfer et al. 2021).

A majority of cities have health boards and/or housing boards, both of which I classify as weak boards. Health boards include boards of health, emergency medical services, mental health, medical districts, hospital oversight, health, education, housing equality, and more. Housing boards include boards focused on public housing, affordable housing, fair housing, and homelessness, and various bodies that oversee housing trusts or low-income loans. These boards regularly are staffed with people who have backgrounds in these areas, including public health and medical personnel on health boards and affordable housing advocates and tenants on housing boards.[4]

Does the presence of a health board or a housing board shape whether cities adopted COVID restrictions or eviction moratoria in the early months of the pandemic? I find no evidence that the presence of these weak boards influences policy in times of crisis (see Table 7.1, top pane): cities with public health boards did not use those boards to assist in making more aggressive decisions about COVID policy in the early days of the pandemic. Early COVID restrictions were equally likely to emerge from cities that had public health boards (42%) and those that did not (44%).

Similarly, housing boards did not seem to effectively increase the likelihood that a city passed an eviction moratorium; cities were equally likely to adopt moratoria whether they had an affordable housing board or not. In New Orleans, the city's eviction moratorium originated in the city's courts, which shut down all eviction hearings for a month until the state issued its own moratorium. And, despite housing advocates pressuring the HANO and its board, there was no direct action to protect those living in govern-

TABLE 7.1. THE PRESENCE OF HEALTH AND HOUSING BOARDS DOES NOT INFLUENCE COVID OR HOUSING POLICY OR OUTCOMES

	City adopted any early COVID restrictions (%)	City vaccine rate (%)
Health board	42	82
No health board	44	79
	City adopted eviction moratoria (%)	City eviction rate (%)
Housing board	23	9
No housing board	20	11

Notes: Predicted values from a multilevel logistic regression model with controls and clustered errors at the state level. I draw from research on government reactions to the COVID-19 pandemic for guidelines on controls (Gadarian, Goodman, and Pepinsky 2021; Holman, Farris, and Sumner 2020b; Farris, Holman, and Sullivan 2022; Funk 2020), which include the partisanship, gender, and race of the mayor; the ideology score for the city (Tausanovitch and Warshaw 2013), median income, COVID rates, share of renters in the city, and whether the state where the city is located had enacted similar policies.

ment-subsidized housing from eviction until the state intervened (PBS 2022; Kasakove 2020). Cities with housing boards and without housing boards had very similar rates of eviction filings (9 percent and 11 percent, respectively); the differences emerge when scholars compare eviction filings before and after a moratorium (Callison, Finger, and Smith 2022).

Do local boards have any effect on actual policy output? In short, no. I examine county-level vaccine uptake rates for the entire set of cities and eviction rates for the group of cities where the Eviction Lab collected data.[5] Again, I estimate models with a full set of controls and present the predicted values for cities with and without health and housing boards. I also do not find any evidence that a health board is associated with shifting policy outcomes. Cities with health boards and without health boards had statistically indistinguishable rates (82 percent and 79 percent, respectively) of COVID vaccine uptake.

Examining the relationship between weak boards and policy outcomes during a period of crisis does not provide any evidence that these boards intervene during a window of opportunity to shift policy. The (lack of an) effect on health and housing is particularly striking, given that both board's members have backgrounds in health and housing advocacy. For example, in New Orleans, the Housing Authority board has two seats reserved for the City-wide Tenants Council and housing advocates regularly sit on the board. In Los Angeles, the Public Health Commission's entire membership was composed of doctors and public health professionals. These boards also regularly discussed health and housing issues associated with the COVID-19 pandemic. The Housing Authority of New Orleans (HANO) board worked to issue COVID-19 guidelines for renters, property owners, and tenants in public housing, but did not independently act to stop those in New Orleans's public housing from facing eviction. And the Los Angeles Public Health Commission was active on COVID-related issues, holding hearings and drafting reports on the pandemic well into 2023. Yet, these activities did not influence how elected officials made policy related to housing or health during the pandemic.

Women's Equality and Policymaking on Low-Salience Issues

I next consider whether boards can, at minimum, provide information on low-salience issues. Issue salience is the degree to which people engage around a political issue; often, issues with a low salience for voters are not considered important enough for political resources to be used to solve them (Mullin 2009; Moniz and Wlezien 2020; Lusvardi 2022), even if some voters consider the issue to be highly important. Scholars who investigate the idea of descriptive representation often point out note that raising the salience of issues that are important to a minority group but not the majority is a core role played by members of that minority group in political office (Curry and Haydon 2018; Badas and Stauffer 2018; Campbell 2016). Boards may play this role—elevating discussions, increasing the visibility of issues that elected members of the local government might not know or care about, and demonstrating clear policy solutions to those issues.

At the same time, the presence of a weak board may be a weak or trivial substitute for other, more visible forms of political power. A broad range of scholarship has shown the importance of women's descriptive representation in elected office (Barnes and Holman 2018, 2020a; Swers 2013), including at the local level (McBrayer and Williams 2022; Holman 2015, 2017; Funk 2015). Women's representation in political office sends powerful signals about the legitimacy of the office (Clayton, O'Brien, and Piscopo 2019; Stauffer 2021), in part because women engage in work to elevate the voices of those marginalized from politics (Holman 2015; Kathlene 1994).

To test whether policy changes in symbolic and substantive areas are associated with the presence of particularly kinds of boards or descriptive representation in elected or appointed office, I turn to the SOW boards in cities. Here, I look specifically at the presence or absence of a commission on the status of women, an SOW board, a women's equity board, or other boards that advocate for women's equality. These boards exist in 43 of the large cities in my data. Unsurprisingly, these boards have the highest share of women members of any board category; 75 percent of the members of these boards are women. Women of color are also well represented on these boards, holding 36 percent of board seats.

I compare the presence of an SOW board to the effect of women's representation as mayors or holding the majority of city council seats, both of which are associated with changes in policymaking at the local level (Holman 2014). A final comparison is with women's representation on boards in the city. That is, does the city change symbolic and substantive policies when women hold positions across weak or strong boards in the city?

Cities created these SOW boards over the last 50 years to address issues of gender equality; many of these boards were created in the 1970s and 1980s at the height of the second wave of women's liberation (Wolbrecht 2000; Wolbrecht and Corder 2019). When mayor Tom Bradley created the Los Angeles Commission on the Status of Women in 1975, his mission was "to advance the general welfare of women and girls in the Los Angeles community and to ensure that all women have full and equal participation in City government." The Denver Women's Commission (created in 1985) has the goals of recommending "procedures, programs or legislation to promote and ensure equal rights and opportunities" for women, to facilitate research on women, and to coordinate and conduct workshops and public hearings on these issues. Some SOW boards focus on specific issues; for example, the Greensboro (North Carolina) Commission on the Status of Women focuses on education and equity, balance and health, women and violence, and leadership through service. Other SOW boards act as a resource for other city boards and departments seeking to study or improve their gender equality. Most SOW boards serve as advisory bodies; few have independent policymaking power.

To understand the impact of a city adopting and filling an SOW board, I examine three sets of outcomes: symbolic policy creation, substantive policy creation, and population outcomes. I start with a low bar: Does the SOW commission in a city increase the likelihood that the city will adopt symbolic policies relating to gender equity? One key role that boards may play is by elevating the importance of symbolic policymaking. Political science often focuses on the connection between descriptive representation and symbolic representation—that is, whether someone views political institutions with more trust when the person sees someone who looks like them or shares a key group membership with them (Hayes and Hibbing 2017; Badas and Stauffer 2018; Stauffer 2021; Clayton, O'Brien, and Piscopo 2019). One way such representation might matter is that descriptive representatives are able to translate their physical presence into the production of symbolic policymaking (Rouault 2017). These symbolic policies can serve to represent the interests of those excluded from power or as an indicator of future substantive policies (Conlan, Posner, and Beam 2014).

A city adoption of the CEDAW (Convention on the Elimination of All Forms of Discrimination Against Women, first discussed in this book in the Section III introduction) resolution is a symbolic action: there is not an enforcement mechanism, and the city is not responsible for completing any specific steps to address gender equality.[6] It thus represents an easy place for a commission to raise the salience of the issue and lobby for action from elected leaders. In some cities, this might even involve the commission drafting the ordinance or resolution for the elected leaders to adopt. Many of the early campaigns for cities to adopt the Cities for CEDAW resolutions emerged from city-level SOW commissions. For example, San Francisco, the initial city to adopt a full CEDAW resolution, in 1998, did so largely because of work by members of the SOW commission in the city. In other cities, SOW boards worked collaboratively with an elected official to draft the resolution. Further, some cities that do not have standing SOW boards have passed CEDAW ordinances and resolutions, providing variance in the outcome that allows me to test whether SOW boards are associated with an increased likelihood of CEDAW adoption and compare this to other representational factors such as the presence of a woman mayor or women on the city council.

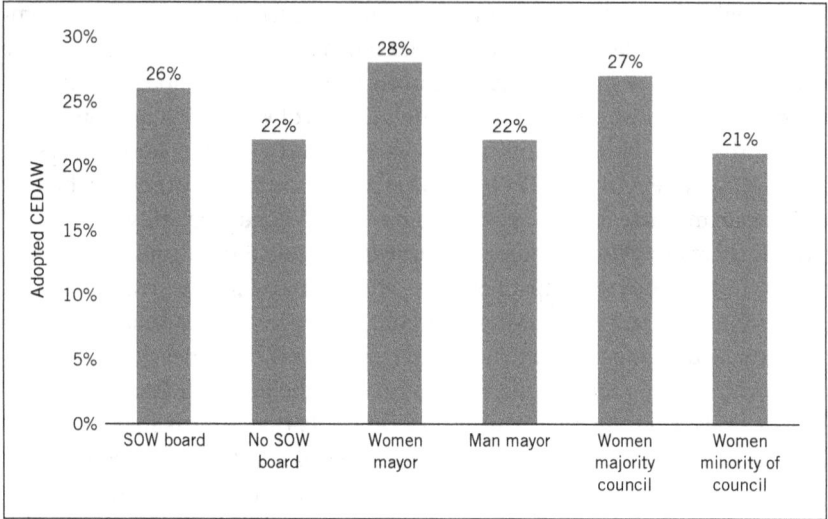

Figure 7.1 Adoption of CEDAW Resolutions by Board and Representation Characteristics. *Note: Predicted values from full models with controls for city demographics, politics, and board characteristics. Ordinary least squares models with clustered errors at the state level.*

I find some evidence of a positive relationship (see Figure 7.1): cities with an SOW board are slightly more likely to have enacted CEDAW resolutions (26%) compared to cities without an SOW board (22%), a difference that is statistically significant in a model with a full set of controls. At the same time, this 4 percent gap is smaller than the gap between cities with a woman mayor (28%) and not (22%) or a majority of women on the city council (27%) or not (21%).

When I look at women's representation on all boards in these cities, I also find a positive relationship (see Figure 7.2). As the share of women on boards in the city increases from low levels to high levels, so does the probability that the city adopts a CEDAW resolution. Moving from one standard deviation below the mean of women's representation to one standard deviation above is associated with a corresponding increase of adoption from 25 percent to 30 percent. But once I disaggregate women's representation on weak and strong boards, the association is driven by women's representation on powerful boards. Women's representation on weak boards has no statistical relationship with CEDAW adoption, while women's strong board representation is associated with a 12 percent increase in rate of adoption.

Members of these board offered nuanced evaluations of the board's impact on policy: some members I interviewed discussed the agenda-setting power of the board. "We are successful in bringing issues up to the council,"

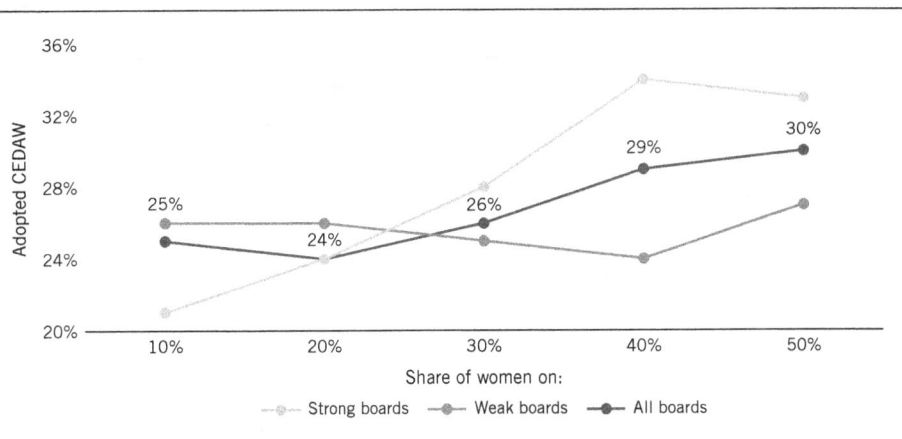

Figure 7.2 Women's Representation on Strong Boards Increases CEDAW Resolutions.
Note: Predicted values from full models with controls for city demographics, politics, and board characteristics. Logistic regression models with clustered errors at the state level.

said one board member, while another defined the successes of the board as "identifying new and creative ways to make [city] work better for women." Others expressed frustration; one member, who said she was resigning from the board soon, told me, "We don't DO anything. We just talk talk talk. I don't have time for that." Other women noted how outside the power structure their board was: "It doesn't seem like there's open communication between us and [the city's mayor]—I know he appointed me but I've never met him and I don't know that he even remembers we exist."

These comparisons suggest that SOW boards are not the only path by which a city might adopt a symbolic policy toward gender equality. Indeed, it appears that places that elect women to office and appoint women to powerful boards are those that are making symbolic policy on gender equality. The presence of a specific board does matter, but it can easily be replaced by other forms of representation in elected or appointed office to achieve the same outcome. Later in the chapter, I consider the ways that these factors might interact to shape policy adoption.

Boards and Substantive Policies:
The Case of #MeToo

Does the presence of specific boards matter for substantive policymaking? I examine whether a city adopted one of three policies relating to workplace sexual misconduct at the height of attention on these issues during #MeToo, a global movement aimed at addressing sexual harassment, assault, and misconduct (Holman and Kalmoe 2021a, 2021b; Costa et al. 2020; Castle et al. 2020). As I discuss in the Section III introduction, I examine three #MeToo city policy outcomes: Did the city adopt an antiharassment policy for city employees? Did the city ban automatic arbitration and NDAs for sexual misconduct? And did the city set up policies that protect employees from misconduct by elected officials? Some cities adopted all three of these policies, while others adopted a single policy or none. To simplify analysis, I present whether the city adopted any policy at all from 2019 forward; results do not vary substantially if I look instead at a count of policies or at each policy individually.

As I did with the CEDAW resolutions, I examine the relationship between an SOW board and the adoption of any of these sexual harassment policies alongside women's presence in the office of mayor and as a majority of the city council. I also compare this to women's representation on boards overall in the city, and on weak boards and strong boards. I again estimate a full set of models and present the substantive effects in figures. To simplify analysis, I present whether the city adopted any policy at all from 2016 forward; I consider cities as having adopted these policies only if they newly adopted a policy or substantially revised a policy in the period after the fall of 2016 to the spring of 2022.

In comparison to the CEDAW resolutions, I see no effect for the presence of an SOW board on the adoption of sexual harassment policies but I see significant and substantively meaningful effects for the presence of a woman mayor or majority of women on the city council. These effects (see Figure 7.3) include an increase of passage of 27 percent between a male mayor and

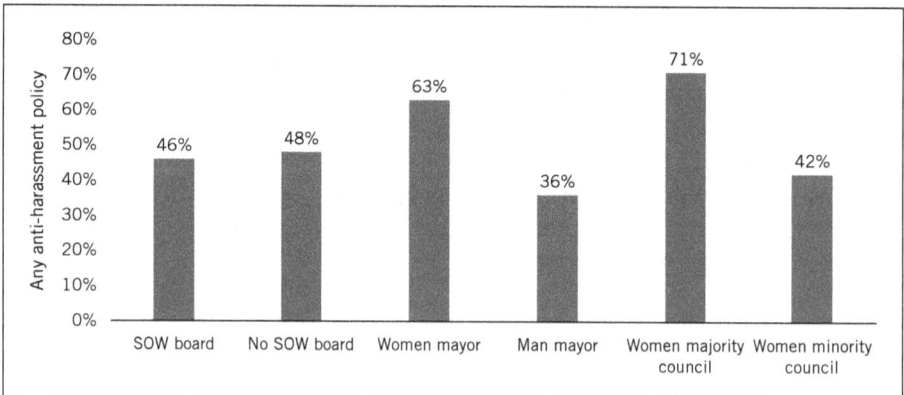

Figure 7.3 Women's Representation in Elected Office Increases Passage of Sexual Harassment Policies, but the Presence of an SOW Board Does Not. *Note: Predicted values from full models with controls for city demographics, politics, and board characteristics. Ordinary least squares models with clustered errors at the state level.*

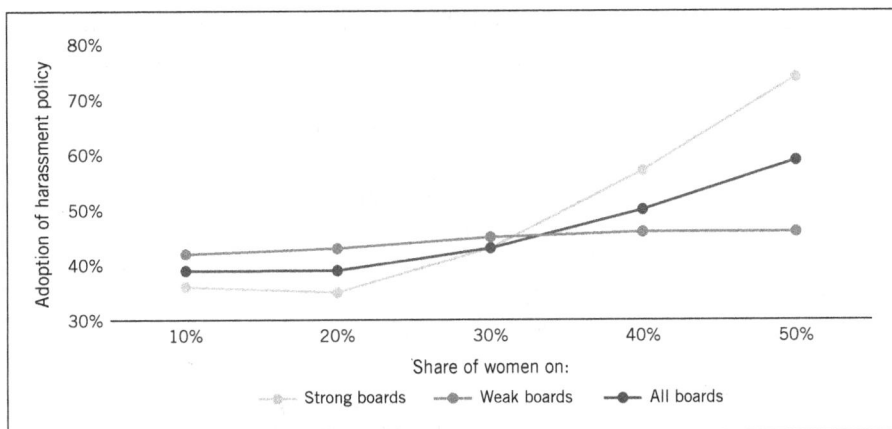

Figure 7.4 The Share of Women on Strong Boards Increases Adoption of Harassment Policies. *Note: Predicted values from full models with controls for city demographics, politics, and board characteristics. Logistic regression models with clustered errors at the state level.*

a female mayor, or a 42 percent increase in probability between a city council that has a majority of women members compared to one that has a minority of women members.

Comparing the rate of adoption of harassment policies across women's representation on all boards, weak boards, and strong boards, I again find that women's representation on strong boards is far more impactful than women's board representation overall or on weak boards (see Figure 7.4). Moving from a low level to a high level of women's representation on strong boards is associated with a dramatic increase in the likelihood that the city adopted at least one of the antiharassment policies; in comparison, women's representation on weak boards has no significant or substantive effect on the city's policy adoption.

Boards and Substantive Policies: Minority Empowerment and Ban the Box

In 2018, the Greater Tulsa Area African-American Affairs Commission met for the first time; the city had long had boards for Hispanic Affairs, Indian Affairs, and Women's Affairs, but it had resisted calls to create a similar board for African Americans in the city. After her election in 2016, city councilwoman Vanessa Hall-Harper organized community groups toward the creation of the board. She argued, "The reason for having an African American affairs commission is to have a central main frame to advocate for issues such as education, economy, health and the political wellbeing of those in the community" (Hutchins 2017). In response to these pressures, Tulsa mayor Dewey Bartlett created the 23-member board in 2017 (Brockman 2018).

Like SOW boards, cities rarely vest minority empowerment boards with independent powers. The Greater Tulsa Area board is advisory but has big plans; as one of the chairs noted, "I don't want this to be a commission in name only. I want to set goals, and I want to accomplish them. I want success" (Brockman 2018). The commission has since set a strategic plan and carried out a series of events, from art exhibits to expungement clinics. Yet, the board is also stymied by the lack of official power; the members acknowledge this. The chair, again: "There are some issues and problems that we will not be able to effectively address given our role, responsibility and vested powers but we will work to identify solutions to problems that exist within the African-American community" (Brockman 2018). In contrast to Tulsa, Baltimore created an Interracial Commission in the 1930s (*Maryland Historical Magazine* 1962)[7]; this commission existed on and off until the 1980s (Thomas 2016), when it appears to have simply been forgotten about and gone unstaffed until it stopped appearing in city records.

Just as cities adopted SOW boards in response to a variety of calls for change from women and feminist organizers, cities also adopted minority empowerment boards in response to critiques about the exclusion of people of color from important policy decision-making arenas. As the Tulsa and Baltimore examples show, the timeline of adoption of these boards is quite long—ranging more than 40 years from the first created board to the most recent in my Large Cities Dataset.

Nearly one in three Americans have a criminal record, with a disproportionate share found among African Americans, particularly African American men (Lageson 2022). People with criminal records are less likely to be employed full time, participate less in politics, and are less engaged with civic culture (García-Castañon et al. 2019; H. L. Walker 2020; Owens and Gunderson 2023). One cause of this disengagement is that governments target previously incarcerated individuals with specific administrative burdens and "penal harm"; for example, a city might ban individuals with criminal records from applying for certain occupational licenses or employment. The Ban the Box movement emerged as a direct challenge by the previously incarcerated and their support networks to a specific form of this discrimination: that applications for employment and housing required applicants to reveal whether they had a criminal conviction on their record and would immediately discard the applications of those individuals who selected yes. Typically, city-level BTB policies ban asking about criminal backgrounds at the initial stage of application and for public employment only.

TABLE 7.2. CITIES WITH MINORITY EMPOWERMENT COMMISSIONS HAVE HIGHER LIKELIHOOD OF ADOPTING BAN-THE-BOX (BTB) POLICIES (AND VICE VERSA)			
	BTB policy (%)		Minority commission (%)
No minority commission	22	No BTB policy	38
Minority commission	35	BTB policy	51
Note: Post hoc predicted probabilities from model with full controls.			

In this section I ask, Is the adoption of a city-level BTB policy more likely in cities with boards that might advocate for such a policy? Given that criminal justice reforms have a disproportionate impact on Black community members, that Black elected leaders represent Black interests more strongly, that the Black community is more supportive of criminal justice reforms (Broockman 2013; Eckhouse 2019; Bobo and Gilliam 1990), and that Black mayors are more likely to be in power when a city passes a BTB policy (Owens and Gunderson 2023), I test whether the presence of a Black or minority empowerment board is associated with an increased likelihood of a city adopting a BTB policy. See Table 7.2.

The answer to whether minority empowerment commissions are associated with BTB policy adoption is both yes and no. In many cities, the story here is complicated, as the creation of minority empowerment boards and criminal justice reform commissions can occur concurrently with a city adopting a BTB policy. For example, Tulsa adopted a BTB policy in 2016, two years before the creation of the Greater Tulsa Area African-American Affairs Commission. Thus, if I ignore dates of creation (which, honestly, are often very hard to nail down precisely for many commissions), the presence of a minority empowerment board is associated with a statistically significant increase in the probability that a city adopts a BTB policy. But adopting a BTB policy is also statistically associated with a city creating a minority empowerment board or a criminal justice reform commission.

The big takeaway is that cities that do one of these things (create and staff minority empowerment commissions) do the other (adopt BTB policies) as well. This is particularly true for cities that created minority empowerment commissions in the last 20 years. Is this surprising? No, it's not. As I show in Section I of the book, the root causes for the creation of a minority commission (the representation of people of color in elected office, group power in the community, pressure on elected officials) are the same as others find when looking at the adoption of BTB policies (Owens and Gunderson 2023).

How well do boards meet the expectations for representation when it comes to either symbolic policy or substantive policy? Taking these three case studies—of COVID policymaking, of CEDAW and sexual harassment policies, and of Ban the Box policies—together, the presence of a board dedicated to advancing the equality of a particular group may be associated with symbolic policies, but to achieve substantive outcomes, a group needs representatives in positions of power, not just symbolic figureheads.

Why Are Strong Boards More Successful at Producing Policy?

Why is it that representation on strong boards is associated with both symbolic and substantive policy, but the presence of a particular kind of weak board is not? One clear possibility is that strong boards have better relationships with those who actually make policy in cities, including city staff and elected officials. In Chapter 6, I showed that donors to elected officials are better represented among strong board members. Here in Chapter 7, I focus on the relationship between board strength and city staff and the interactive relationship between boards and elected representatives.

Staff and Decision-Making by Boards

"I just ask the staff to do it for me" was the response by one economic development board member to my question of how he navigated making policy. Why do some boards help cities make decisions and others do not? For many boards, the answer is that some cities employ a full-time bureaucrat who works for the city and works with the chair, president, or membership of the board to prepare an agenda for the board to consider. But, like many other institutional factors, the staff assigned to these boards takes a different role and function for strong and weak boards. I read the meeting minutes of every board in 2018 in Richmond, obtained via a public records request for the meeting minutes. Within these minutes, I looked at three factors: whether a staff member was present at the meeting; if a staff member was present, how many were present; and how many times the staff member spoke during the meeting.

As expected, the role of staff varies across weak and strong boards. For strong boards in Richmond, staff members are universally present at every single board meeting. For weak boards, staff members are present at two-thirds of meetings, with a minimum of 25 percent of meetings. Thus, staff members do not completely ignore weak board meetings but often they interact only infrequently with the members at meetings. These differences also appear in the number of staff who attend meetings: for weak boards, the average number of staff is 1.1; only rarely does more than one staff member attend a meeting. In comparison, an average of three staff members attends each strong board meeting. Finally, staff members are much more likely to speak at strong board meetings: staff members appear in the meeting minutes an average of 5.5 times per meeting at strong board meetings and an average of 1.3 times per meeting at weak board meetings. The most common occurrence of staff appearing in the meetings is a formal note that a staff member from a particular department is at the meeting. Interestingly, several board members on strong boards brought up connections to other offices that they have held, such as school board or corporate board memberships, as examples of how they learned to effectively use staff. "When I was on the school board, the superintendent and their staff—they were amazing. They helped us develop the agenda, what to focus on. When I moved to [current strong board], I asked the staff to do the same thing. Later I realized that was maybe out of line? My wife sits on [weak board] and they don't seem to have a staff. But maybe she just doesn't ask?" Another board member noted, "Like when I sat on [corporate board], the staff are really guiding us." These qualitative responses suggest that the relationship between board members and staff is the product both of who sits on these boards and the availability of staff.

Connections between Elected and Appointed Officials

Another path by which boards influence policy is via their connections to elected officials. While this poses a problem for inference because it is difficult to disentangle the effect of the board from the effect of the elected leader, such connection also offers an opportunity to understand the interactive effect of boards and representation. I return to the symbolic CEDAW resolutions and the substantive antiharassment policies. If elected leaders shape policy in conjunction with boards, then I should find accelerated effects of representation and board characteristics. Responses from board members echo this: one SOW board member noted, "We worked and worked on a childcare policy, but it wasn't really until [city council member] started paying attention to the issue that we could make real headway on the policy." Another pointed to a "meeting of the minds" between the board and the mayor as the key to accomplishing change.

Evidence of collaborative work is clear with the CEDAW resolutions: when I examine adoption by the presence of a board and the gender of the mayor and the city council, as well as the share of women on strong boards, there is a positive interactive effect with an SOW board. The presence of a woman mayor and an SOW board increases the probability of adopted CEDAW to 33 percent, while a majority woman council increases the probability to 31 percent. In the absence of an SOW board, these elected representatives are not associated with increased probabilities of adopting the resolution (see Figure 7.5). Similarly, the rate of adoption of a CEDAW resolution is positively associated with the interaction between women holding

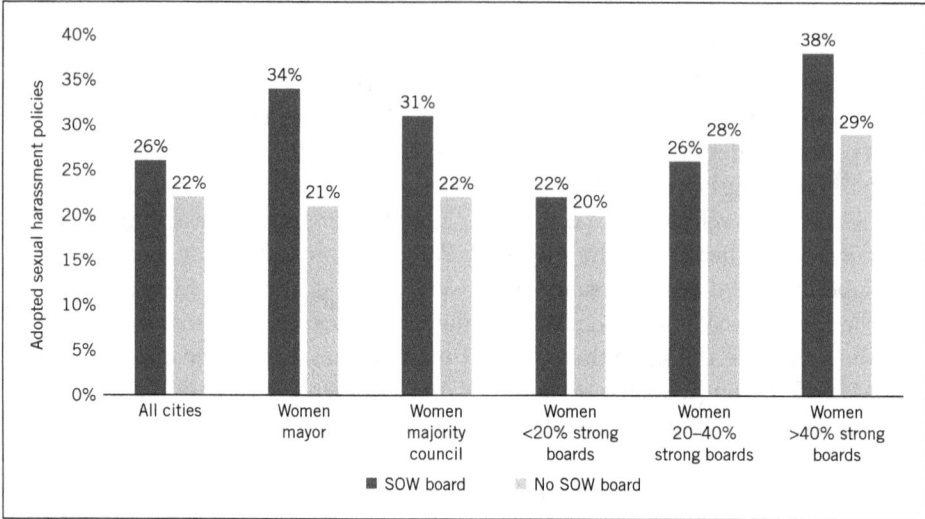

Figure 7.5 Women's Representation on Strong Boards Increases CEDAW Resolutions.
Note: Predicted values from full models with controls for city demographics, politics, and board characteristics. Logistic regression model with clustered errors at the state level.

more than 40 percent of positions on strong boards and the presence of an SOW board.

Women's representation across all strong boards is also positively associated with adopting a CEDAW resolution, but only in cities with a woman mayor (see Figure 7.6). CEDAW adoption rates in cities without a woman mayor do not vary by the share of women on strong boards. But in cities with a woman mayor, women's share of strong board appointments more than doubles the probability of adoption.

Do these interactive patterns also hold for substantive policy? I turn back to the adoption of sexual harassment policies in the #MeToo era. Unlike with CEDAW resolutions, I find no evidence that SOW boards increase substantive policymaking on gender equity policies (see Figure 7.7). While women's representation in elected office and women's representation on strong boards do continue to be associated with the passage of antiharassment policies, the presence or absence of an SOW board does not seem to increase the probability that a city will adopt one or more of the antiharassment policies. This is not to say that these boards do not matter when it comes to antiharassment policies; it is possible that cities with SOW boards did not adopt policies in the #MeToo era because these cities had adopted these policies well before the #MeToo era.

In comparison to the SOW board null effects, I do see that women's representation on strong boards interacts with representation to influence

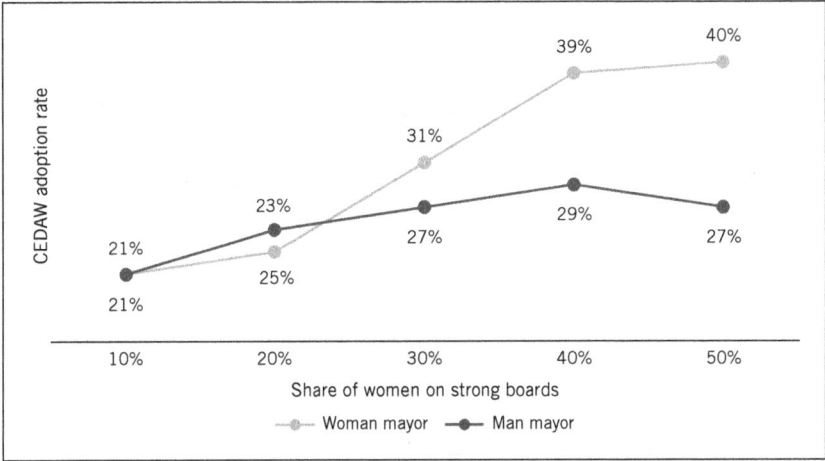

Figure 7.6 Women Mayors and Women on Strong Boards Increase CEDAW Resolutions. *Note: Predicted values from full models with controls for city demographics, politics, and board characteristics. Logistic regression models with clustered errors at the state level.*

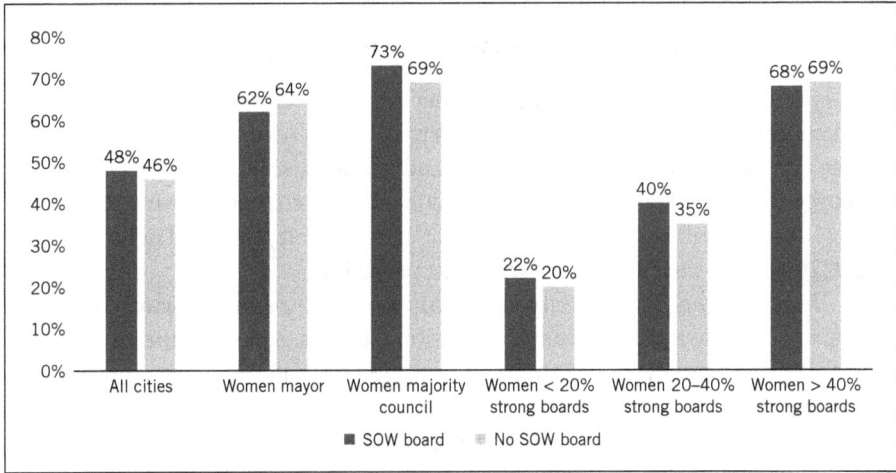

Figure 7.7 Elected Representation of Women Increases Antiharassment Policies. *Note: Predicted values from full models with controls for city demographics, politics, and board characteristics. Logistic regression models with clustered errors at the state level.*

harassment policy. In Figure 7.8, I show that women's representation on strong boards is positively associated with adopting policies under mayors who are men. But women's representation has the largest substantive effect under a woman mayor, where the probability of adopting at least one policy more than doubles as the share of women on strong boards increases.

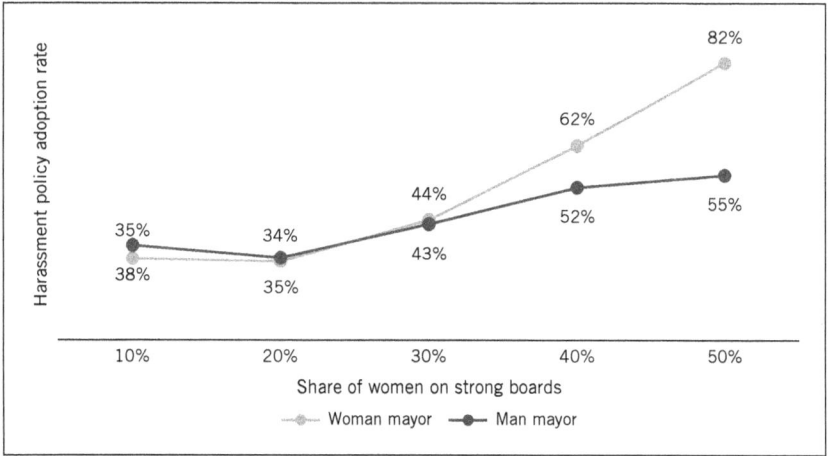

Figure 7.8 Women on Strong Boards in Cities with a Woman Mayor Adopt More Antiharassment Policies. *Note: Predicted values from full models with controls for city demographics, politics, and board characteristics. Logistic regression models with clustered errors at the state level.*

Boards and the Possibility of Policymaking

In January 2021, Sarah Williams, a former police officer in Lincoln, Nebraska, asked the city council to make changes to the city's sexual harassment policies after she suffered a sexual assault and gender discrimination as an employee of the city (Bischof 2021). Eventually, the city council, which was composed of six men and one woman (but had a woman mayor), acted in February 2022 to revise the city's antiharassment procedure.

Lincoln is not the only city to act only after victims came forward about abuses. In Milwaukee, the city's Common Council expanded the city's antiharassment policy in 2022 to include elected officials after a set of women came forward with evidence that the city's attorney systematically discriminated against women and regularly made sexually suggestive comments about women's bodies (Seehafer News 2021). The Common Council, which was 32 percent women at the time of passing the policy, had previously dealt with a mayor resigning because of sexual misconduct.

Neither Lincoln nor Milwaukee has an SOW board, nor do they have a majority of women on the city council. Women hold less than 30 percent of seats on all boards in both cities, and less than 25 percent of strong board seats. And in both cities, it took women suffering irreversible harm at the hands of city employees or elected officials before the city would pass antiharassment claims. In comparison, cities like Vancouver, Washington, Fort Collins, Colorado, and Cedar Rapids, Iowa, also passed antiharassment policies in the post–#MeToo era without needing to first face public shaming and law-suits. All these cities have women mayors and a majority of women on strong boards.

What do these findings mean for how local governments make policy in the United States? For democracy and representation? And for the work that many members of these boards put in to improve their communities? One central finding is that representation via weak boards is not a replacement for electoral representation or representation on boards with power. But because women, people of color, and women of color are underrepresented in elect-ed office and on strong boards, this deprives residents of cities of appropriate representation.

The interplay between the presence of women in elected office and the presence of women on boards suggests that there are cities in the United States where women have more power—and places where they have less power. Like the "women friendly districts" identified by scholars studying women's rep-resentation in Congress (Ondercin 2022; Palmer and Simon 2010), there ap-pear to be "women-friendly" cities, with higher levels of women's represen-tation in elected and appointed office, that then generate policies that are important for women's lives in those cities. Perhaps increasing women's repre-sentation on boards—or even creating new boards that address gender equal-ity—is a step toward creating a women-friendly city. Or perhaps it requires a deeper change in cities.

The COVID-19 pandemic also laid bare severe and persistent structural inequities in the United States. Particularly glaring was how the country's long history of systemic racism and sexism interacted with harmful economic consequences, such that people of color, women, and women of color faced compounding challenges associated with part-time labor, more job precarity, and work that required face-to-face engagement (Wenham, Smith, and Morgan 2020; Albanesi and Kim 2021). Local policymaking in response to COVID-19 reflected the gendered and racialized power structures in each city (Farris, Holman, and Sullivan 2022). Future research might consider how COVID-19 led to some elected leaders strategically using boards as policymaking de-vices, as well as when health boards and affordable housing boards actually shape policy.

A Veneer of Democracy

Years before I embarked on the long process of writing a book on appointed boards, I found myself talking to "Dave"[1] in our Florida beach town.[2] Dave, an artist and former porn director, excitedly informed me about his recent appointment to our town's Public Art Advisory Board. In many ways, his appointment made sense. In a world of bland subdivisions, McMansions, and retirement communities, Dave, and his bar[3] full of art, stood out. The only issue, according to Dave, was that the city held the twice-a-month public art board meetings at 10 a.m., a "super early" time for someone with his schedule. Years later, the town's arts board would come under fire from the public for choosing to terminate an agreement with a nonprofit organization that ran a museum and an events center. One resident, upset over the decision, saw it as undemocratic: "Three people got to decide for the 68,000 people who live in this town without bothering to talk to the community or even address whatever their concerns were" (Villanueva-Marquez 2021).

Weak Boards, Strong Boards, Deliberation, and Democracy

Throughout this book, I argue that two forms of boards exist: strong boards, which make policy, and weak boards, which do not. But boards may serve other roles in their communities beyond policymaking and advising. Perhaps, for example, the deliberative structure of boards could result in democratic gains even without policy impact. To improve citizen engagement and the quality of democracy, scholars have long promoted deliberative democracy mechanisms (Barber 1985; Gutmann and Thompson 1998; Mansbridge 1983; Collins 2018), including focusing on increasing citizen participation in government, gathering feedback from a community's residents, and sharing the decision-making capacity of government across a larger set of individuals (Zhang and Liao 2011; Portney and Berry 2010; Einstein, Palmer, and Glick 2019).

These participatory mechanisms often focus on the process of deliberation, rather than just policy outcomes. In his work examining deliberation in local government Jonathan Collins outlines the basic criteria for a truly deliberative body: initial disagreement, diversity, pursuit of the common good, information exchange, collective decision-making, and justification (Collins 2018). Appointed boards meet many of these requirements: they make decisions about issues where there is some disagreement (Habermas 1984), and the decisions should occur among a diverse and representative set of individuals (Fishkin 1991; Mansbridge 1983) who exchange information and are interested in a common good (Benhabib 1996; Barber 1985; Chambers 2003). The final decisions, whatever they may be, are collective and are justified to the public (Dryzek 2001; Collins 2018).

The issue, however, is that while boards generally meet these standards, each board rarely individually meets them. That is, while boards collectively meet the criteria for democratic deliberation, once I break the entities into weak boards and strong boards, these standards apply to only one type of board or another. Do boards discuss issues where there is some disagreement? Do they come to collective decisions? Yes, weak boards do discuss (often, at length) issues where there is disagreement (see Chapter 5), but they do not seem to come to collective decisions. On strong boards, there is rarely disagreement among the board members, even if the public at large is split on the issue at hand, but there is decision-making. As one newspaper story noted, "It was a relatively short but eventful meeting for the Planning Board," where the "events" consisted of making successive decisions about development in the city (Crandall 2023). Reviewing a year of the hearings of economic development boards in six cities (81 meetings in total), I found one meeting where the entire board did not vote to approve a project. Members of these boards do engage in due diligence: they read materials, they ask questions, and then they universally approve the projects brought before them. Even those issues that inspire passionate activism from the community (Einstein, Glick, and Palmer 2019; Einstein, Palmer, and Glick 2019; Einstein et al. 2023), such as housing and zoning decisions, rarely feature sincere deliberation among members of the board, just among the public. Strong boards feature decision-making without deliberation.

In comparison, weak boards often have deliberation within the board itself; these include long meetings to discuss issues ranging from housing discrimination to the racist legacy of redlining to gender equality in hiring practices. For example, when I estimate the length of meetings, both human relations commissions and human rights commissions have meetings that last an average of 174 minutes—nearly two and a half hours long. Much of this time is spent in deliberation, but these commissions rarely make decisions. The goals of the Human Relations Commission of Durham, North Carolina, include "promoting dignity for all citizens of Durham." The commission's 2022 year-end report notes the commission's successes as "listened to our neighbors," participated in a National Night Out program, and viewed presentations from five different city entities. That is it. Examining meeting minutes shows that the commission's 17 members each spent more than 15 hours in commission meetings over the year and that much of each meeting involved deliberation over key issues associated with affordable housing, racial equality, and policing. But according to the board itself, as told in its annual report, or via a reading of the board's meeting minutes, this deliberation did not produce any key decisions. Weak boards feature deliberation without decision-making.

Does it matter, though, if only some kinds of boards meet each criterion for a deliberative body? Deliberation is a valuable outcome on its own. But I would echo earlier scholars in their concerns about the segregated nature of boards. In their deep investigation of how cities created policy in response to Model Cities and other federal mandates, Bachrach and Baratz (1970, 70–71) note, "The appointments, which were easily justified on the grounds that important public posts should be filled only by the most highly qualified persons, not only denied Negroes participation in the making of important decisions, but also all but foreclosed the possibility that their grievances could be heard." In other words, Black isolation from the political system was made more complete and their political apathy fortified through what may be called a "sustaining nondecision," or one that "prevents an overt challenge to the existing political process and the allocation of values it produces" (Arnstein 1969). Sally Nuamah's (2022) evaluation of how Black communities react to sustained conflict over school closures suggests that this "veneer of democracy" can promote further retreat from political life and disillusionment with the system.

Boards and Transparency

The final criterion is perhaps the most difficult for boards to meet: that final decisions, whatever they may be, are collective and justified to the public (Dryzek 2001; Collins 2018). This criterion touches on a central tenant of democracy: transparency, where citizens must be able to gain knowledge about the "operations and actions" of democratic institutions in an organized and accessible manner (Fung 2013). Of particular importance is the ability of citizens to access information about policy and the outputs of government— that is, when and how the government makes decisions (Hollyer, Rosendorff, and Vreeland 2011; Meijer 2003). Advocates for deliberative democracy and the inclusion of the public in policymaking argue that deliberative structures can also serve to educate and persuade the public about the policy at hand (Beierle 1999; Walters, Aydelotte, and Miller 2000).

Local appointed boards fail to meet both the "operations and the policy standards of transparency," in that few people are aware of how each board makes decisions or whether a board is even able to make policy decisions. I do not blame city residents for their lack of knowledge. In most cities, finding the outcomes of a board decision is a mazelike process, where individuals would need to know where to look for agendas and meeting minutes and how to read these documents. And that is the best-case scenario, wherein a city actually posts those documents in a timely manner. Board members themselves acknowledge this in interviews: one zoning board member told me that they were not "sure that anyone [in the community] knows anything about the zoning board. When we meet or what we meet about. What we do." The board member went on: "But also, why would the average resident care? We don't make it easy. We don't make it worth their time."

If boards are deliberative via this criterion, then the public would, at a bare minimum, need to be aware of what boards do and how they operate. But this is not the case. Here, I examine empirically whether residents of cities have any knowledge about boards or their activities. Recall, from the beginning of the book, AOC's call for the creation of police oversight boards. I use the Black Lives Matter protests and an uptick in interest in police accountability to attempt to understand how and when individuals know about appointed boards. As I discuss in the Section III introduction, I surveyed individuals who lived in large cities and asked them whether their city had a police oversight board; then I asked those who answered yes to select the powers of the board. I consider the first question to be easier: people who pay only nominal attention to local politics might know whether their city has such a structure. The second part is a tougher test, as only those who pay very close attention to local politics and police oversight might know the rules about the design and power of these institutions (see Figure 8.1).

Given the public discussions in the spring and summer of 2021 of civilian oversight boards following the murder of George Floyd by Minneapolis police, asking about these boards is a best-case scenario. But even asking about boards that had recently been a part of a broad national discussion about criminal justice reform resulted in a low accuracy rate. Of the whole sample,

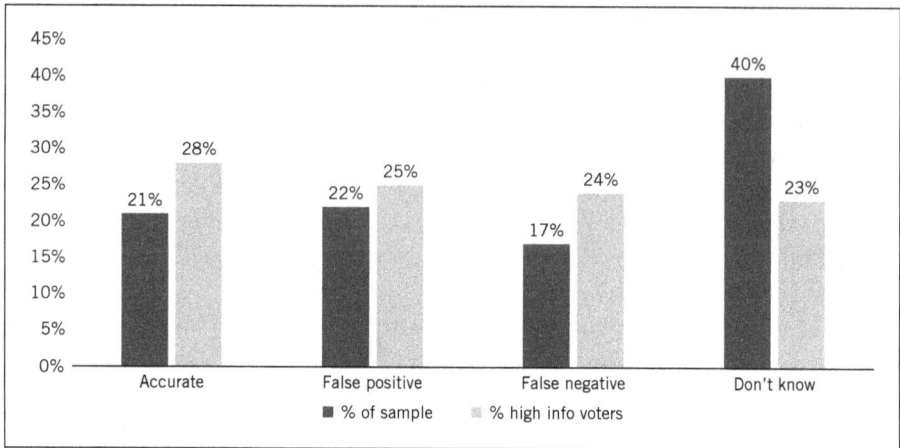

Figure 8.1 City Residents Are Not Knowledgeable about the Presence of Boards.
Note: Survey of LUCID respondents in large cities.

the most common answer is "don't know" (40%) and only one in five respondents (21%) answered correctly about whether the city had a civilian oversight board. Interestingly, respondents got the answer wrong in both directions; that is, people thought that there was a board when their city did not actually have a board, and they did not know about a board when their city did have one.

The (lack of) knowledge about boards also extends to high-information voters. Here, I identified high-information voters by asking respondents to tell me if they had voted in their last municipal elections (yes, no, not sure), to recall what date that election was held on (open-ended), and to provide the name of their mayor (open-ended) (Sumner, Farris, and Holman 2020). Among the much smaller group of individuals who reported they had voted and gave correct (or close to correct[4]) information for the latter two questions ($N = 243$), rates of knowing about their cities' civilian oversight board are higher (28%). But false positives and false negatives also increased, with high-information voters seemingly more likely to guess about their city's boards.

For those who answered correctly, did they know about the details of the board? In short, no. Three-quarters (73%) of participants who accurately said their city had a civilian oversight board attributed more power to the board than the board actually was granted.[5] As I discuss in Chapter 4 (and as Krishnamurthy [2023] finds with a larger set of boards), civilian oversight boards overwhelmingly take the form of either a "monitor" or an "investigator."[6] People are optimistic about the power of their city's oversight boards. Most respondents, including the high-knowledge respondents, said that their board had "investigator" powers when in fact their city's board has monitor powers. Respondents were also often wrong about the membership of the boards: very few respondents correctly identified that current and former police officers could serve on their city's board, and most assumed that membership was drawn from active community groups.

Even highly engaged members of the community are often unaware of what boards do or how boards operate. In a survey of civically engaged women in Richmond, Virginia (Holman, Iyer, and Wolbrecht 2023), respondents expressed frustration with the "mazelike nature of local politics." Interviews with current board members in large cities confirm this; board members on weak boards noted that they "didn't even know" before they joined that "it's all talking and nothing happens." Others noted that "some of these boards don't actually get to make real change" and that "people there may not want to actually do anything." Others were more suspicious: "It is almost like [the city] doesn't WANT us doing anything." In comparison, members of strong boards noted that they did not anticipate that they "would be making these kinds of big dollar decisions" or that "we just decide things. And that's it. Shouldn't there be some kind of check?" Other members of strong boards took pride in their ability to make important decisions and to participate fully in the policymaking process. The lack of transparency about what boards exist, who sits on those boards, and how someone might be appointed to a board position privileges those with insider knowledge and fails basic tests for transparency in democracies.

Trust and Legitimacy

Central to concerns about a decline of democracy has been a crisis of legitimacy and trust, where the public views political institutions as suspicious, illegitimate, and untrustworthy. A legitimate and trusted political system is one in which the participants grant authority to the government and are willing to acquiesce to the government's commands (Spencer 1970; Rawls 2005). Trust in government and views of government legitimacy have a wide set of downstream positive outcomes. Individuals who trust government are more likely to comply with government rules and participate in voluntary efforts to support the government (Levi, Sacks, and Tyler 2009; T. Tyler 2006). Legitimacy can smooth the process of policy change and acceptance, particularly when the government chooses a policy that cuts against individual preferences (Weatherford 1992).

Even though people know much less about their local government than their state or national governments, trust and legitimacy are higher for local governments than for state and national governments (Leland et al. 2021; Cooper, Knotts, and Brennan 2008; Beshi and Kaur 2020). Some attribute this to the immediacy of local government (i.e., people can see local government policy in action all around them). Others point to the inability of local residents to accurately attribute blame to local government as a mechanism that reduces trust and views of legitimacy (de Benedictis-Kessner 2018; Trounstine 2013). At the local level, police misconduct and killings, financial mismanagement, corruption, and the perception of insider dealings all damage trust in local government (T. Tyler 2006; Ares and Hernández 2017; Rocha Beardall 2022; Bakker and Dekker 2012; Zhang and Kim 2018; Cordis and Milyo 2016; Macdonald and Stokes 2006). For example, Silva and colleagues (2022) find that poor performance by the police in a community lowers trust in local government across all racial groups.

It is possible that decisions made by an elected or appointed board might influence perceptions of trust and legitimacy . . . or maybe not. Looking at presidential commissions, Miller and Reeves (2017) find no differences in the acceptance of a decision or support for the administration. Similarly, research finds little evidence that the public is more or less supportive of presidential action when it is unilateral (i.e., the president decides alone) or via an appointed commission (Goehring and Lowande 2024). Low levels of information about local government (de Benedictis-Kessner 2018), a lack of understanding or curiosity about the functioning of local institutions (Bernhard and Freeder 2020), and a general opaqueness from off-cycle elections and low levels of electoral competition (Anzia 2011; de Benedictis-Kessner 2017; Farris and Holman 2024) do not suggest differing results at the local level compared to the presidential level. Here, I directly test whether decisions made by appointed or elected leaders influence views of government.

Appointed versus Elected Bodies and Views of Government

Can boards increase trust in local government and views of government legitimacy? Here, I turn to an experimental evaluation of trust and legitimacy to understand the effects. I examine attitudes toward police reform and affordable housing through the lens of board policy action. Both represent current debates in local politics in the United States, issues that are regularly handled by both boards and city councils, and issues where I can probe government legitimacy. And these boards differ in strength: planning boards regularly produce housing policy and are strong boards with independent authority, while I classify police oversight boards as weak boards as they rarely have independent power. These are also current issues that local communities grapple with and debate, with deep consequences for the lives of people who live in cities.

Does knowledge about (or supposed knowledge about) an oversight board influence perceptions of government legitimacy and trust? Maybe! Returning to the survey I presented earlier in the chapter, those individuals who believed that their city had a police oversight commission were more likely to say that they trusted local government (0.52 on a 0–1 scale) than those who did not believe that there was such a board (0.40, $p < .05$). But being right about the presence of that board is not similarly associated with higher levels of trust; those who correctly guessed that their city had an oversight board trust their local government at rates similar (0.45) to the rates of those who correctly guessed that their city did not have an oversight board (0.46). But many of the factors that go into whether someone *believes* that their city has an oversight board or not (or correctly *knows* their city has an oversight board or not) might also explain trust in government, including race, age, education, homeownership, gender, efficacy, and experiences with police violence (Silva et al. 2022; Abney and Hutcheson 1981; Emig, Hesse, and Fisher 1996; Holman and Lay 2020; Morris and Shoub 2023). I thus turn to an experimental approach to test the relationships between board action and trust and legitimacy.

Understanding whether appointed boards making housing and policing decisions shapes views about trust and legitimacy has external validity rooted in actual government decisions (McDermott 2011): boards often make decisions about these policy issues, including decisions that run counter to the broader interests of the public. As previously discussed, local boards play a central role in throttling the supply of new housing in many cities (Einstein, Glick, and Palmer 2019; Einstein, Palmer, and Glick 2019) and police oversight boards are rarely granted the power to change police policy and outcomes (Ferdik, Rojek, and Alpert 2013). I thus examine whether people's trust in local government and views of government legitimacy increase or decrease when policy decisions about local housing and police are made by elected officials or an appointed board.

Appointed versus Elected Decision-Makers

I start with this basic comparison: Does attributing a policy action on policing or housing to an elected board versus to an appointed board shift trust or legitimacy? Given that the control condition is a "good times" condition (Merolla and Zechmeister 2013, 2009; Holman, Merolla, and Zechmeister 2017), that is, a positive story about a rescued dog, I expect that both of the treatments will see declines in trust and legitimacy. And indeed, people are more trusting in this "good times" condition as both measures of trust and legitimacy are lower among the treatment conditions compared to the con-

TABLE 8.1. TRUST AND LEGITIMACY DO NOT VARY ACROSS APPOINTED VERSUS ELECTED DECISION-MAKERS

	Control	Elected	Appointed
Trust in local government	0.55	0.51	0.50
	(0.03)	(0.02)	(0.04)
Government legitimacy	0.62	0.52	0.53
	(0.03)	(0.04)	(0.03)

Note: Results from Experimental Study 1. Standard errors in parentheses. See Section III introduction for more information.

trol ($p < .05$, see Table 8.1). But I do not find that attributing the policy action to an appointed board reduces or improves views more than when an elected body makes these decisions.

Disagreeable Decisions by Boards or Elected Officials

What about if someone disagrees with the outcome of a decision by a body? At its core, this is the idea of government legitimacy: that you will abide by a government action, even when you disagree with the choice made by a political body. In Experimental Study 2, I consider whether presenting someone with a decision that is directly counter to their preferences shapes views of legitimacy and trust, and whether elected boards versus appointed boards making those decisions further shapes these views. As discussed in the introduction to Section III, all respondents were first asked to share their preferences about defunding the police and about allowing a project to bypass environmental standards in order for affordable housing to be constructed.

To test whether legitimacy-threatening behavior from an elected board versus an appointed board shapes views of government, I again use policing and housing. These serve as useful issues for this approach because public opinion on these policies is quite divided. Public opinion about defunding the police is decidedly divided in the United States; for example, in a 2020 poll, 41 percent of respondents supported "defunding the police in your community to spend more on other local services" while 50 percent of respondents opposed the statement (NBC 4 2020). Similarly, the public is divided on whether existing structures to hold police accountable for misconduct are effective: a 2023 survey found that 54 percent of those surveyed believed the police in their community are doing an excellent job or a good job at holding officers accountable when misconduct occurs, compared to 43 percent who see the police as doing an "only fair" job or a poor job (Pew Research Center 2023; Wilke et al. 2023). The public also holds divided opinions about the appropriate way to change the supply of housing, with nearly half of re-

TABLE 8.2. PEOPLE TRUST APPOINTED BOARDS LESS WHEN THEY DISAGREE WITH DECISIONS			
	Control	Elected	Appointed
Trust in local government	0.55	0.47	0.42
	(0.04)	(0.04)	(0.03)
Government legitimacy	0.53	0.50	0.41
	(0.03)	(0.02)	(0.04)

Note: Results from Experimental Study 2. Standard errors in parentheses. See Section III introduction for more information.

spondents in a 2019 poll favoring relaxing environmental standards in order to construct more housing, while nearly half were opposed to relaxing the standards (PPIC 2019).

Decisions that are counter to one's interests reduce trust and legitimacy, particularly if those decisions are made by an appointed board (see Table 8.2). Again, I find that those in the control condition (reading a story about a fairy garden assembled during COVID) had more trust in local government and a higher assessment of legitimacy ($p < .01$) than those in the appointed condition (as expected), but I do not find a significant drop among those in the elected condition.[7] I also find that government legitimacy is significantly lower among those who received the appointed treatment as compared to the elected treatment ($p < .05$); trust is also lower among those in the "appointed" treatment group versus the "elected" treatment group, but the difference is not statistically significant to the 0.05 level.

Elected and Appointed Bodies Refusing to Act

One core status quo–defending function of many appointed boards is to table, or refuse to further consider, a particular action if it runs counter to the interests of the city or the city's leaders. Does the decision by an elected board or an appointed board to not take a specific policy action (when intervention is possible) shape trust and legitimacy? Again, I compare the two treatments to a control condition where a local teen persevered to win a poetry contest (see Table 8.3). Reactions are as they were in the first study: individuals reading about the failure to act are similarly likely to reduce their trust and perceptions of legitimacy for both elected and appointed officials ($p < .05$ for both measures and both treatments as compared to the control). These are the largest drops in substantive effect that I find across the four studies.[8] Unlike in Study 2, I do not find that appointed leaders' failure to make decisions reduces trust and legitimacy significantly more than such failure by elected leaders.

Democratic theories point to the importance of deliberation, but it remains unclear if this matters in shaping views of government. That is, does

TABLE 8.3. PEOPLE DISLIKE BOTH APPOINTED AND ELECTED BODIES WHO REFUSE TO ACT

	Control	Elected	Appointed
Trust in local government	0.51	0.38	0.35
	(0.04)	(0.04)	(0.03)
Government legitimacy	0.54	0.41	0.38
	(0.04)	(0.04)	(0.03)

Note: Results from Experimental Study 3. Standard errors in parentheses. See Section III introduction for more information.

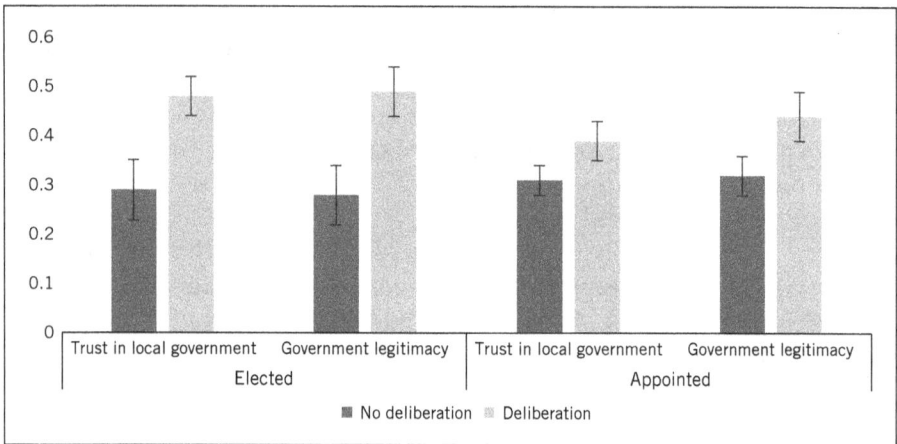

Figure 8.2 A Lack of Deliberation Reduces Trust and Legitimacy, Especially with Elected Leaders. *Note: Results from Study 3. See Section III introduction for study details.*

it matter to the public if an elected or appointed body spends time deciding about a policy issue? Deliberative structures increase trust in government, as do perceptions of policymaking as the product of deliberation (Collins 2018, 2021; Boulianne 2019; Asen 2013). In Experimental Study 3, respondents in either of the treatment conditions were also randomly assigned to be prompted with the information that the elected or appointed body spent "significant time deliberating" over the issue or "made the decision quickly." The information about deliberation came prior to questions about trust and legitimacy.

People do like decision-making bodies more when they deliberate and dislike them when they do not deliberate, but this applies more to elected decision-makers than to appointed ones. Evaluations of elected bodies vary more when information about deliberation is provided: trust and legitimacy both drop significantly ($p < .01$), with a substantively large gap, as shown in Figure 8.2. There is also a significant gap for appointed bodies ($p < .01$), but the substantive effect is far smaller than for elected leaders.

Descriptive Representation and Appointed
versus Elected Decision-Makers

Does it matter who is in the room when a decision is made? Political leadership in the United States is unrepresentative of the broader population, especially when we examine gender, race, and class (Holman 2015, 2017; Shah 2014; Barnes, Beall, and Holman 2021; Kirkland 2022; Scott et al. 2022). Who deliberates and makes decisions is also important for trust and legitimacy. Differences between the backgrounds of members of the decision-making bodies and the backgrounds of the citizenry also reduce legitimacy (Clayton, O'Brien, and Piscopo 2019; Bos 2015; Bos, van Doorn, and Nelson 2018; Hinojosa and Kittilson 2020; Clark 2019). In legislatures, the failure to accurately reflect society's demographics undermines the legitimacy of governing bodies. For example, Clayton, O'Brien, and Piscopo (2019) show that people perceive legislative decisions as less legitimate if women were underrepresented or not involved in the process. Similarly, Arnesen and Peters (2018) find that individuals are more willing to accept a decision when it is made by a group of people "like them" on various dimensions, including race/ethnicity and gender.[9] And members of government bodies see increasing descriptive representation as having consequences for legitimacy. Former Supreme Court justice William Brennan argued that "the sole end of making the Court diverse and reflective of America's heterogeneity was to foster legitimacy for it in the eyes of the American people" (quoted in Ifill 1997, 139). Thus, if a majority-Black group makes decisions, this may increase views of government legitimacy and trust, particularly among Black people.

As I show in Chapter 6, while boards are more representative of their communities than elected leaders are, the share of women and people of color is not evenly distributed across weak and strong boards. It is not just those who hold office who are unrepresentative; homeowners, older residents, and wealthy residents dominate public exchanges and deliberations. For example, political scientists Katherine Einstein, Max Palmer, and David Glick (2019) studied public deliberations on the construction of new housing in Massachusetts and found that older, white homeowners made up the vast majority of commentators at public meetings; because this group already has access to housing, they regularly block efforts to increase the supply of housing, particularly affordable housing.

In Experimental Study 4, I examine whether descriptive representation on elected and appointed boards influences views of trust and legitimacy. Here, there's substantial evidence from other venues that descriptive representation should matter; that is, people do view governments that have people who look like them or share life experiences with their group as more legitimate and trustworthy (Clayton, O'Brien, and Piscopo 2019; Mansbridge 1999; Stauffer

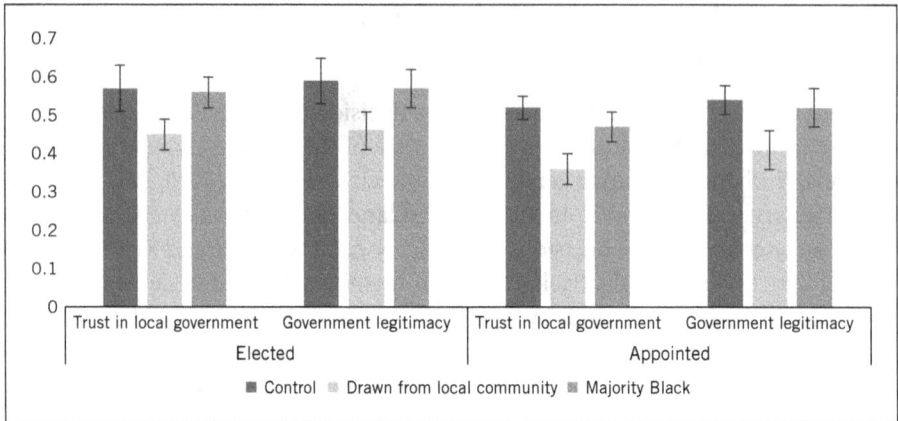

Figure 8.3 Descriptive Representation Increases Legitimacy and Trust for Both Elected and Appointed Boards. *Note: Results from Study 4. See Section III introduction for study details.*

2021). Indeed, political actors not of the group will often encourage representation by members of specific groups in order to appear as if they care about the substantive issues of that group (Weeks 2018, 2022; Valdini 2019).

Descriptive representation of Black members both on city councils and on appointed boards and commissions increases perceptions of government legitimacy and trustworthiness (see Figure 8.3). Given that the decision here is counter to the respondent's stated preferences, the higher levels of trust are particularly important. Indeed, compared to the control condition (a juggling competition), those in the "Majority Black" decision treatment had particularly high levels of legitimacy and trust.

Do these values vary by the race of the respondents? Recall that I oversampled Black respondents in Experimental Study 4, allowing me to compare how Black and white respondents viewed these actions. Hayes and Hibbing (2017) find that descriptive representation of Black members of the community in decision-making boards can increase both Black and white support for a policy, but particularly a policy that does not favor Black members of the community. My results confirm their findings in a different arena and policy: I find that both Black and white community members view actions by city council members and boards as more legitimate when a majority Black members make the decisions, but that Black members view majority Black decisions as particularly legitimate. Figure 8.4, which presents the difference in trust and legitimacy between the "representative of the community" and majority Black treatments, shows that the majority Black treatment increases positive feelings toward the government across all groups and decision-making bodies. But for Black respondents, trust and legiti-

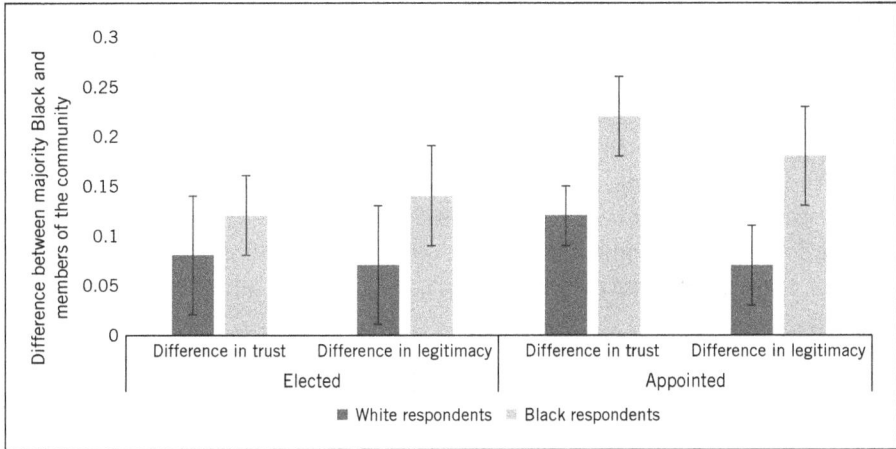

Figure 8.4 Descriptive Representation Increases Trust and Legitimacy for Both Black and White Respondents. *Note: Results from Study 4. See Section III introduction for study details.*

macy are particularly high after the respondents read about a majority Black appointed board making these decisions.

Open-Ended Responses

In Studies 3 and 4, I asked respondents to provide open-ended explanations for their evaluations of trust and legitimacy after reading about the elected or appointed officials' decisions.[10] I then hand-coded these responses[11] and used a roBERTa-Base model to assess the positive and negative sentiments of the text responses (Wang 2023; Muddiman, McGregor, and Stroud 2019; Russell, Macdonald, and Hua 2023). The written responses contained similar levels of negative sentiment and positive sentiment in both the appointed and elected conditions, and rarely mention the construction of the decision-making body in the responses. Responses have more negative than positive sentiment. For example, in Experimental Study 3, these negative comments include how ordinary voices and social movements do not seem to matter: "No one in government seems to care about anything anymore," "What does BLM matter if this shit happens," and "Police are gonna just shoot people I guess." Other respondents specifically mentioned how consistent they saw the decision with other actions by cities: "I wouldn't trust them to anything else because that's just what people in power do" and "No ordinary people are protected by government that's clear." In Experimental Study 4, the responses were particularly negative when the decision-making body was described as majority Black, including from Black respondents, including describing them as "sell out's," as "unforgiveable," and as "the worst . . . pretending to serve everyone. I've never gotten help from the government, not when it is filled with these kinds of people."

These studies suggest little positive link between boards making decisions and increased levels of trust in local government or views of government legitimacy. If anything, people trust local government less and view it as less legitimate when boards make decisions, rather than elected officials. Even if boards are meeting some standards for deliberation, the public does not view these actions as paying dividends in terms of trustworthiness or legitimacy.

Boards and Trust in Government and Government Legitimacy

In this chapter, I've focused on the question of whether the inclusion of boards in decision-making by governments has the potential to increase positive feelings toward local government more generally. Overall, I find few differences between how people view decisions made by appointed boards compared to those by elected officials. People usually respond negatively to the government making unpopular decisions (or failing to make them).

Across the studies, I focused on understanding the ways that boards might overcome a challenge that is central to government legitimacy and trust: that on a regular basis, governments must make decisions that individuals disagree with. Does it matter if a board (compared to elected officials) makes these unpopular decisions? The answer is generally no. People are less trusting and view government as less legitimate when it makes decisions they disagree with, and it does not necessarily matter who makes that decision. How might this vary if the issues were less salient? Much of what local governments do is quiet, uneventful policymaking, the government of the mundane. It is possible that people would be more trustworthy of board action on this form of policymaking.

But I do find that descriptive representation matters—both Black and white respondents are more favorable toward their local government when a majority Black body makes an unpopular decision. And Black respondents have particularly positive attitudes toward their local government after appointed boards that are majority Black make these decisions. Here, I have focused on only one group and one level of representation; it is possible that providing more information about the levels of representation and those representatives would matter further for government legitimacy and trust.[12]

9

POLITICAL INSTITUTIONS
AND THE POSSIBILITY
OF POLITICAL CHANGE

In April 2019, Mike Steele, a member of the Fort Worth, Texas, Human Relations Commission (HRC), posted a Facebook meme featuring a picture of Donald Trump and the message "FEELING CUTE. MIGHT SHOVE A BUNCH OF ILLEGALS UP PELOSI'S ASS LATER. IDK."[1] This message, posted on the board member's public Facebook page, was one of several hundred with similar messages that were predominately pro-Trump, anti-immigrant, anti-trans, or anti-Muslim posts. After Emily Farris, an associate professor of political science at Texas Christian University,[2] tweeted about how these messages were inconsistent with the HRC's mission,[3] Fort Worth's mayor, Betsy Price, called for Steele's resignation (Russell 2019). When asked, Mayor Price noted that the HRC was "largely a standalone body" (Ranker 2019b). A subsequent media investigation revealed that community members had previously brought Steele's posts to the attention of several city council members with no response. Mr. Steele refused to resign (Russell 2019), writing in a statement:

> As a disabled combat veteran of the first Gulf War and a former Watauga councilman of ten years, my public service on the Fort Worth Human Relations Commission is more than a duty—it is a calling. As a proud father of a LGBT son, I vehemently reject the defamatory comments posted about me on social and local media. I believed Mayor Betsy Price earlier today when she said, "We must respect freedom of speech. We must remember that many Americans have fought and

died for the freedoms we cherish today." Some may not agree with my message, but I followed policies and procedures set forth by the city. I do not intend to resign. I have fought foreign enemies, and I will fight domestic social media mobs.

Given Steele's refusal, Fort Worth had three options: at their next meeting (more than a month away) the city council could vote to remove him, the HRC could vote to expel him with a two-thirds vote, or the city council could decide not to renew his position when his term expired in four months. Ultimately, the HRC voted to remove Steele from the board (CBS DFW 2019).

As elected leaders in Fort Worth grappled with how to deal with a racist member of an antiracism commission, the questions became these: what purpose does this board serve for the city? Does it matter if someone with racist, anti-LGBTQ, and nativist views sits on a board whose goal is to pro-vide "information and services related to basic human rights, including en-forcement of the city's anti-discrimination ordinance and federal housing, employment and accommodation laws . . . [and] strives to help create a welcoming community for all people by providing resources and outreach efforts at promote basic human rights and facilitate harmonious relation-ships among Fort Worth's diverse population"?

In this book, I argue that cities create, fill, and support two kinds of ap-pointed boards: strong boards and weak boards. I take a historical-institu-tionalist perspective, where I see institutions as produced by historical strug-gles; these institutions persist because they serve as a tool to maintain power imbalances in society that favor white men who have political and econom-ic resources. In creating planning, zoning, public service oversight, and eco-nomic development boards, cities generated a set of policymaking bodies. These strong boards are autonomous, quasi-legislative, or quasi-judicial; have real policymaking power and independence; and are deeply connected to elected leaders and city staff. By design and network, the membership of these boards is largely composed of white people, men, and those with access to economic resources. The boards produce policy consistent with the status quo: homeowners and developers prefer higher costs for housing, and so do zoning and planning boards. Businesses want tax incentives, and so do eco-nomic development boards. Members of these boards describe their work as "routine" and "easy," while others call it "important" and "meaningful." A member of an economic development board expressed some discomfort with the decisions of the board, saying that their work "feels a little too important to be left up to amateurs, you know?"

After experiencing a variety of challenges to their political power during upheavals like the civil rights movement, cities created another set of boards, including those that oversee social services, minority incorporation, and criminal justice reform. These weak boards have little independent power, with institutional rules that are designed to promote deliberation but not decision-making. Mr. Steele is generally the exception here: these boards are filled with earnest individuals who care deeply about the issues at hand. These individuals often have backgrounds that are relevant to the board and are likely to be women, people of color, and women of color. Yet, despite the well-meaning nature of these volunteers, their work does not affect policy change, even though individuals join these boards with the goal of influencing policy: board members report their motivation as "bringing new voices to the policy making process," "representing the community's interests as the city makes decisions," and "changing who gets heard by those in power." Unfortunately for these community members, the boards they sit on do not affect policy in any substantive way, even if the members of these boards would prefer outcomes that are different from the status quo. The members of these boards often recognize this, discussing the "futility" and the "stalled" and "wasteful" nature of their work on the board.

To make the case that the system of boards in U.S. cities is two-tiered, I present three sets of evidence. In Section I, I start with a political development approach, using archival materials, contemporary reporting, and secondary sources to understand when and why cities created boards. In Section II, I move to a largely quantitative evaluation of what boards look like today, using current data from boards and examining their power, size, and membership. Finally, in Section III I examine whether board strength, policymaking, and membership matter, both in terms of policy and in terms of how people view their local governments.

Section I
In the first set of chapters of the book I ask this: How did we get to this point where cities in the United States universally use boards as governance institutions? In Chapters 2 through 4, I use a political development approach, concentrating on three questions: Under what conditions did cities create boards? How do critical junctures in urban history shape the creation, power, policymaking, and membership of boards? And how did boards contribute to inequality (particularly racial inequality) in cities? Chapters 2–4 focus on key durable shifts in urban politics. In Chapter 2, I discuss how machine politics and the Progressive movement dramatically changed urban politics and used boards to do so; in particular, both machines and Progressives attempted to use boards as mechanisms for thwarting their political opponents. In Chapter 3, I identify how the politics of racial exclusion and racism in cities in response to the civil rights movement prompted the privatization of some services in the hands of strong boards and the creation of weak boards across the country. And in Chapter 4, I focus on the rise of neoliber-

alism and economic development boards in response to the Reagan Realignment. The chapter and the section end with modern board creation, focusing on the creation and use of police oversight boards in response to police violence and misconduct and the Black Lives Matter movement.

Section II
In the next set of chapters, I ask: What consequences for power, representation, and policy arise from the creation of these weak and strong boards? In Chapter 5, I show the distribution of weak boards and strong boards by legal authority. Using information on decision rules and board size, I show that weak and strong boards differ in their membership size and rules; this results in strong boards' capacity for making decisions quickly, while weak boards' design promotes deliberation but not decisions. In Chapter 6, I consider membership, showing that women and people of color are underrepresented on strong boards but that they hold a significant share of seats on weak boards. Using New Orleans board membership as a case study, I show (1) how the demographics of a city matter in shaping the race and gender of board members and (2) that political donors are more likely to be represented on boards generally, but on strong boards specifically.

Section III
In the final section of the book, I ask: Do boards matter for policy or democracy? In Chapter 7 I bring these findings together to examine urban policy-making around gender and racial equity issues. Further, examination of COVID-19 policy and housing policy shows that while a particular kind of weak board in a city does not influence policy, the membership of marginalized groups on strong boards is associated with positive policy outcomes. Finally, in Chapter 8, I ask: Are these boards good for democracy? Focusing on the elements of knowledge, transparency, deliberation, trust, and government legitimacy, I use evaluations of board behavior, survey data of city residents, and a series of experiments to show that boards do not broadly increase the quality of local democracy.

Boards and Big Ideas about Local Politics

"There is a New Orleans Civil Service Commission meeting scheduled today. The http://nola.gov calendar includes a zoom link that leads to a Google map address in Fort Worth, Texas. There is no agenda posted." So tweeted Ben Meyers, a local political reporter in New Orleans in 2021. As I discussed at the beginning of Chapter 3, the Civil Service Commission in New Orleans is a powerful entity: its duties include quasi-judicial power to "make rules which have the force and effect of law" and to "serve as the court for all employee appeals of disciplinary actions." The commission also has legislative capacity to adopt rules and establish policies to "regulate the conduct of labor and management" of public employees. How will the public know what this board is doing or how they are making decisions if there is no agenda for the meeting or no access to the meetings themselves?

Transparency, Knowledge, and Local Boards

But media attention to local politics generally and to local boards specifically is the exception, not the rule, in today's journalism environment. Newspapers have been decimated by declining funds and staff, by consolidations and hostile takeovers from hedge fund companies. Coverage of local politics is one of the topics that has suffered the most (Darr, Hitt, and Dunaway 2019; Kalmoe et al. 2018; McGregor, Mourão, and Molyneux 2017). I watched a year of meeting videos in several cities and did not see a single local reporter at any meeting. I do not blame reporters for this; most of what boards do is deeply boring and unimportant (especially for weak boards). Even with a robust local news environment, this serves as a barrier to reporters paying attention even in communities with more newspapers and reporters.

The lack of information that residents have about boards is at least partially due to incompetence in how some cities provide information about boards. New York City has 111 boards, but little to no information is available on any of them and more than half of the links on the city's website are broken. Similarly, Baltimore, Maryland, Newark, New Jersey, and Colorado Springs, Colorado, had little to no information on the internet about their boards, the boards' members, or what the boards do, and these cities refused to answer questions via email or phone. Some cities purposefully shield this information: St. Paul, Minnesota, and multiple cities in Virginia informed me that I was not privy to information about who sat on boards because I was not a resident of their city or state. But when residents of those cities volunteered to ask for this information for me, the cities were similarly not forthcoming: three cities in Virginia ignored Freedom of Information Act requests from their own residents, and St. Paul told the resident who requested information about board members that that is "private information."

Sometimes even elected officials are unable to access information about who sits on boards and commissions. In New Orleans in 2015, the legislative director for a councilmember noted the importance of gender balance in appointments. When I offered into engage in an analysis of the gender balance of boards, the legislative director asked if I "could construct a list of members of boards during my report writing?" This was because the councilmember herself did not have and could not find a full list of board members. It was not just that the list needed to be assembled but that it was impossible to assemble because New Orleans did not keep a central list of who serves on appointed boards and commissions.[4] After 2015, the New Orleans mayor's office improved the information about boards and regularly posted up-to-date information about appointees. That is, until last year, when the city stopped posting information and left out-of-date appointee names on the city's website. As of this writing in September 2023, over 50 people listed on the website had expired terms.

If transparency is indeed "a self-evident good in Western society" (Etzioni 2010, 389), then cities are falling far short of this public good. Scholars often make the parallel between the rise of demand for public transparency and societal changes about expectations of transparency from medical practitioners, food manufacturers, and financial institutions: we used to tolerate a fair amount of "not knowing," but we do so no longer (Schudson 2015, 2020; Etzioni 2010). Future work might examine what the factors are that contribute to a city being more or less transparent with its board information, and whether outside interventions by organizations that focus on appointments[5] might increase transparency around who is appointed, when, and why.

Organized Groups, Elected Leaders, and Accountability

What has this study of the creation, use, membership, and effect of local boards contributed to our understanding of urban politics more generally? Theorists of urban power have long argued that conflict and cooperation between political coalitions or organized groups tells us much about how cities create policy and allocate power (Stone 1989; Shefter 1992; Dahl 1961; Logan and Molotch 1987; Anzia 2022; Benjamin 2017a). Some of these authors imply a kind of fairness: if less-resourced groups simply organize themselves better, they should be able to access policymakers and the levers of policy control. But those groups must operate within the institutions that exist or take on the heavy lift of changing or creating new institutions. And the institutions that exist, as I show, are heavily biased toward protecting the status quo and are designed to explicitly privilege the voices that are already the loudest in local politics or the voices of those who have connections to political insiders. Boards are one tool that those in power use to allocate resources to their inner circle and to exclude those they deem undeserving.

Boards offer those in power a way of subverting even those well-organized groups that are well-liked and supported in a city. In a 2021 poll of New Orleanians, respondents rated firefighters (73% approval) more positively than the New Orleans Police Department (50% approval), the mayor's office (36%), or the city council (61%). The positive views of firefighters are not new;

for example, they enjoyed 75 percent approval in 2013. Despite the positive views from the public, however, the city's firefighters have had a rough couple of decades. A drawn-out conflict between the mayor's office and the New Orleans Firefighters Union (Mozzone 2020) left the firefighters without a contract from 2012 to 2021 and had the mayor publicly denouncing the union's efforts (Stein 2023a).[6]

Some of the firefighter's problems stem from financial issues that originate with the New Orleans Firefighters' Pension and Relief Fund (NOFFPF) board. The NOFFPF board "manages the fund and all money donated, paid, or assessed for the relief or pensioning of disabled, superannuated, and retired members of the fire department, their widows and minor children, or widowed mothers, and for the payment of death benefits." Five of the seven members of the board are current or retired firefighters, who serve alongside the city's director of finance and a single member appointed by the mayor.[7] The NOFFPF board meets monthly or more often and makes decisions about the pension investments, as detailed as buying and selling certain funds and approving changing in beneficiaries.

Given the board's diligent work and attention, one would hope that the pension fund would operate carefully and in a manner that benefits the firefighters in New Orleans. But the pension fund has struggled to meet demands. In 2013, a government report identified debt to the firefighters' pension as "a serious problem" with "no quick fix" (BGR 2013); a later intervention by a local coalition of business leaders eventually bailed out the struggling fund. Add fraud to this: in 2020, the federal government arrested an accountant for embezzling more than $930,000 from the fund. He had successfully convinced the NOFFPF that a five-million-dollar investment was not profitable and had diverted the payouts from the investment to himself to pay for gambling, other personal debts, and home improvements (Wilkinson 2022). In 2021, the union finally negotiated a $15 minimum wage for firefighters through lobbying the New Orleans Civil Service Commission and the city council, bypassing the mayor (IAFF 2021; Truong 2021). The mayor has repeatedly pointed to the NOFFPF as the mechanism through which firefighters in the city should advocate their claims, even though the board does not address contracts or fair pay for firefighters.

One might ask, How does such a well-liked group of city workers who provide an essential, basic, lifesaving service to the city struggle so much with funding wages and pensions? In this book, I point to the role of appointed boards as serving status quo–enforcing and power-consolidating roles in local politics, even against groups that have salience, political power, and organization. Those interested in the power of organized groups in cities might investigate how and when groups might use boards as a diversionary tactic to obscure their actual goals.

Political Development and Path Dependency

This book draws deeply on the idea that choices made when institutions are created constrain that institution deep into the future (Mahoney 2000; Koelble 1995). Like many urban politics scholars before me (Davies and Trounstine 2012), I believe that institutions matter in shaping who lives in cities, what cities physically look like, and how urban policy operates. By using a political development approach, I hope I have convinced readers that boards are not created randomly but are instead the product of strategic political actions by those in power. Further, the choices made about the (varying) institutional design of these boards and how elected officials appoint people to boards and interact with members influence the policymaking power of the boards and their impact today. Boards fit well into the "new institutionalism" framework of urban politics (Lowndes 2001; Lowndes and Roberts 2013), which argues that the "rules of the game" play a crucial role in structuring political life (Chappell and Waylen 2013).

In examining the role of history in shaping what boards look like today, I have become increasingly convinced of the power of path dependency in influencing today's cities. At its core, path dependency means that institutions, once created, persist and become increasingly difficult to change (Mahoney 2000). As a result, even the smallest choice (say, how many members a board has) can have a very long-term influence. But institutions can be amended and changed; unfortunately, as I show, choices about reform are made in ways that reinforce the status quo and keep those in power, in power.

Understanding the ebbs and flows of organizations over time is hard; we are dependent on the records that are kept and often we cannot access complete information about how institutions function, particularly given the informal nature of many processes. Of particular importance is understanding not just the rules but also the "rules-in-place" or the way things are actually done (E. Ostrom 1999). Future work might consider engaging in a deep case study of policy change, such as Gains and Lowndes' (2022) investigation of police governance and policy change around violence against women and girls. Other work might consider how micro- and macro-level processes of institutions interact via boards to produce and constrain urban policy (Guarneros-Meza 2009).

Recommendations for Reforming Boards

Can anything be done about the veneer of democracy created by appointed boards and commissions in local government in the United States? I outline several tools that cities, states, groups, and individuals might use to reform local appointed boards and commission.

Some states and local governments have taken the diversity of boards much more seriously, instituting gender, race, ethnicity, or neighborhood quotas. When Los Angeles mayor Eric Garcetti established gender, race, and ethnicity quotas for boards in the city, he connected this to women's ability to access positions of power and influence: "Our progress is clear: my administration achieved gender parity on our boards and commissions for the first time in history; more women are in positions of power and influence than ever before." And, as I discuss in Chapter 5, he was successful: Los Angeles now has gender, race, ethnicity, and neighborhood parity in board appointments. Other cities might seek similar options; states might use Iowa's approach (McQueen 2021; Hannagan and Larimer 2010; Hannagan, Larimer, and Hibbing 2017) and dictate gender equality on all city and county boards and commissions. But as I outline in Chapter 8, if the representation of women and people of color remains concentrated among weak board members, even a quota might not produce the policy change that advocacy organizations and individuals seeking equality have in mind. Further, as Shannon McQueen's (2021) analysis of Iowa's gender balance legislation shows, these quotas may influence only the bodies that they directly apply to, with no spillover effects to elected office.

One solution to issues with transparency would be to require that cities provide up-to-date information about their boards and appointments, clear instructions about the appointment process, and information about the specific requirements and responsibilities of each board. In California, the state legislature began (in 2017) requiring that cities post "at least once per calendar year" a list of all board appointments and vacancies, and guidance as to the process of appointment. As a result, I could easily identify which boards exist and who sits on those boards, with far lower rates of missingness for my California Cities Dataset than for the Large Cities Dataset. Other states might consider passing similar laws as a mechanism for transparency and as a way to equalize the experience of trying to get access to information about local boards across local governments.

While my work has focused entirely on the creation and use of boards in local politics in the United States, there are clear parallels to other kinds of appointed bodies. Work on appointed boards in other countries, particularly other federal government structures, suggests similar uses of boards as tools to give the allusion of democracy (Hendriks, Bolitho, and Foulkes 2013). State-level commissions are common and are often plagued with issues that are similar to what I have observed at the local level. And academics reading this book will recognize similarities among administrative governance models at American (and beyond) universities, where committee work is highly variable in importance and is often used to distract from actual change. As is the case in cities, university faculty and staff often settle for deliberation without decision-making.

Cities—and others—could decide to radically change the structure of local appointed boards and commissions: What if all boards had similar levels of power? Were of the same size? Had the same rules for appointment? Or what if cities used a lottery system to randomly draw applicants to serve on boards? What if cities engaged in deep work to recruit new members of the community to serve on boards? Alternatively: What if cities got rid of all appointed boards and simply provided elected officials with better staff and resources so that an elected group of individuals made these decisions and could be held accountable for their positions and policies? What if a different world were possible?

NOTES

CHAPTER 1

1. Ocasio-Cortez (2020). AOC continued with a second tweet: "3. What does mental healthcare look like in your city? Too often our prisons are used to discard ppl struggling w mental health, housing. Invest in the latter. 4. Healthcare, living wage, housing & education guarantees. Without them we feed the cycle. What are your ideas?"

2. Throughout the book, I refer to these as appointed boards and commissions, boards, commissions, appointed boards, and appointed commissions. There is no legal difference between a board and a commission, and unless I specifically note a difference, all the boards and commissions in this book are made up entirely of appointed members. Please consider these alternative terms to refer to the same entities.

3. Minneapolis Municipal Code §172.10, "Police Conduct Oversight System Established."

4. As much as an inch of concentrated rainfall in some areas of New Orleans can prompt street flooding and an overrun of the pumping systems.

5. The S&WB relies on a combination of modern 60-Hz electricity and self-generated (via turbines) 25-Hz power; this latter source of power dates to the early 1900s. As one councilmember noted, "The combined age of the turbines is 379 years old" (SWBONO 2022). One of the turbines was hand-wound by Thomas Edison after New Orleans contracted with the Edison Electric Illuminating Company in 1886 to build a source of power for the city's drainage pipes (Schneller 2016).

6. Allegations range from people fixing bills of friends and relatives to double-billing to unusually high rates of pay for the system's executives.

7. The S&WB's billing system is antiquated and regularly involves the misapplication of very large water bills. The S&WB has been unwilling to engage in widespread reforms of their system (Myers 2023a).

8. For example, the FBI raided the SWBONO's plumbing department after a local news report identified widespread double-dealing (Hammer 2021).

9. An investigation into fraud led to the discovery of "what one employee described as a 'secret sex room.' One employee provided a video of it, showing couches, a refrigerator, a microwave, a TV and a shelf full of framed photos of nude women" (Stein 2023b).

10. The S&WB has been under a federal consent decree since 1998 for violating the Clean Water Act; the city's drinking water problems include saltwater intrusion, killer brain-eating amoebas, and lead, among other dangerous contaminants (Subbaraman 2019; Fox 2015).

11. For example, in their piece measuring local land use regulations, Gyourko, Saiz, and Summers (2007) include whether approval is needed from a "Local Planning commission," a "Local zoning board," a "County Zoning Board," or an "Environmental Review Commission" for development projects. Approval from at least one of these local boards is required by 81 percent of cities for projects that require a zoning change and by 76 percent of cities for projects even when a zoning change is not required.

12. My research approach differs significantly from the existing research on local boards. In his study of small-city boards in six states, John Baker (2015) uses surveys of board members and elected and appointed members of local government to understand the motivations of people who serve on these boards. Other scholars also survey or interview elected officials and board members (Dougherty and Easton 2011; Rebori 2011; Houghton 1988; Collins 2018) or use case studies of individual types of boards (Hendriks, Bolitho, and Foulkes 2013; Fung 2001; Einstein, Glick, and Palmer 2019).

SECTION I INTRODUCTION

1. In this case, employees of the city grew in number and power and demanded more institutional rules and protections (Anzia and Trounstine 2022).

2. The Civil Service Commission has five seats. The city council selects four of the members from a list of candidates prepared by one of four local universities (each university nominates three people); one member is a city employee nominated by fellow employees and confirmed by the council. The city charter dictates that the order of the list determines who is nominated if the city council does not take action within 30 days—the first person listed is appointed to the committee.

3. Cities in the United States are founded at different points in time (from St. Augustine, Florida, which was founded in 1565 to St. George, Louisiana, whose white residents voted themselves a modern segregated suburb in 2019) and go through key points of change and development in a staggered fashion. For this reason, creating anything close to a chronological history of urban development necessitates the exclusion of some cities and a focus on others.

CHAPTER 2

1. For example, New Haven, Connecticut, created a "Proprietors of Common and Undivided Grounds" Board in 1641 to distribute local land. The board still exists today and has been called "a sort of geriatric Skull and Bones Society, a secret society open to membership only upon invitation of those deemed acceptable to current members . . . a colonial vestige that is governed by folks elected in secret and holding office for life" (P. Bass 2017).

2. Little else is known about Hodges, other than he was the youngest mayor to serve (at age 28) and he had a generous hand with the drink (Simon 1993). Hodges died at age 35 from unknown causes.

3. Erie's (1990, 525) classification of Los Angeles as an "Entrepreneurial regime" also begins in 1880.

4. Previously named the Public Works Committee, the Public Works Board oversaw both street paving and street repair, along with other infrastructure decisions (Kassel 1929).

5. The Los Angeles Library Board was also created during this time (Hansen, Gracy, and Irvin 1999). These boards predated and survived changes from the 1889 freeholder's charter, which created six city departments that overlapped with existing boards (police, fire, education, libraries, health, and parks).

6. The commission could "adopt rules and regulations for the government thereof; it may establish, promulgate, and enforce proper rules, regulations, and orders for the good government of the police force." Honestly, this board had a ridiculous selection process: "Members shall be elected in the month of July, by the two branches of the city council, in the following manner, to wit . . . [one branch of the city council] shall [make the] selection, by a viva voce vote, which shall be recorded in their minutes, and a copy . . . forwarded . . . to the joint meeting, eighteen persons, three from each ward, who are voters in said city, and who shall be freeholders, and who shall not hold any office, state, municipal, or federal; the names of which eighteen persons shall be certified by the city council by the president of the board of public interests as the person from who the police commissioners are to be elected, together with the recorded vote for said board of public interest as above required. From the eighteen names thus sent in to the council by the board of public interests, the council, meeting in join session, shall proceed to elect six—one from each ward—no person shall be elected who shall not receive a majority in each branch of the council of the whole number of members elected to each branch; and in case there is no election, or those decline to act under the first nomination thus made, or whenever there is a vacancy, the board of public interest shall, in like manner, proceed to nominate to the council three times as many persons from the ward in which the vacancy occurred, as there are vacancies, and said vacancies shall be filled as above described." Charter of the City of Richmond, Virginia, 1885, pages 30–31.

7. New Orleans Council Series 1806, 1864, 1886.

8. Perhaps the most useful for political machines were election boards, which facilitated a variety of underhanded and corrupt schemes to suppress votes of opponents and elevate votes for the machine (Allswang 1977).

9. Or the "crowd of illiterate peasants," so named by Andrew White, a Progressive activist and first president of Cornell University (Judd 1979).

10. New Orleans's Progressive movement happened far later: reformers emerged as a powerful public force in the mid-1940s, reaching their peak power with the election of Chep Morrison in 1945 (Parker 1998). Even at this later date, Mayor Morrison used boards as a tool in his reformer efforts, including attempting to remove members from several powerful boards and the creation of a new set of boards. Progressive reformers in the city engaged in the same patterns as political machines: using their networks and campaign structures as the primary pool from which they drew board appointees.

11. Wilson advocated for the commission form of government in public speeches, in writing, and when he was governor of New Jersey.

12. You didn't think I'd write a book without talking about sheriffs? See Farris and Holman (2024) for lots more on sheriffs.

13. When Progressives failed to reform cities through local action, state governments provided a path, often via mandated boards for oversight and regulation. Progressives in New Jersey were able to lobby for a requirement that all city budgets gain approval from a state-appointed tax and civil service board (though local political machine bosses would later subvert the tool).

14. Political machines and corrupt individuals co-opted boards and commissions as a tool for local control and incentives. For example, Frank Hague, political machine boss and mayor of Jersey City, New Jersey, wanted to increase taxes on corporations in the city. Luckily for him, he had connections to the Democratic governor and arranged for "his men" to be appointed to the tax and civil service boards, which were supposed to provide a check on the taxation power of the local government (Erie 1990).

15. Hartford, Connecticut, is credited with creating the first board specifically focused on planning in 1907, but earlier boards exist in cities that aim to regulate land use. For example, Massachusetts dictated that Boston create a board of survey in 1891 to make "plans showing the location of highways which the present and future interests of the public require" (Scott 1971). Planning boards, such as Hartford's Planning Board in 1910, engaged in what they called "making decisions today in light of tomorrow's needs."

16. The committee that assisted Hoover in crafting the legislation included a city planner and Edward Bassett, who had helped form the first planning board in Brooklyn. He had also overseen a 1913 commission in New York to regulate skyscrapers that "marked the beginning of comprehensive zoning in the United States." Bassett later traveled from state to state, proselytizing about comprehensive zoning plans and the commissions that would be created with them (Knack 1996; Bassett 1939, 116).

17. Annexation of land surrounding cities caused great turmoil as roads did not meet up, neighborhood "characters" did not align (i.e., white and Black neighborhoods were too close together), and resulted in the uneven provision of public services like water and sewage systems (Brownell 1975).

18. The organizations included the Association of Commerce, the Board of Trade, the Cotton Exchange, the Contractors and Dealers Exchange, the Real Estate Agents Association, the New Orleans Federation of Clubs, the Young Mens' Business Club, and the Central Trades and Labor Council.

19. A lawsuit finally pushed the Playground board to fully integrate public facilities in 1952 (C. Bass 1960).

20. As Sivulka (1999, 4) notes, women were motivated by very real problems in their communities, like "an enormous foul-smelling pile of manure."

21. Created in 1692, the Overseers of the Poor had 12 members, each from a ward, whose responsibility it was to remove children from unsuitable parents or take on orphans and "bind them out to appropriate masters" (Boston Public Library, n.d.).

22. By 1923, the Los Angeles District of the General Federation of Women's Clubs had 172 separate clubs in affiliation (Steinhauer 2010).

23. When a member of the planning commission resigned, the commission chair moved that "the Friday Morning Club be communicated with [a] relative to a successor to Mrs. Hutchinson," suggesting that the women's club had a reserved seat on the commission. Los Angeles Planning Commission, executive subcommittee, August 5, 1924.

24. Los Angeles Planning Commission, executive subcommittee, October 14, 1924.

25. These objections were voiced despite the Park Service designing the campground to physically separate the white and Black areas, provide different watersheds for the campers by race, and even name the white and Black campgrounds separately (W. E. O'Brien 2015).

26. Cities across Virginia, as well as Winston-Salem and Greenville in North Carolina, and Atlanta, Georgia, had all passed similar laws by the time the Supreme Court struck down Baltimore's ordinance (Massey and Denton 1988, 52).

27. As Silver notes, "Planning was regarded as an important means to regulate developments in [Richmond's] sizable Black community to ensure continued race separation" (1984, 11).

28. Los Angeles Planning Commission, first assembled meeting, June 16, 1920.

29. Los Angeles Planning Commission, first assembled meeting, June 16, 1920.

CHAPTER 3

1. Los Angeles Playground and Recreation Commission, July 23, 1925.

2. Including the Hooper and Sons Western Avenue Tract Protective Association, the Hollenbeck Heights Improvement Association, the Eagle Rock Chamber of Commerce, the Kiwanis Club of Eagle Rock, the Ninth District Chamber of Commerce, Mrs. Edna McMillan, the White Home Owners' Protective Association, F. W. Kringel, the Citizens and Tax Payers Protective League Inc. (signed by Eva Craft).

3. Note from the Kiwanis Club of Eagle Rock, August 15, 1929.

4. Note from the Eagle Rock Chamber of Commerce, August 15, 1929.

5. Black residents were allowed to use Exposition Park Pool on Monday afternoons, Arroyo Seco Pool on Wednesday afternoons, and North Broadway Pool on Friday afternoons.

6. Los Angeles Playground and Recreation Commission, September 10, 1925.

7. Los Angeles Playground and Recreation Commission, August 20, 1925.

8. At a meeting after the first month that the segregationist policies were in place, the Playground and Recreation Commission received a report from the superintendent "on the uses of the municipal swimming pools on days allotted for colored groups." The report noted low usage and "further reported that the group of colored people which had requested special use on Sunday, August 23, had failed to make any extensive use of the pool which was set aside for their special use, and that owing to the setting aside of this pool on this occasion the general public had been barred and several hundred people were not given service." Los Angeles Playground and Recreation Commission, August 27, 1925. When petitioned to create "separate swimming pools in Exposition Park," the commission responded that "there are not enough negroes in that vicinity to warrant a separate pool for their use." To justify this decision, the commission simply cited the above report for that single day in 1925 when a "group of colored people which had requested special use on Sunday, August 23, [1925] had failed to make any extensive use of the pool which was set aside for their special use, and that owing to the setting aside of this pool on this occasion the general public had been barred and several hundred people were not given service." Los Angeles Playground and Recreation Commission, August 29, 1929; citing report from August 27, 1925.

9. Los Angeles Playground and Recreation Commission, September 10, 1925.

10. The use of boards represents policy diffusion (Bromley-Trujillo et al. 2016), where cities learned about the institutional structures from each other, from new policy challenges arising in cities, and from efforts by federal and state governments to create boards.

11. Los Angeles Planning Commission, March 17, 1927. Eventually the planning commission allowed for a single property to be converted from residential-only to mixed-use.

12. Zoning boards had also been allowing a "steady industrial encroachment into . . . Negro zones," which further restricted the quality of housing available for Black residents of cities (Meyer 2000).

13. Los Angeles Playground and Recreation Commission, report to commission on August 15, 1929, from Forrester B. Washington's article in *The Annals*, "a monthly publication of the American Academy of Political and Social Science."

14. Los Angeles Playground and Recreation Commission, August 15, 1929.

15. In 1931, the commission asked the city attorney to "take the necessary steps to appeal said judgement." The city attorney refused, advising the "Board of Playground and Recreation Commissioners to admit all persons of African descent to the use and enjoyment of all bathhouses and swimming pools owned and operated by the City of Los Angeles." Los Angeles Playground and Recreation Commission, March 5, 1931.

16. Los Angeles Playground and Recreation Commission, June 18, 1931, and June 23, 1931. The board considered this so important that they met again the next day so that two missing members could attend and the board as a whole could vote unanimously on the resolution.

17. No Black clergy appeared before the board, partially out of strategic efforts and partially because of a view by the Black clergy that the white clergy needed to engage in efforts on their own: "There were no Negros around when you white people messed up this thing. Now, you white folks straighten it out" (Alan Dent, president of Dillard University, as quoted in Rogers 1993, 36).

18. Letter from Arthur Chapital to Mayor Schiro, January 17, 1963.

19. Letter from Rev. Milton Upton to Mayor Schiro, February 3, 1964.

20. Letter from Mayor Schiro to William LaGarde, July 15, 1963.

21. As reported in Haase 2014, footnote 86.

22. Letter, published in the *Times Picayune* on July 18, 1963.

23. Letter from Thomas Heier Jr., CAO to Mayor Victor Schiro, April 23, 1964. Thomas Heier, in a letter to the mayor, notes, "As you know, this is a 28 member committee and the degree of success which can be achieved with the Housing Improvement Program will be largely dependent on the public acceptance and support generated by members of your advisory committee." Heier goes on to recommend 22 members for appointment, including Dr. Leonard Burns, with the note "Negro" next to his name (and only his name).

24. Appointment notes from Mayor Schiro's files, 1964, 1965, and 1966.

25. Letter from Archbishop Philip Hannan to Mayor Schiro, September 1968.

26. Letter from George Soule to Mayor Schiro, October 28, 1966.

27. Letter from E. L. Barthelemy to Mayor Schiro, November 29, 1966.

28. An alternative view is that the state controls the uprising via coercive control, or the threat or implementation of sanctions against the group, or beneficent control, where the government provides material resources to the group (Piven and Cloward 1971). The production of criminal justice (as a means of coercion) and welfare policy (as a means of beneficence) by the federal government in the 1960s and 1970s fit with this view of the outcome of protests. That is not to say that the state control view and the group-based interests view cannot cohabitate in a single period!

29. Cities across the country also created a variety of new boards, including Human Relations Commissions, in response to these pressures (Martinez-Ebers and Calfano 2020). Tom Bradley, who served on the Los Angeles City Council before his election as the city's first Black mayor, had "regularly and fruitlessly beseeched the city council and mayor to establish a Human Relations Commission" (Sonenshein 2006, 67).

30. Some of the variation in assessment of the success of these boards relates to the author and audience of these assessments.

31. Press release, Mayor's Office, June 11, 1968.

32. Letter from Paul Sanzenbach to Mayor Schiro, May 5, 1969.

33. Letter from Mayor Schiro to Paul Sanzenbach, May 7, 1969.

34. The inclusion of Black members on the CIA was a direct result of the lobbying efforts of SOUL (the Southern Organization for Unified Leadership), which gained a seat on the commission in exchange for voter mobilization efforts in the Black community.

35. The board's initial membership consisted of Walter Barnett, a white attorney and head of the New Orleans Property Owners Association (an association of white property owners who engaged in political efforts to resist rent control, encourage easy eviction processes, and lobby against property tax increases [Committee on Banking and Currency, U.S. Senate 1949]); Thomas Heier, the city's white chief administrative officer; Edgar Stern Jr., a wealthy white investor who headed the Council for a Better Louisiana (a state-wide coalition of business leaders); Laurance Eustis Jr., a white former state senator who served as the director of several banking and investment companies; Mark Smith III, an white engineer who chaired the New Orleans Federal Savings and Loan Association; Lawrence Wheeler, a Black politician and lawyer who was active in Black voter registration and turnout efforts, and Andrew Peter Sanchez Sr., a Black teacher who was the vice chair of the Lower Ninth Ward Neighborhood Council and an active member of the Southern Organization for Unified Leadership (SOUL).

36. A U.S. congressional representative, F. Edward Hebert, called the project "increased governmental regimentation by the centralized socialistic government in Washington" in an op-ed.

37. When Black families attempted to move into a set of homes in Detroit, "a mob of 700 armed white men and women had barricaded the entrance to the project." A police presence of 200 officers told the first Black man to arrive that he "had better turn around and go back" (Meyer 2000, 69).

38. Noting high rates of distrust in the police, a 1966 ACLU report stated, "At best, the citizen is torn over whether he has confidence in the police. At worst, the man in blue is a sworn enemy."

39. Both New York and Chicago already had some version of a police oversight commission, and the Wickersham Commission, established in 1928 by the Los Angeles Bar Association, argued that every police agency should have an independent authority (Prenzler 2016; Prenzler and Ronken 2001; Fairley 2020).

40. The CCPM also took (unsuccessful) action to oppose a stop and frisk ordinance under consideration by the city council. The New Orleans City Council passed the "Stop and Frisk" ordinance by a 6–0 vote in 1968.

41. Ernest Nathan Morial, "Inaugural Address," May 1, 1978.

CHAPTER 4

1. Richmond was able to create the Economic Development Authority because Code of Virginia §15.2–49 grants cities, towns, and counties the ability "to appoint an industrial advisory committee or similar committee or committees to advise the authority, consisting of such number of persons as it may deem advisable." The Richmond ordinance allocates the following powers: the Economic Development Authority is "empowered to acquire, own, lease and dispose of properties to promote industry and develop trade by inducing manufacturing, industrial and commercial enterprises to locate in, or, remain in this commonwealth for the benefit of the inhabitants of the Commonwealth, for the

increase of commerce and for the promotion of safety, health, welfare, convenience and prosperity of the citizens of the Commonwealth."

2. Members of the Economic Development Authority received tickets to Washington Redskins (now the Washington Commanders) games as a thank-you for being "such good ambassadors" for the team.

3. Henrico County is the county that surrounds Richmond. It was unclear "what is happening" in Henrico that the board wants to avoid.

4. As far as I could tell, no members of the board brought anyone to the next meeting.

5. This proliferation was largely due to early model legislation from the American Legislative Exchange Council (Hertel-Fernandez 2014, 2019).

6. There are also challenges associated with assessing the impact of programs because of the selection process: programs were selected for funding from the federal government in part because they already had pilot programs that produced similar outcomes (Boyle 1995).

7. Conger has been active in antifascist efforts in Charlottesville. She was fired from her job writing a local-politics column in a newspaper for a story about the connections between Charlottesville police and white supremacists involved in the 2017 deadly "Unite the Right" march (Conger 2019a; Thompson 2017). She was also described as an "undercover anti-fascist" by *Rolling Stone* magazine (Kroll 2021).

8. Conger eloquently encapsulates my theory in her evaluation of Charlotteville's boards: "The Planning Commission is a well-oiled machine, packed with policy knowledge. The Human Rights Commission is pulling itself back together after a few years lost in the wilderness" (Conger 2019b).

9. Conger also notes, "i can't claim to be a policy expert, but i'm sometimes the member of the public in the room" on her Patreon "About" page.

10. @socialistdogmom, Twitter [X], December 9, 2021, https://twitter.com/socialist dogmom/status/1469094219361009668.

11. NACOLE and advocates also emphasize that oversight boards should have the final decision on both disciplining officers and creating policies.

12. The commission identified street names, parks, and places in New Orleans named after (1) members of the Confederacy, (2) participants in the attempt to overthrow the government of Louisiana in 1874 (Battle of Liberty Place), (3) participants in the denial of the 14th and 15th Amendments at the Louisiana Constitutional Convention of 1989, and (4) participants in the passage of the New Orleans housing segregation act of 1924.

13. The 2014 Consent Decree is not the only consent decree for the city: the Orleans Parish sheriff also operates under a consent decree (Faia 2014); nor is it the first time the NOPD has been under a consent decree (Piliawsky 1985).

SECTION II INTRODUCTION

1. I grew up in Josephine County, Oregon, less than 100 miles from Grants Pass. Grants Pass was the big town with a bowling alley and a movie theater—a mere hour fifteen from my house.

2. For many years, the Grants Pass tag line was "It's the Climate"; this climate also allows for individuals to sleep outside much of the year. This, combined with high levels of poverty, dying industry, escalating housing costs, and the failure of national, state, and local homeless policy has led to an escalation of the unhoused population in Southwest Oregon (Willison 2021; Willison et al. 2023; Willison et al. 2021; Dake 2020). Grants Pass was also famously a "sundown town" where Black residents were unwelcome, includ-

ing Black members of the U.S. Army who were stationed in the area in the 1940s for training (Loewen 2005; Maynard 2016).

3. Ms. Blake would pass away the next year and the case was renamed for another plain-
tiff, Gloria Johnson.

4. We obtained at least board and membership information on 68 of the largest cities
and 302 of California's 451 cities via the method.

5. For seven cities, the email addresses provided by the city for the person in charge
of boards were broken. In those cases, and when we did not receive a reply from the board
person, we contacted the city clerk.

6. For example, the city clerk of Virginia Beach, Virginia, informed us that they do
not need to honor out-of-state FOIA requests and so would not provide information on
board members.

7. Occasionally, the function of the board was not clear from the name and a description was not available. In those cases, I attempted to identify the function through minutes or agendas; failing that, the issue area of the board is simply not coded.

8. That planning boards are found in almost all cities in both the Large Cities Dataset and the California Cities Dataset is not surprising: planning boards are often the only
boards dictated by state law and they were the focus of early federal and state intervention. In California, the state dictated in 1925 that all city governments have a planning
board. In my evaluation, only one city with available data is in direct violation of this law;
basically, all cities (even those with fewer than five boards) have a planning board.

9. There are also 74 inactive boards, which I do not include in my evaluations. These
boards exist on some lists or in legislation but are not active or currently staffed with members.

10. For example, Cincinnati's Board of Health requires that "not more than four of these
[10] members shall be professional providers of health services. The remaining members
shall represent consumers of health services and citizens at large," while the Community
Development Advisory Board sets requirements for all 17 seats on the board. I would code
the prior as a 44 percent requirement of professional backgrounds and 100 percent of the
latter, even though the Cincinnati Board of Health has four vacant seats and so only 12
percent of the members are professional providers of health services.

CHAPTER 5

1. Los Angeles Planning Commission, general meeting, April 7, 1925.

2. Los Angeles Planning Commission, general meeting, April 7, 1925.

3. Los Angeles Planning Commission, general meeting, April 7, 1925.

4. Louisiana Act No. 191 of 1914, House Bill No. 358.

5. The ability of local boards to make decisions about appeals to local laws was a point
of contention in drafting the 1928 Standard City Planning Enabling Act at the federal level.
Bassett, one of the committee members, wanted to allow local boards of adjustments to
"hear and decide appeals from and review any order, requirement, decision, or determi-
nation made by an administrative official." Others on the committee saw this as an opportunity for corruption and wanted it changed to give the board power only in excep-
tional circumstances. A compromise emerged, whereby local boards would have discretion
to authorize variances if strict enforcement would cause a hardship. This language is
present in a variety of quasi-judicial boards' authority-granting ordinances today.

6. In this circumstance, decisions by the Design Review Board require approval on the
city council's consent agenda, but without discussion or amendment. Indeed, if the city

council wishes to amend the Design Review Board's decisions, they must ask the Design Review Board to reconsider the action in whole—the city council cannot ask for a particular amendment.

7. Richmond Code 2004, §2–843; Ord. No. 2005-260-252, §1, 11–28–2005; Ord. No. 2010–175–168, §1, 9–27–2010; Ord. No. 2017–100, §1, 6–12–2017; Ord. No. 2017–143, §1, 10–9–2017.

8. Usually via Robert's Rules of Order.

9. See Chamberlin (1974) for discussion of a debate about the degree to which the size of a body shapes its willingness to provide a public good.

10. Comprehensive, representative survey data on local issues is very rarely available; the Kinder Houston Area Survey, fielded for more than 20 years, asks about a variety of local issues in the Houston area.

11. I draw on responses from the Kinder Houston Area Survey to estimate the probability (P) of enough members of the board agreeing, given a Binomial distribution, Y rules (where Y is either majority or consensus), and n members of the board. For each figure, I estimate the probability that in a group of n, $P(X \geq n/2 + 1) = 1 - P(X \leq n/2)$, where X has a Binomial distribution of $B(n, 1/2)$ for majority rule and $B(n, 1/1)$ for consensus rule.

12. The city's Human Relations Commission started with 28 members. Although the board focused on racial relations, it "accomplished no fundamental reform of the city's socio-economic structure" (Germany 2011, 145). While the HRC initially was tasked with evaluating police violence, meeting minutes note that "citizen review boards, at one time recommended by the American Civil Liberties Union, have been dropped because this met with severe opposition from the police" (minutes of Human Relations Committee, July 1, 1968).

13. The board was tasked with organizing progress toward seven "milestones," with committees for each goal and for each neighborhood, so the 18-member board soon created 13 subcommittees. As a result, the HRC moved on to other issues.

14. Sandy Krasnoff was a New Orleans attorney and victim's rights advocate.

15. Year of creation and membership based on city ordinance.

16. Author interview, April 2019.

17. Recall that I coded these characteristics using an organic coding method developed from reading a broad set of board membership requirements that cities had set out for their boards. Going back to Cincinnati's Community Development Advisory Board, which requires that the board be comprised of "3 members from Community Council/Neighborhood Leadership, 1 member each from City Planning, Human Services, Trades/Labor, Low Income Advocate, Housing Authority, Small Business Advocate, Real estate community, Developer, Lenders, Corporate community, Community development Corporation, and 4 members from the Cincinnati city council." In this circumstance, 6 percent of Cincinnati's Community Advisory Board would be coded as city employees (the City Planning seat), 35 percent business (businesses, real estate, developers, lenders, corporate), 18 percent citizens (community council), 18 percent nonprofit (community development, housing authority), and 24 percent elected officials.

18. In some cities, the mayor is an "ex officio" member of every board. Unless the mayor is explicitly listed as a member, I do not count them in the board numbers.

19. I use a multilevel model to estimate the difference in the share of the board that will have a particular requirement, with board strength and population as independent variables. I then calculate the estimated probabilities for weak and strong boards through post hoc predicted values from these models.

20. The mayor appoints 11 members (with city council approval) from the following: "Three from list of six names submitted by Greater New Orleans Tourist & Convention Commission, Inc.; Four from list of eight names submitted by Greater New Orleans Hotel/Motel Association; One from list of two names submitted by Greater New Orleans Black Tourism Network, Inc.; One from list of two submitted by Preservation Resource Center; One from list of two submitted by New Orleans East Economic Development Foundation; One from list of two submitted by Louisiana Restaurant Association." If you count the seat from the Greater New Orleans Black Tourism Network as an identity seat instead of development, the diversity score increases to 51 percent.

21. The full requirements include the following: "The Mayor or their designee serves as Chairman; The two councilmembers at-large or their designees; One district councilmember is selected by the City Council; The Superintendent of Police or his/her designee; The District Attorney or his/her designee; One Criminal District Court Judge appointed by the Criminal District Court Judges en banc or his/her designee; The Clerk of the Criminal District Court or his/her designee; One Juvenile Court Judge appointed by the Juvenile Court Judges en banc or his/her designee; One Municipal Court Judge appointed by the Municipal Court Judges en banc or his/her designee; One Traffic Court Judge appointed by the Traffic Court Judges en banc or his/her designee; The City Attorney or his/her designee; The Chief Administrative Officer of the City of New Orleans or his/her designee; The Orleans Parish Sheriff or his/her designee; The Chief Defender of the Orleans Public Defender Program or his/her designee; The Coroner for Orleans Parish or his/her designee; The Director of the Juvenile Justice Intervention Center or his/her designee; The District Administrator for the Probation and Parole New Orleans District Office or his/her designee; The Regional Manager of the Office of Juvenile Justice/Jefferson Regional Office or his/her designee; The following citizen members are appointed by the Mayor and subject to approval by the Council: One member of the New Orleans Business Council from a list of three recommendations of its chairman; One member of Total Community Action from a list of three recommendations of its chairman; One member of Women with a Vision from a list of three recommendations by its president; and Three additional citizen representatives at-large."

22. Even more striking is the difference between the Criminal Justice Council's 70 percent background diversity score and the Industrial Development Board, whose entire membership is composed of people from development backgrounds, resulting in a background diversity score of 0 percent.

23. Given that 95 percent of applicants for board memberships forwarded to the council were approved, I present the share of board members; shares of applicants look nearly identical.

CHAPTER 6

1. Uptown New Orleans is one of the richest and whitest neighborhoods in New Orleans. Located on high ground, the neighborhood is sometimes called the "sliver by the river" or, following Hurricane Katrina, when the neighborhood did not experience flooding losses like most of the rest of the city, the "Isle of Denial" (as poet Andrei Codrescu noted), "because as soon as you leave the French Quarter and uptown, you're in this vast ruin" (Codrescu 2006).

2. As the letter noted, "Chep [the mayor's nickname], you will recall Jack married Libby Lykes and because of the Lykes interests around the world it is believed by members of

the Park and Park Board that they could use Lykes to help the Park in the way of animals, plants, flowers, etc. as well as getting the interest of the Lykes Foundation and other friends interested in Audubon Park."

3. Letter dated December 12, 1960.

4. Mayor Morrison appointed someone's mother to the Audubon Commission because the son had sent $100 to help "defray the costs of the second primary" and had made this appeal: "Since I have never asked you to do anything of this sort for me previously, I would appreciate your looking into the matter [of appointing my mother] and advising me what be done." Letter from Jay Weil Jr. to Mayor Morrison, February 24, 1958.

5. The participation of Black activists on boards was often the source of conflict within community organizations. "Many militants who now call the poverty program 'mickey-mouse' but got considerable experience on the CAP [Community Assistant Program] payroll" (Hallman 1974, 11).

6. Vappie told investigators that the mayor had appointed him to the board after he told her that he had recently received a graduate degree: "I had a talk with my boss, which is the mayor. I was asking her how would one start their career outside of law enforcement in another civil service—another capacity of serving the public. And she made mention of various boards; the NOPD, HANO being one of the boards. And when the HANO position came available, I was asked if I would be interested." He later confirmed that the mayor had asked him if he would be interested in the HANO position (Zurik and Sauer 2022).

7. The lion's share of research on patronage focuses on bureaucratic appointments, especially how elected officials reward followers in clientelist systems, where leaders directly exchange votes for payments or access to government resources (Oliveros 2021), but patronage can be motivated by an interest in shaping public policy or rewarding supporters for their actions or resources during elections (Kopecký et al. 2016). It is the latter two motivations of patronage that I focus on in relation to board appointments. Political machines did use direct clientelism at key points in urban political history, so board appointments largely fall into the two categories of rewarding supporters and pursuing policy.

8. Letter from Mayor Morrison to Bob Wall, March 7, 1960.

9. Letter from Morey Sear to Mayor Morrison, September 20, 1960. Morey Sear was a local lawyer who served as special counsel to the New Orleans Aviation Board and went on to serve as a U.S. magistrate judge and then as a federal district court judge. He was very active in local politics from 1950 on until his death in 2004.

10. Any political candidates includes all local, state, and federal candidates from 2016 to 2022.

11. I include donations to any of the 17 candidates who ran for mayor in 2017 and any of the 14 candidates who ran in 2021.

12. The women in the sample are highly educated (median education: a master's degree), high-income (median income: more than $200,000 a year), and highly informed about local politics (for example, every single respondent got the name of the mayor correct).

SECTION III INTRODUCTION

1. One resident noted that residents of Lakeview felt particularly betrayed: "To feel like, regardless of what neighborhood you're from, the city just, they just don't care. That's how we feel."

2. In comparison, the Audubon Area Zoning Association, which was founded in the late 1940s and "promotes the safe, family friendly ambiance that is the hallmark of the neighborhood," charges $25 per year. Audubon Area Zoning Association, "About," http://www.audubonarea.org/, last accessed November 7, 2024.

3. Letter from Mayor Morrison to Charles Winter, Teamsters Local No. 270 representative, March 10, 1959.

4. "It was a real pleasure for me to speak to you briefly at the Rex Ball and if I can *ever be of service* to you on a committee or commission, please do call on me." Letter from Karl Everett Ashburn, professor of economics and finance, Loyola University of the South, to Mayor Schiro, February 26, 1966 (emphasis in original). In another letter, Professor Ashburn says, "My dear Mayor Schiro—I keep up with your many and complex duties and capable administration and appropriate and wise decisions in the press and over TV and I strongly feel you are making New Orleans really great, Mayor! I would place you in the same category as the late Mayor La Guardia of New York City. . . . On April 18, I had a very gracious letter from you stating that you hoped in the near future to be able to utilize my talents and energies as a member of one of your public boards or advisory committees but I have not heard from you since then on this particular matter. I would still be honoured to serve you and the city of New Orleans on one of your boards or commissions." Letter from Karl Everett Ashburn, professor of economics and finance, Loyola University of the South, to Mayor Schiro, August 30, 1966.

5. Letter from Robert Wall (executive secretary to the mayor) to Mayor Morrison, September 2, 1958.

6. This includes cities that engaged in a substantial revision of existing policies.

7. While attitudes about police funding and zoning rules are relatively balanced (for example, 45 percent of people oppose defunding the police and 46 percent of people oppose relaxing zoning standards), these attitudes are not perfectly balanced. As a result, the treatment groups are not uniform.

8. While I asked all respondents about their trust in state and national governments, I focus on the trust in local government measure in this chapter. The trust in state and national governments measures are less affected by the treatments, but are still lower than in the control condition.

CHAPTER 7

1. It is very common in New Orleans for elected leaders to crash vehicles—a city council member, Jared Brossett, crashed his city-owned car after drinking heavily and subsequently attended rehab and left office; a former congressional representative, Cedric Richmond, was released after crashing his car in a single-car accident, without screening for drugs or alcohol. Former city councilmember Oliver Thomas was arrested after crashing his car while driving with a suspended license; Thomas had previously spent several months in jail for corruption and bribery charges. One of the current at-large city council members, Helena Moreno, was involved in a fatal car crash in 2002, but submitted to blood and breath tests, which determined that she had not been impaired while driving.

2. If a government vehicle owned by the Orleans Parish Communication District is involved in a crash, the Standard Operating Procedure 1.3.1, Section IX(e) says, "The operator of the OPCD vehicle(s) must take a drug and alcohol test as soon as possible. The Director of Human Resources should be contacted for the name and location of the testing facility." But after Mr. Morris's wreck, he changed the policy to read, "*If injuries are re-*

ported, the operator of the OPCD vehicle(s) must take a drug and alcohol test as soon as possible. The Director of Human Resources should be contacted for the name and location of the testing facility" (emphasis added for comparison). The document was altered four days after the wreck, by Morris himself (Hammer 2023).

3. This is distinct from the systemic agenda, which involves "all issues that are commonly perceived by members of the political community as meriting public attention and as involving matters within the legitimate jurisdiction of existing governmental authority" (Cobb and Elder 1972, 85).

4. Both sets of boards have larger shares of women members (Health: 48%; Housing: 45%) and women of color (Health: 17%; Housing: 22%) than the overall average board.

5. I measured rates on January 1, 2023, for COVID vaccines and June 1, 2023, for eviction rates.

6. As Och (2018) notes in her evaluation of City for CEDAW adoptions, an ordinance involves three elements: "(1) gender analysis of city operations and laws; (2) establishment of a CEDAW oversight body; and (3) financial underwriting of CEDAW initiatives." But most cities simply adopt resolutions, not ordinances, and these resolutions have very little substance; for example, the Columbia, South Carolina, resolution is that the city "supports the elimination of all forms of discrimination and violence against women and girls, promoting the health and safety of women and girls, and supporting their being afforded equal academic, economic, social cultural and business opportunities in the City of Columbia."

7. The city's commission was created in response to the state's commission of the same name, which was created in 1927 (Martinez-Ebers and Calfano 2020).

CHAPTER 8

1. Name changed. All other details are accurate.

2. Delray Beach has had several nicknames: it was named as the best small town in America and West Delray was called "heaven's waiting room" for many years because of the large number of retirement communities.

3. A bar where he sold his art, including a very large, intimate nude of his wife in the woman's bathroom, right across from the toilet.

4. I counted anyone as being correct about the election date if they were within two weeks of the election day. Nothing changes if I extend that bandwidth to a month. If someone got either the first name or last name of their city's mayor correct, they were marked as correct.

5. People who thought their city had a board when the city did not have one attributed similar amounts of power to this nonexistent board as those who lived in cities that did have boards.

6. As I discuss at length in Chapter 4, "investigator" boards have more autonomous power, with independent resources and the ability to sanction and discipline individual members of law enforcement, while "monitor" boards are advisory, providing policy guidance without enforcement power (although clearly there are gradations between the two poles).

7. The base levels of trust and legitimacy are lower than in the first experiment. This is not altogether unsurprising, given that the study took place during the COVID-19 pandemic, which (rightfully) shaped government trust and legitimacy (Gadarian, Goodman, and Pepinsky 2021).

8. Unlike in Experimental Study 2, I am not providing people with a decision that they would explicitly disagree with (i.e., I did not first ask about their preferences on policy misconduct sanctions or affordable housing). Instead, respondents just read a newspaper article about the city's failure to hold a bad actor responsible for their misconduct. But when I did ask about their support for or opposition to six questions on criminal justice reform or affordable housing provision and can compare the responses among those who support police reform and affordable housing provision to the responses of those who do not. The loss in trust and legitimacy is accelerated among those who are the strongest supporters of police reform and affordable housing, but even those who do not endorse police and housing reform reduce their assessments of trust and legitimacy after the treatment, with no difference between appointed or elected decision-makers.

9. Political parties seem to be aware of this—for example, both Democrats and the Republicans overrepresent women in images they post on social media (Bos, van Doorn, and Nelson 2018).

10. Specifically, I asked for the respondents' trust ratings. After they answered this question, I asked: "Why is it that you trust local government? Please provide specific examples."

11. I removed all information about which condition the respondent was assigned; then I read through each response, looking for specific mentions of boards, appointments, elections, candidates, elected officials, representation, and related terms.

12. In their investigation of descriptive representation, Hayes and Hibbing note that "the level of descriptive representation necessary to achieve positive evaluations of decision-making might be conditional on the issue" (2017, 44). Future work might integrate their findings and my work to understand whether any representation matters or if the descriptive representation of groups much reach a particular level to influence attitudes.

CHAPTER 9

1. Other comments included a post suggesting a civil war between states based on partisanship, a picture of a gun part with the message "Those who do not know what this is should not start a civil war with those who do," several posts making fun of transgender individuals, and lots of anti-Obama posts.

2. Emily Farris is also my longtime collaborator and good friend!

3. Farris noted on Twitter [X], "As an officer of the city serving on a commission dedicated to eliminating prejudice and discrimination, Mr. Steele's posts are completely out of line with the mission of the Human Relations Commission" (Ranker 2019a).

4. For many years, the application for board membership in New Orleans was available only in the program WordPerfect, a file format that has been almost entirely phased out of use since the late 2000s.

5. An example is the Appointments Project by United WE, which "works to empower women and strengthen communities by improving the gender diversity of civic boards and commissions" ("Appointments Project" 2023).

6. As union president Aaron Mischler notes, "We never had as many problems except for in the past eight to ten years. That's when all the problems started. When [former mayor] Landrieu took over, it was just a nonstop shit show. And it's being carried on in the new administration" (Stein 2023a).

7. The member "must be domiciled and an elector of the city."

WORKS CITED

Abney, Glenn, and John Hutcheson. 1981. "Race, Representation, and Trust: Changes in Attitudes After the Election of a Black Mayor." *Public Opinion Quarterly* 45 (1): 91–101.

Abramovitz, Mimi. 2017. *Regulating the Lives of Women: Social Welfare Policy from Colonial Times to the Present*. Taylor & Francis.

Adams, Brian. 2004. "Public Meetings and the Democratic Process." *Public Administration Review* 64 (1): 43–54.

Advisory Commission on Intergovernmental Relations. 1989. "Significant Features of Fiscal Federalism." U.S. Government Printing Office.

Albanesi, Stefania, and Jiyeon Kim. 2021. "The Gendered Impact of the COVID-19 Recession on the US Labor Market." National Bureau of Economic Research.

Ali, Abdinasir K., and George L. Wehby. 2022. "State Eviction Moratoriums during the COVID-19 Pandemic Were Associated with Improved Mental Health among People Who Rent." *Health Affairs* 41 (11): 1583–89.

Aligica, Paul D., and Vlad Tarko. 2012. "Polycentricity: From Polanyi to Ostrom, and Beyond." *Governance* 25 (2): 237–62.

Allswang, John M. 1977. *Bosses, Machines, and Urban Voters*. John Hopkins University Press.

Andronovich, Gregory, and Gerry Riposa. 1996. "Urban Empowerment Zones: Linking Interests and Administrative Capacity." Paper presented at the 26th annual meeting of the Urban Affairs Association, New York, March.

Anthony, Jerry. 2023. "Housing Affordability and Economic Growth." *Housing Policy Debate* 33 (5): 1187–205.

Anzia, Sarah F. 2011. "Election Timing and the Electoral Influence of Interest Groups." *The Journal of Politics* 73 (2): 412–27. https://doi.org/10.1017/S0022381611000028.

———. 2013. *Timing and Turnout: How Off-Cycle Elections Favor Organized Groups*. University of Chicago Press.

———. 2022. *Local Interests: Politics, Policy, and Interest Groups in US City Governments*. University of Chicago Press.

———. 2024. "Public Schools and Their Pensions: How Is Pension Spending Affecting U.S. School Districts?" *Education Finance and Policy* 19 (4): 586–611. https://doi.org/10.11 62/edfp_a_00412.

Anzia, Sarah F., and Rachel Bernhard. 2022. "Gender Stereotyping and the Electoral Success of Women Candidates: New Evidence from Local Elections in the United States." *British Journal of Political Science* 52 (4): 1544–63.

Anzia, Sarah F., and Jessica Trounstine. 2024. "Civil Service Adoption in America: The Political Influence of City Employees: Civil Service Adoption in America." *American Political Science Review.* https://doi.org/10.1017/S0003055424000431.

"Appointments Project." 2023. United WE. https://united-we.org/ap-overview.

Archer, Allison M. N., and Cindy D. Kam. 2020. "Modern Sexism in Modern Times: Public Opinion in the #Metoo Era." *Public Opinion Quarterly* 84 (4): 813–37.

Ares, Macarena, and Enrique Hernández. 2017. "The Corrosive Effect of Corruption on Trust in Politicians: Evidence from a Natural Experiment." *Research & Politics* 4 (2). https://doi.org/10.1177/2053168017714185.

Armstrong, Brenna, Tiffany D. Barnes, Diana Z. O'Brien, and Michelle M. Taylor-Robinson. 2022. "Corruption, Accountability, and Women's Access to Power." *Journal of Politics* 84 (2): 1207–13.

Arnesen, Eric. 1994. *Waterfront Workers of New Orleans: Race, Class, and Politics, 1863–1923.* University of Illinois Press.

Arnesen, Sveinung, and Yvette Peters. 2018. "The Legitimacy of Representation: How Descriptive, Formal, and Responsiveness Representation Affect the Acceptability of Political Decisions." *Comparative Political Studies* 51 (7): 868–99.

Arnstein, Sherry R. 1969. "A Ladder of Citizen Participation." *Journal of the American Institute of Planners* 35 (4): 216–24.

Asen, Robert. 2013. "Deliberation and Trust." *Argumentation and Advocacy* 50 (1): 2–17.

Audubon Area Zoning Association. 2024. "About." http://www.audubonarea.org/. Accessed November 7, 2024.

Audubon Nature Institute. 2024. "Audubon Board." https://audubonnatureinstitute.org/audubon-board.

Bachrach, Peter, and Morton Baratz. 1970. *Power and Poverty: Theory and Practice.* Oxford University Press.

Badas, Alex. 2019. "The Applied Legitimacy Index: A New Approach to Measuring Judicial Legitimacy." *Social Science Quarterly* 100 (5): 1848–61.

Badas, Alex, and Katelyn E. Stauffer. 2018. "Someone like Me: Descriptive Representation and Support for Supreme Court Nominees." *Political Research Quarterly* 71 (1): 127–42.

Baker, John. 2015. *Government in the Twilight Zone.* SUNY Press.

Baker, Paula. 1984. "The Domestication of Politics: Women and American Political Society, 1780–1920." *American Historical Review* 89:620–47.

Bakker, Linda, and Karien Dekker. 2012. "Social Trust in Urban Neighbourhoods: The Effect of Relative Ethnic Group Position." *Urban Studies* 49 (10): 2031–47.

Baldwin, James. 1966. *Unnameable Objects, Unspeakable Crimes.* Chicago: Johnson Publishing.

Baldwin, J. Pemberton. 1904. "New Orleans under a Partisan Administration." In *The Chicago Conference for Good City Government and the Tenth Annual Meeting of the National Municipal League,* 143–53. Chicago: National Municipal League.

Barari, Soubhik, and Tyler Simko. 2023. "LocalView, a Database of Public Meetings for the Study of Local Politics and Policy-Making in the United States." *Scientific Data* 10 (1): 135.

Baratz, Morton. 1970. "The Community Action Program in Baltimore City, 1965–67." In *Power and Poverty: Theory and Practice*, edited by Peter Bachrach and Morton Baratz. Oxford University Press.

Barbaro, Michael, and Megan Twohey. 2016. "Crossing the Line: How Donald Trump Behaved with Women in Private." *New York Times*, May 14, 2016.

Barber, Benjamin. 1985. "Strong Democracy." *Ethics* 95 (4): 940–41.

Barber, Michael, Daniel M. Butler, and Jessica Robinson Preece. 2016. "Gender Inequalities in Campaign Finance." *Quarterly Journal of Political Science* 11 (2): 219–48.

Barnes, Tiffany D. 2016. *Gendering Legislative Behavior: Institutional Constraints and Collaboration in Argentina*. Cambridge University Press.

Barnes, Tiffany D., Victoria Beall, and Mirya R. Holman. 2021. "Pink Collar Representation and Policy Outcomes in U.S. States." *Legislative Studies Quarterly* 46 (1): 119–54.

Barnes, Tiffany D., and Mirya R. Holman. 2018. "Taking Diverse Backgrounds into Account in Studies of Political Ambition and Representation." *Politics, Groups, and Identities* 7 (4): 829–41.

———. 2020a. "Essential Work Is Gender Segregated: This Shapes the Gendered Representation of Essential Workers in Political Office." *Social Science Quarterly* 101 (5): 1827–33.

———. 2020b. "Gender Quotas, Women's Representation, and Legislative Diversity." *Journal of Politics* 82 (4).

Barnes, Tiffany D., and Diana Z. O'Brien. 2018. "Defending the Realm: The Appointment of Female Defense Ministers Worldwide." *American Journal of Political Science* 62 (2): 355–68.

Barnes, Tiffany D., and Gregory W. Saxton. 2019. "Working-Class Legislators and Perceptions of Representation in Latin America." *Political Research Quarterly* 72 (4): 910–28.

Bass, Charlotta A. 1960. *Forty Years: Memoirs from the Pages of a Newspaper*. Self-published.

Bass, Paul. 2017. "Green Proprietors Enter 21st Century." *New Haven Independent*, January 20, 2017. https://www.newhavenindependent.org/article/tgreen.

Bassett, Edward Murray. 1939. *Autobiography of Edward M. Bassett*. Harbor Press.

Bates, Laurie J., and Rexford E. Santerre. 1994. "The Determinants of Restrictive Residential Zoning: Some Empirical Findings." *Journal of Regional Science* 34 (2): 253–63.

Beauregard, Katrine. 2017. "Quotas and Gender Gaps in Political Participation among Established Industrial European Democracies." *Political Research Quarterly* 70 (3): 657–72.

Beckman, Norman. 1970. "Legislative Review—1968–1969: Planning and Urban Development." *Journal of the American Institute of Planners* 36 (5): 345–59.

Behrman, Martin. 1914. *New Orleans: A History of Three Great Public Utilities: Sewerage, Water and Drainage and Their Influence Upon the Health and Progress of a Big City*. Brandao Print.

Beierle, Thomas C. 1999. "Using Social Goals to Evaluate Public Participation in Environmental Decisions." *Review of Policy Research* 16 (3–4): 75–103.

Béland, Daniel, Gregory P. Marchildon, Anahely Medrano, and Philip Rocco. 2021. "COVID-19, Federalism, and Health Care Financing in Canada, the United States, and Mexico." *Journal of Comparative Policy Analysis: Research and Practice* 23 (2): 143–56.

Benfer, Emily A., David Vlahov, Marissa Y. Long, Evan Walker-Wells, J. L. Pottenger, Gregg Gonsalves, and Danya E. Keene. 2021. "Eviction, Health Inequity, and the Spread of COVID-19: Housing Policy as a Primary Pandemic Mitigation Strategy." *Journal of Urban Health* 98 (1): 1–12.

Benhabib, Seyla. 1996. "Toward a Deliberative Model of Democratic Legitimacy." In *Democracy and Difference: Contesting the Boundaries of the Political*, edited by Seyla Benhabib, 67–94. Princeton University Press.

Benjamin, Andrea. 2017a. "Coethnic Endorsements, Out-Group Candidate Preferences, and Perceptions in Local Elections." *Urban Affairs Review* 53 (4): 631–57.

———. 2017b. *Racial Coalition Building in Local Elections: Elite Cues and Cross-Ethnic Voting*. Cambridge University Press.

———. 2022. "PACs Rule Everything around Me: How Political Action Committees Shape Elections and Policy in the Local Context." *Interest Groups & Advocacy* 11 (2): 278–302.

———. 2023. "A Woman Whose Father Didn't Graduate from High School Can Become This City's First Female African American Mayor." In *Political Black Girl Magic: The Elections and Governance of Black Female Mayors*, edited by Sharon D. Wright Austin, 141–161. Temple University Press.

Benjamin, Andrea, and Sydney L. Carr. 2022. "Does Incumbency Matter? Black Voter Support for Non-Incumbent POC Democratic Candidates in the 2018 Congressional House of Representative Elections." *National Review of Black Politics* 3 (1–2): 2–16.

Benjamin, Andrea, and Alexis Miller. 2019. "Picking Winners: How Political Organizations Influence Local Elections." *Urban Affairs Review* 55 (3): 643–74.

Benoit, William. 2017. "Image Repair on the Donald Trump 'Access Hollywood' Video: 'Grab Them by the P*ssy.'" *Communication Studies* 68 (3): 243–59.

Bernhard, Rachel, and Sean Freeder. 2020. "The More You Know: Voter Heuristics and the Information Search." *Political Behavior* 42 (2): 603–23.

Bernhard, Rachel, and Mirya R. Holman. 2025. *Gendered Jobs and Local Leadership*. Cambridge University Press.

Berry, Jeffrey M., Kent E. Portney, and Ken Thomson. 1993. *The Rebirth of Urban Democracy*. Brookings Institution Press.

Besco, Randy, and Erin Tolley. 2022. "Ethnic Group Differences in Donations to Electoral Candidates." *Journal of Ethnic and Migration Studies* 48 (5): 1072–94.

Beshi, Taye Demissie, and Ranvinderjit Kaur. 2020. "Public Trust in Local Government: Explaining the Role of Good Governance Practices." *Public Organization Review* 20: 337–50.

BGR. 2013. "Sound the Alarm: New Orleans Firefighter Pension Woes and the Legislative Session." Bureau of Government Research. https://www.bgr.org/report-index/new-orleans-firefighter-pension-woes-and-legislative-session/.

Birkland, Thomas A. 1998. "Focusing Events, Mobilization, and Agenda Setting." *Journal of Public Policy* 18 (1): 53–74.

———. 2006. *Lessons of Disaster: Policy Change after Catastrophic Events*. Georgetown University Press.

Bischof, Bayley. 2021. "Former Lincoln Police Officer Brings to Light Alleged Sexual Harassment and Discrimination within the Department." *1011Now*, December 14, 2021. https://www.1011Now.com.

Blee, Kathleen M. 2009. *Women of the Klan: Racism and Gender in the 1920s*. University of California Press.

Bobb, Merrick. 2003. "Civilian Oversight of the Police in the United States." *Louisville University Public Law Review* 22:151.

Bobo, Lawrence, and Franklin D. Gilliam Jr. 1990. "Race, Sociopolitical Participation, and Black Empowerment." *American Political Science Review* 84 (2): 377–93.

Bos, Angela L. 2015. "The Unintended Effects of Political Party Affirmative Action Policies on Female Candidates' Nomination Chances." *Politics, Groups, and Identities* 3 (1): 73–93.

Bos, Angela L., Bas W. van Doorn, and Kjersten Nelson. 2018. "Who Is in the Picture? The Gender Composition of Images of Congress in Party Caucus Twitter Feeds and Online Media." *Politics, Groups, and Identities* 6 (4): 788–801.

Bostdorff, Denise M., and Steven R. Goldzwig. 2005. "History, Collective Memory, and the Appropriation of Martin Luther King, Jr.: Reagan's Rhetorical Legacy." *Presidential Studies Quarterly* 35 (4): 661–90.

Boston Public Library. n.d. "Boston Overseers of the Poor Indentures and Related Materials, 1734–1805." Digital Commonwealth, Massachusetts Collections Online. Boston Public Library.

Boulianne, Shelley. 2019. "Building Faith in Democracy: Deliberative Events, Political Trust and Efficacy." *Political Studies* 67 (1): 4–30.

Boustan, Leah Platt. 2007. "Black Migration, White Flight: The Effect of Black Migration on Northern Cities and Labor Markets." *Journal of Economic History* 67 (2): 484–88.

Boyd, Gabrielle R. 2023. "Cities for CEDAW: A Critical Evaluation of Three Gender Reports." PhD thesis, University of Cincinnati.

Boyer, M. Christine. 1986. *Dreaming the Rational City: The Myth of American City Planning*. MIT Press.

Boyle, Robin. 1995. "Empowerment Zones: Picking the Winners." *Economic Development Quarterly* 9 (3): 207–11.

Bratton, Kathleen A. 2006. "The Behavior and Success of Latino Legislators: Evidence from the States." *Social Science Quarterly* 87 (5): 1136–57.

Breiman, Leo. 2001. "Random Forests." *Machine Learning* 45 (1): 5–32.

Brockman, Anne. 2018. "Unified Voice: The Greater Tulsa African-American Affairs Commission." *TulsaPeople Magazine*, May 30, 2018. https://www.tulsapeople.com/tulsa -people/june-2018/unified-voice-the-greater-tulsa-african-american-affairs-commis sion/article_b76e8349-a1ed-55da-aa26-28154b2ced3f.html.

Bromley-Trujillo, Rebecca, J. S. Butler, John Poe, and Whitney Davis. 2016. "The Spreading of Innovation: State Adoptions of Energy and Climate Change Policy." *Review of Policy Research* 33 (5): 544–65.

Broockman, David E. 2013. "Black Politicians Are More Intrinsically Motivated to Advance Blacks' Interests: A Field Experiment Manipulating Political Incentives." *American Journal of Political Science* 57 (3): 521–36.

Brown, Nadia E. 2014. *Sisters in the Statehouse: Black Women and Legislative Decision Making*. Oxford University Press.

Brown, Nadia E., Christopher J. Clark, Anna M. Mahoney, Orly Siow, and Michael G. Strawbridge. 2024. "Intersectional Identity and Representative Politics." *Politics & Gender* 20 (3): 727–33.

Brown, Nadia E., and Sarah Allen Gershon. 2023. *Distinct Identities*, 2nd ed. Routledge.

Brownell, Blaine A. 1975. "The Commercial-Civic Elite and City Planning in Atlanta, Memphis, and New Orleans in the 1920s." *Journal of Southern History* 41 (3): 339–68.

Browning, Rufus P., Dale Rogers Marshall, and David H. Tabb. 1984. *Protest Is Not Enough: The Struggle of Blacks and Hispanics for Equality in Urban Politics*. University of California Press.

———. 1986. "Protest Is Not Enough: A Theory of Political Incorporation." *PS* 19 (3): 576–81.

———. 1997a. "Can People of Color Achieve Power in City Government? The Setting and the Issues." In *Racial Politics in American Cities*, 2nd ed., edited by Rufus P. Browning, Dale Rogers Marshall, and David H. Tabb. Longman.

————. 1997b. "Has Political Incorporation Been Achieved? Is It Enough?" In *Racial Politics in American Cities*, 2nd ed., edited by Rufus P. Browning, Dale Rogers Marshall, and David H. Tabb. Longman.

Buchanan, James M. 1979. "The Potential for Taxpayer Revolt in American Democracy." *Social Science Quarterly* 59 (4): 691–96.

Buchanan, James M., and Gordon Tullock. 1962. *The Calculus of Consent*. University of Michigan Press.

Buenker, John D. 1973. *Urban Liberalism and Progressive Reform*. Scribner.

Burke, Tarana. 2019. "About." Me Too Movement. https://metoomvmt.org/about/.

Burns, Peter F. 2003. "Regime Theory, State Government, and a Takeover of Urban Education." *Journal of Urban Affairs* 25 (3): 285–303.

————. 2006. *Electoral Politics Is Not Enough: Racial and Ethnic Minorities and Urban Politics*. SUNY Press.

Burns, Peter F., and Matthew O. Thomas. 2004. "Governors and the Development Regime in New Orleans." *Urban Affairs Review* 39 (6): 791–812.

————. 2015. *Reforming New Orleans: The Contentious Politics of Change in the Big Easy*. Ithaca, NY: Cornell University Press.

Busso, Matias, Jesse Gregory, and Patrick Kline. 2013. "Assessing the Incidence and Efficiency of a Prominent Place Based Policy." *American Economic Review* 103 (2): 897–947.

Button, James W. 2014. *Blacks and Social Change: Impact of the Civil Rights Movement in Southern Communities*. Princeton University Press.

Cairney, Paul, and Adam Wellstead. 2021. "COVID-19: Effective Policymaking Depends on Trust in Experts, Politicians, and the Public." *Policy Design and Practice* 4 (1): 1–14.

Callison, Kevin, Davida Finger, and Isabella M. Smith. 2022. "COVID-19 Eviction Moratoriums and Eviction Filings: Evidence from New Orleans." *Housing and Society* 49 (1): 1–9.

Calvo, Ernesto, and Iñaki Sagarzazu. 2011. "Legislator Success in Committee: Gatekeeping Authority and the Loss of Majority Control." *American Journal of Political Science* 55 (1): 1–15.

Camou, Michelle. 2014. "Labor-Community Coalitions Through an Urban Regime Lens: Institutions and Ideas in Building Power from Below." *Urban Affairs Review* 50 (5): 623–47.

Campanella, Richard. 2006. *Geographies of New Orleans: Urban Fabrics before the Storm*. Lafayette Press.

Campbell, Rosie. 2016. "Representing Women Voters: The Role of the Gender Gap and the Response of Political Parties." *Party Politics* 22 (5): 587–97.

Capers, Gerald M. 1938. "Yellow Fever in Memphis in the 1870's." *Mississippi Valley Historical Review* 24 (4): 483–502.

Cargile, Ivy. 2015. "Latina Issues: An Analysis of the Policy Issue Competencies of Latina Candidates." In *Distinct Identities: Minority Women in U.S. Politics*, edited by Sarah A. Gershon and Nadia E. Brown. Routledge.

Carrier, Anastasiia. 2024. "While the Police Oversight Board Struggled for Access to Police Records, Its Attorney Was Also Representing the City." *Charlottesville Tomorrow*. June 14, 2024.

Carrigan, Jo Ann. 1988. "Mass Communication and Public Health: The 1905 Campaign against Yellow Fever in New Orleans." *Louisiana History: Journal of the Louisiana Historical Association* 29 (1): 5–20.

Carroll, Susan J., and Kira Sanbonmatsu. 2013. *More Women Can Run: Gender and Pathways to the State Legislatures*. New York: Oxford University Press.

Cassese, Erin C., and Mirya R. Holman. 2019. "Playing the Woman Card: Ambivalent Sexism in the 2016 Presidential Race." *Political Psychology* 40 (1): 55–74.

Castle, Jeremiah J., Shannon Jenkins, Candice D. Ortbals, Lori Poloni-Staudinger, and J. Cherie Strachan. 2020. "The Effect of the #MeToo Movement on Political Engagement and Ambition in 2018." *Political Research Quarterly* 73 (4): 926–41.

CBS DFW. 2019. "Fort Worth Human Relations Commission Recommends Member's Removal Over 'Inappropriate Facebook Posts.'" *CBS DFW*, July 15, 2019. https://www.cbsnews.com/texas/news/fort-worth-human-relations-commission-recommends-members-removal-disrespectful-inappropriate-facebook-posts/.

Chamberlin, John. 1974. "Provision of Collective Goods as a Function of Group Size." *American Political Science Review* 68 (2): 707–16.

Chambers, Simone. 2003. "Deliberative Democratic Theory." *Annual Review of Political Science* 6 (1): 307–26.

Chappell, Louise, and Georgina Waylen. 2013. "Gender and the Hidden Life of Institutions." *Public Administration* 91 (3): 599–615.

Checkoway, Barry, and Jon Van Til. 1978. "What Do We Know about Citizen Participation? A Selective Review of Research." In *Citizen Participation in America*, edited by Stuart Langton, 25–42. Lexington Books.

Childs, Sarah. 2006. "The Complicated Relationship between Sex, Gender and the Substantive Representation of Women." *European Journal of Women's Studies* 13 (1): 7–21.

City News Service. 2023a. "LA Planning Commission OKs USC's Plan to Develop New Sports Stadium." *Patch Los Angeles*, September 14, 2023. https://patch.com/california/los-angeles/la-planning-commission-oks-uscs-plan-develop-new-sports-stadium.

———. 2023b. "LA Planning Commission to Vote on Proposal to Fast-Track Affordable Housing." *NBC Los Angeles*, November 16, 2023. https://www.nbclosangeles.com/news/local/la-planning-commission-to-vote-on-proposal-to-fast-track-affordable-housing/3270143/.

City of Detroit. 1973. "Charter of the City of Detroit." https://detroitmi.gov/sites/detroitmi.localhost/files/2018-05/ctiy_of_detroit_proposed_charter_revisions_0.pdf.

City of Grants Pass v. Johnson. 2024. US Supreme Court. 603 U.S. (2024).

Clark, Cal, and Janet Clark. 1992. "Federal Aid to Local Governments in the West: An Irony of the Reagan Revolution." *Review of Policy Research* 11 (1): 91–99.

Clark, Christopher J. 2019. *Gaining Voice: The Causes and Consequences of Black Representation in the American States*. Oxford University Press.

Clayton, Amanda, Cecilia Josefsson, and Vibeke Wang. 2017. "Quotas and Women's Substantive Representation: Evidence from a Content Analysis of Ugandan Plenary Debates." *Politics & Gender* 13 (2): 276–304.

Clayton, Amanda, Diana Z. O'Brien, and Jennifer M. Piscopo. 2019. "All Male Panels? Representation and Democratic Legitimacy." *American Journal of Political Science* 63 (1): 113–29.

Clemens, Elisabeth. 1993. "Organizational Repertoires and Institutional Change: Women's Groups and the Transformation of American Politics, 1890–1920." *American Journal of Sociology* 98 (4): 755–98.

CNN. 2023. CNN Poll, Question 20, 31120466.00019. SSRS. Cornell University, Roper Center for Public Opinion Research, 2023, Survey question. https://doi.org/10.25940/ROPER-31120466.

Cobb, R, and C Elder. 1972. *Participation in American Politics: The Dynamics of Agenda Building*. Johns Hopkins University Press.

Cobbina-Dungy, Jennifer, Soma Chaudhuri, Ashleigh LaCourse, and Christina DeJong. 2022. "'Defund the Police:' Perceptions among Protesters in the 2020 March on Washington." *Criminology & Public Policy* 21 (1): 147–74.

Codrescu, Andrei. 2006. "Poet Contemplates Future of New Orleans." *WHQR*, February 27, 2006. https://www.whqr.org/2006-02-27/poet-contemplates-future-of-new-orleans.

Cohen, Elisha, Anna Gunderson, Kaylyn Jackson, Paul Zachary, Tom S. Clark, Adam N. Glynn, and Michael Leo Owens. 2019. "Do Officer-Involved Shootings Reduce Citizen Contact with Government?" *Journal of Politics* 81 (3): 1111–23.

Cohen, Rachel M. 2023. "Cities Are Asking the Supreme Court for More Power to Clear Homeless Encampments." *Vox*, October 10, 2023. https://www.vox.com/2023/10/10/23905951/homeless-tent-encampments-grants-pass-martin-boise-unsheltered-housing.

Cole, Leonard. 1976. *Blacks in Power*. Princeton University Press.

Cole, Richard L., Delbert A. Taebel, and Rodney V. Hissong. 1990. "America's Cities and the 1980s: The Legacy of the Reagan Years." *Journal of Urban Affairs* 12 (4): 345–60.

Collins, Jonathan E. 2018. "Urban Representation through Deliberation: A Theory and Test of Deliberative Democracy at the Local Level." *Journal of Urban Affairs* 40 (7): 952–73.

———. 2021. "Does the Meeting Style Matter? The Effects of Exposure to Participatory and Deliberative School Board Meetings." *American Political Science Review* 115 (3): 790–804.

Colonnelli, Emanuele, Mounu Prem, and Edoardo Teso. 2020. "Patronage and Selection in Public Sector Organizations." *American Economic Review* 110 (10): 3071–99.

Colten, Craig E. 2002. "Basin Street Blues: Drainage and Environmental Equity in New Orleans, 1890–1930." *Journal of Historical Geography* 28 (2): 237–57.

———. 2006. *An Unnatural Metropolis: Wresting New Orleans from Nature*. LSU Press.

Committee on Banking and Currency, U.S. Senate. 1949. "Rent Control Legislation: Hearings Before a Subcommittee of the Committee on Banking and Currency, United States Senate," Eighty-First Congress, First Session, on S. 434, S. 600 and S. 888, Bills Pertaining to Rent Control Legislation. March 3–4, 7–10, and 11, 1949. U.S. Government Printing Office.

Conger, Molly. 2019a. "I Lost My Job for Keeping Charlottesville Police Accountable. I'd Do It Again." *Guardian*, August 19, 2019. https://www.theguardian.com/commentisfree/2019/aug/19/charlottesville-police-molly-conger-newspaper.

———. 2019b. "Worth the Wait: We Need the Police Civilian Review Board." *C-VILLE Weekly*, April 24, 2019. https://www.c-ville.com/worth-the-wait-we-need-the-police-civilian-review-board.

——— @socialistdogmom. 2021. "i remain utterly uninspired by the police civilian review board, but i must do my duty." Twitter [X], December 9, 2021. https://web.archive.org/web/20211210000403/https://twitter.com/socialistdogmom/status/1469094219361009668.

Conlan, Timothy J., Paul L. Posner, and David R. Beam. 2014. *Pathways of Power: The Dynamics of National Policymaking*. Georgetown University Press.

Conroy, Meredith. 2018. "Strength, Stamina, and Sexism in the 2016 Presidential Race." *Politics & Gender* 14 (1): 116–21.

Conyers, John. 1981. "Police Violence and Riots." *Black Scholar* 12 (1): 2–5.

Coon, Arthur F. 2023. "Another Call for CEQA Litigation Reform? Second District Rejects NIMBY Group's CEQA, Coastal Act, and Land Use Challenges." *CEQA Developments*, March 21, 2023. https://www.ceqadevelopments.com/2023/03/21/another-call-for-ceqa

-litigation-reform-second-district-rejects-nimby-groups-ceqa-coastal-act-and-land
-use-challenges-affirms-judgment-upholding-approval-of-zoning-compliant-and-ceq/.

Cooper, Christopher A., H. Gibbs Knotts, and Kathleen M. Brennan. 2008. "The Importance of Trust in Government for Public Administration: The Case of Zoning." *Public Administration Review* 68 (3): 459–68.

Cooper, Hannah L. F., and Mindy Fullilove. 2016. "Editorial: Excessive Police Violence as a Public Health Issue." *Journal of Urban Health* 93 (S1): 1–7.

Cordis, Adriana S., and Jeffrey Milyo. 2016. "Measuring Public Corruption in the United States: Evidence from Administrative Records of Federal Prosecutions." *Public Integrity* 18 (2): 127–48.

Costa, Mia, Trevor Briggs, Ajaipal Chahal, Jonathan Fried, Rijul Garg, Sophia Kriz, Leo Lei, Anthony Milne, and Jennah Slayton. 2020. "How Partisanship and Sexism Influence Voters' Reactions to Political #MeToo Scandals." *Research & Politics* 7 (3). https://doi.org/10.1177/2053168020941727.

Cox, Karen L. 2003. *Dixie's Daughters: The United Daughters of the Confederacy and the Preservation of Confederate Culture.* University Press of Florida.

Crain, W. Mark, and Robert D. Tollison. 1977. "Legislative Size and Voting Rules." *Journal of Legal Studies* 6 (1): 235–40.

Crandall, Brian. 2023. "Planning Board Recap: Warm Welcome Given to West End Supportive Housing." *Ithaca Voice*, June 28, 2023. https://ithacavoice.org/2023/06/planning-board-recap-board-gives-warm-welcome-to-w-end-supportive-housing/.

Crawford, Nyron N. 2019. "Of Suspicious Minds: Race, Scandal, and the DC Mayoralty." *Journal of Urban Affairs* 41 (5): 679–99.

Crepaz, Markus. 1996. "Consensus Versus Majoritarian Democracy: Political Institutions and Their Impact on Macroeconomic Performance and Industrial Disputes." *Comparative Political Studies* 29 (1): 4–26.

Croly, Jane Cunningham. 1898. *The History of the Woman's Club Movement in America.* H. G. Allen.

Crowder, Kyle. 2000. "The Racial Context of White Mobility: An Individual-Level Assessment of the White Flight Hypothesis." *Social Science Research* 29 (2): 223–57.

Crowder-Meyer, Melody. 2013. "Gendered Recruitment without Trying: How Local Party Recruiters Affect Women's Representation." *Politics & Gender* 9 (4): 390–413.

Crowder-Meyer, Melody, Shana Kushner Gadarian, and Jessica Trounstine. 2015. "Electoral Institutions, Gender Stereotypes, and Women's Local Representation." *Politics, Groups, and Identities* 3 (2): 318–34.

Crowder-Meyer, Melody, and Benjamin E. Lauderdale. 2014. "A Partisan Gap in the Supply of Female Potential Candidates in the United States." *Research & Politics* 1 (1). https://doi.org/10.1177/2053168014537230.

Crutcher, Michael. 2001. "Protecting 'Place' in African-American Neighborhoods: Urban Public Space, Privatization, and Protest in Louis Armstrong Park and the Treme, New Orleans." PhD diss., Louisiana State University.

Cunningham, Roger A. 1975. "Rezoning by Amendment as an Administrative or Quasi-Judicial Act: The 'New Look' in Michigan Zoning." *Michigan Law Review* 73 (8): 1341–60.

Curry, James M., and Matthew R. Haydon. 2018. "Lawmaker Age, Issue Salience, and Senior Representation in Congress." *American Politics Research* 46 (4): 567–95.

Cutler, David, and Grant Miller. 2005. "Water, Water, Everywhere: Municipal Finance and Water Supply in American Cities." Working Paper 11096, National Bureau of Economic Research. https://www.nber.org/system/files/chapters/c9982/c9982.pdf.

Dahl, Robert. 1961. *Who Governs? Democracy and Power in an American City.* Yale University Press.

Dake, Lauren. 2020. "How the Big Oregon Timber Deal Came Together, and How It Could Fall Apart." *Oregon Public Broadcasting*, February 14, 2020. https://www.opb.org/news/article/oregon-timber-deal-salem-forests-conservation-logging-legislature/.

Darden, Joe T. 2013. *Detroit Race Riots, Racial Conflicts and Efforts to Bridge the Racial Divide.* Michigan State University Press.

Darr, Joshua P., Matthew P. Hitt, and Johanna L. Dunaway. 2019. "Newspaper Closures Polarize Voting Behavior." *Journal of Communication* 68 (6): 1007–28.

Davies, Jonathan S., and Jessica Trounstine. 2012. "Urban Politics and the New Institutionalism." In *The Oxford Handbook of Urban Politics*, edited by Susan Clarke, Peter John, and Karen Mossberger, 51–70. Oxford University Press.

Davis, Clark. 2002. "An Era and Generation of Civic Engagement: The Friday Morning Club in Los Angeles, 1891–1931." *Southern California Quarterly* 84 (2): 135–68.

de Benedictis-Kessner, Justin. 2017. "Off-Cycle and Out of Office: Election Timing and the Incumbency Advantage." *Journal of Politics* 80 (1): 119–32.

———. 2018. "How Attribution Inhibits Accountability: Evidence from Train Delays." *Journal of Politics* 80 (4): 1417–22.

———. 2021. "Strategic Partisans: Electoral Motivations and Partisanship in Local Government Communication." *Journal of Political Institutions and Political Economy* 2 (2): 227–48.

———. 2022. "Strategic Government Communication about Performance." *Political Science Research and Methods* 10 (3): 601–16.

de Benedictis-Kessner, Justin, Katherine Levine Einstein, and Maxwell Palmer. 2023. "Who Should Make Decisions? Public Perceptions of Democratic Inclusion in Housing Policy." HKS Working Paper No. RWP23-016. https://doi.org/10.2139/ssrn.4487350.

de Benedictis-Kessner, Justin, Daniel Jones, and Christopher Warshaw. 2025. "How Partisanship in Cities Influences Housing Policy." *American Journal of Political Science* 69 (1): 64–77.

de Benedictis-Kessner, Justin, Diana Lee, Yamil Velez, and Christopher Warshaw. 2023. "American Local Government Elections Database." *Scientific Data* 10 (1): 912.

de Benedictis-Kessner, Justin, and Christopher Warshaw. 2016. "Mayoral Partisanship and Municipal Fiscal Policy." *Journal of Politics* 78 (4): 1124–38.

———. 2020. "Politics in Forgotten Governments: The Partisan Composition of County Legislatures and County Fiscal Policies." *Journal of Politics* 82 (2): 460–75.

Deckman, Melissa Marie. 2007. "School Board Candidates and Gender: Ideology, Party, and Policy Concerns." *Journal of Women, Politics & Policy* 28 (1): 87–117.

Desmond, Matthew. 2012. "Eviction and the Reproduction of Urban Poverty." *American Journal of Sociology* 118 (1): 88–133.

Dickson, Lynda F. 1987. "Toward a Broader Angle of Vision in Uncovering Women's History: Black Women's Clubs Revisited." *Frontiers: A Journal of Women Studies* 9 (2): 62–68.

Dil, Cuneyt. 2023. "D.C.'s 'Shadow Mayor' Accused of Sexual Harassment." *Axios*, March 21, 2023. https://www.axios.com/local/washington-dc/2023/03/21/dc-shadow-mayor-john-falcicchio.

Dilworth, Richardson. 2010. "The City in American Political Development." In *A History of the U.S. Political System*, edited by Richard Harris and Daniel J Tichenor. ABC-CLIO.

Doleac, Jennifer L., and Benjamin Hansen. 2017. "Moving to Job Opportunities? The Effect of 'Ban the Box' on the Composition of Cities." *American Economic Review* 107 (5): 556–59.

———. 2020. "The Unintended Consequences of 'Ban the Box': Statistical Discrimination and Employment Outcomes When Criminal Histories Are Hidden." *Journal of Labor Economics* 38 (2): 321–74.

Donovan, Todd, and Max Neiman. 1992. "Community Social Status, Suburban Growth, and Local Government Restrictions on Residential Development." *Urban Affairs Quarterly* 28 (2): 323–36.

Dougherty, George W., and Jennifer Easton. 2011. "Appointed Public Volunteer Boards: Exploring the Basics of Citizen Participation through Boards and Commissions." *American Review of Public Administration* 41 (5): 519–41.

Dovi, Suzanne. 2002. "Preferable Descriptive Representatives: Or Will Just Any Woman, Black, or Latino Do?" *American Political Science Review* 96 (4): 729–44.

———. 2012. *The Good Representative*. John Wiley.

Downs, Anthony. 1991. "The Advisory Commission on Regulatory Barriers to Affordable Housing: Its Behavior and Accomplishments." *Housing Policy Debate* 2 (4): 1095–137.

Dryzek, John S. 2001. "Legitimacy and Economy in Deliberative Democracy." *Political Theory* 29 (5): 651–69.

Du Bois, W. E. B. 1935. *Black Reconstruction in America: An Essay Toward a History of the Part Which Black Folk Played in the Attempt to Reconstruct Democracy in America, 1860–1880*. Harcourt, Brace.

Duffy, John. 1992. *The Sanitarians: A History of American Public Health*. University of Illinois Press.

Dunjee, Roscoe. 1936. "Parks for Negroes, Parks for Whites." *Black Dispatch*, August 13, 1936.

Dunnaway, Nicolle Muller. 2011. "Flowers in Their Beauty: The Phyllis Wheatley Club of New Orleans." Thesis, Southeastern Louisiana University. ProQuest 1502407.

Earl, George. 1903. "Drainage, Sewerage and Water Supply of New Orleans." *JAMA XLI* (17):1016–25.

Eckhouse, Laurel. 2019. "Race, Party, and Representation in Criminal Justice Politics." *Journal of Politics* 81 (3): 1143–52.

Einstein, Katherine Levine, and David M. Glick. 2017. "Cities in American Federalism: Evidence on State–Local Government Conflict from a Survey of Mayors." *Publius: The Journal of Federalism* 47 (4): 599–621.

———. 2018. "Mayors, Partisanship, and Redistribution: Evidence Directly from U.S. Mayors." *Urban Affairs Review* 54 (1): 74–106.

Einstein, Katherine Levine, David M. Glick, and Maxwell Palmer. 2019. *Neighborhood Defenders: Participatory Politics and America's Housing Crisis*. Cambridge University Press.

Einstein, Katherine Levine, David M. Glick, Luisa Godinez Puig, and Maxwell Palmer. 2023. "Still Muted: The Limited Participatory Democracy of Zoom Public Meetings." *Urban Affairs Review* 59 (4): 1279–91.

Einstein, Katherine Levine, and Vladimir Kogan. 2016. "Pushing the City Limits: Policy Responsiveness in Municipal Government." *Urban Affairs Review* 52 (1): 3–32.

Einstein, Katherine Levine, Maxwell Palmer, Stacy Fox, Marina Bernadino, Noah Fischer, Jackson Moore-Otto, Aislinn O'Brien, Marilyn Rutecki, and Benjamin Wuesthoff. 2020. "COVID-19 Housing Policy." Initiative on Cities. Boston University. https://www.bu.edu/ioc/files/2020/10/BU-COVID19-Housing-Policy-Report_Final-Oct-2020.pdf.

Einstein, Katherine Levine, Maxwell Palmer, and David M. Glick. 2019. "Who Participates in Local Government? Evidence from Meeting Minutes." *Perspectives on Politics* 17 (1): 28–46.

Eisinger, Peter K. 1988. *The Rise of the Entrepreneurial State: State and Local Economic Development Policy in the United States.* University of Wisconsin Press.

Ellis, Cliff. 2001. "Interstate Highways, Regional Planning and the Reshaping of Metropolitan America." *Planning Practice and Research* 16 (3–4): 247–69.

Emig, Arthur G., Michael B. Hesse, and Samuel H. Fisher III. 1996. "Black-White Differences in Political Efficacy, Trust and Sociopolitical Participation: A Critique of the Empowerment Hypothesis." *Urban Affairs Review* 32 (2): 264–76.

Englehart, Neil A., and Melissa K. Miller. 2014. "The CEDAW Effect: International Law's Impact on Women's Rights." *Journal of Human Rights* 13 (1): 22–47.

Erie, Steven P. 1990. *Rainbow's End: Irish-Americans and the Dilemmas of Urban Machine Politics, 1840–1985.* University of California Press.

———. 1992. "How the Urban West Was Won: The Local State and Economic Growth in Los Angeles, 1880–1932." *Urban Affairs Quarterly* 27 (4): 519–54.

Ethington, Philip, and David Levitus. 2009. "Placing American Political Development: Cities, Regions, and Regimes 1789–2008." In *The City in American Political Development*, edited by Richardson Dilworth. Routledge.

Etzioni, Amitai. 2010. "Is Transparency the Best Disinfectant?" *Journal of Political Philosophy* 4 (18): 389–404.

Evans, Whittney. 2022. "Charlottesville's Police Oversight Board Still a Work in Progress after Five Years." *Virginia Public Radio*, August 26, 2022. https://www.vpm.org/news/2022-08-26/charlottesvilles-police-oversight-board-still-a-work-in-progress-after-five.

Faber, Jacob William. 2020. "We Built This: Consequences of New Deal Era Intervention in America's Racial Geography." *American Sociological Review* 85 (5): 739–75.

Faber, Jacob William, and Jessica Rose Kalbfeld. 2019. "Complaining While Black: Racial Disparities in the Adjudication of Complaints Against the Police." *City & Community* 18 (3): 1028–67.

Faia, Alexandra E. 2014. "Prison, Politics, and Pointing Fingers: The Issues Plaguing Orleans Parish Prison's Consent Decrees." *Loyola Journal of Public Issue Law* 16:129.

Fairley, Sharon R. 2020. "Survey Says?: U.S. Cities Double Down on Civilian Oversight of Police despite Challenges and Controversy." *Cardozo Law Review De-Novo* 2020: 1–54.

Farenthold, David. 2018. "Trump Recorded Having Extremely Lewd Conversation about Women in 2005." *Washington Post*, October 6, 2018. https://www.washingtonpost.com/politics/trump-recorded-having-extremely-lewd-conversation-about-women-in-2005/2016/10/07/3b9ce776-8cb4-11e6-bf8a-3d26847eeed4_story.html.

Farris, Emily M., and Mirya R. Holman. 2024. *The Power of the Badge.* University of Chicago Press.

Farris, Emily M., Mirya R. Holman, and Miranda Sullivan. 2022. "Representation and Anti-Racist Policymaking in Cities during COVID-19." *Representation* 58 (2): 269–288.

Farris, Emily M., and Heather Silber Mohamed. 2022. "Race and the Rush to Reopen Schools During COVID-19." *Journal of Public Management & Social Policy* 29 (1): 112–36.

Farrow, Ronan. 2017. "From Aggressive Overtures to Sexual Assault: Harvey Weinstein's Accusers Tell Their Stories." *New Yorker*, October 10, 2017. https://www.newyorker.com/news/news-desk/from-aggressive-overtures-to-sexual-assault-harvey-weinsteins-accusers-tell-their-stories.

Ferdik, Frank V., Jeff Rojek, and Geoffrey P. Alpert. 2013. "Citizen Oversight in the United States and Canada: An Overview." *Police Practice and Research* 14 (2): 104–16.

Fischel, William A. 2004. "An Economic History of Zoning and a Cure for Its Exclusionary Effects." *Urban Studies* 41 (2): 317–40.

Fishkin, James S. 1991. *Democracy and Deliberation: New Directions for Democratic Reform.* Yale University Press.

Flammang, Janet A. 1985. "Female Officials in the Feminist Capital: The Case of Santa Clara County." *Western Political Science Quarterly* 38 (1): 94–118.

Fogelson, Robert M. 1968. "From Resentment to Confrontation: The Police, the Negroes, and the Outbreak of the Nineteen-Sixties Riots." *Political Science Quarterly* 83 (2): 217–47.

———. 1993. *The Fragmented Metropolis: Los Angeles, 1850–1930.* University of California Press.

Fording, Richard C. 2001. "The Political Response to Black Insurgency: A Critical Test of Competing Theories of the State." *American Political Science Review* 95 (1): 115–30.

Forester, Summer, Kaitlin Kelly-Thompson, Amber Lusvardi, and S Laurel Weldon. 2022. "New Dimensions of Global Feminist Influence: Tracking Feminist Mobilization Worldwide, 1975–2015." *International Studies Quarterly* 66 (1): 1–12.

Forman, William. 1969. "The Conflict Over Federal Urban Renewal Enabling Legislation in Louisiana." *Louisiana Studies* 8 (Fall): 251–57.

Fortier, Paula A. 2014. "Crescent City Nightingales: Gender, Race, Class and the Professionalization of Nursing for Women in New Orleans, Louisiana, 1881–1950." PhD diss., University of New Orleans.

Fox, Maggie. 2015. "Killer Amoeba Returns to New Orleans Area Tap Water." *NBC News*, July 23, 2015. https://www.nbcnews.com/health/health-news/killer-amoeba-still-lurks -new-orleans-area-tap-water-n397186.

Francis, Megan Ming. 2014. *Civil Rights and the Making of the Modern American State.* Cambridge University Press.

Frederick, Dee. 1949. "'Impossible' to Admit Negroes, Says Texas Park Official; Suit Expected." *Chicago Defender*, May 28, 1949.

Fung, Archon. 2001. "Accountable Autonomy: Toward Empowered Deliberation in Chicago Schools and Policing." *Politics & Society* 29 (1): 73–103.

———. 2006. "Varieties of Participation in Complex Governance." *Public Administration Review* 66:66–75.

———. 2013. "Infotopia: Unleashing the Democratic Power of Transparency." *Politics & Society* 41 (2): 183–212.

Funk, Kendall D. 2015. "Gendered Governing? Women's Leadership Styles and Participatory Institutions in Brazil." *Political Research Quarterly* 68 (3): 564–78.

———. 2020. "Local Responses to a Global Pandemic: Women Mayors Lead the Way." *Politics & Gender* 16 (4): 968–74.

Fussell, Elizabeth. 2007. "Constructing New Orleans, Constructing Race: A Population History of New Orleans." *Journal of American History* 94 (3): 846–55.

Gadarian, Shana Kushner, Sara Wallace Goodman, and Thomas B. Pepinsky, 2021. "Partisanship, Health Behavior, and Policy Attitudes in the Early Stages of the COVID-19 Pandemic." *PLoS ONE* 16 (4): e0249596.

Gains, Francesca, and Vivien Lowndes. 2022. "Identifying the Institutional Micro-Foundations of Gender Policy Change: A Case Study of Police Governance and Violence against Women and Girls." *Politics & Gender* 18 (2): 394–421.

Galster, George C. 1990. "White Flight from Racially Integrated Neighbourhoods in the 1970s: The Cleveland Experience." *Urban Studies* 27 (3): 385–99.

García-Castañon, Marcela, Kiku Huckle, Hannah L. Walker, and Chinbo Chong. 2019. "Democracy's Deficit: The Role of Institutional Contact in Shaping Non-White Political Behavior." *Journal of Race, Ethnicity, and Politics* 4 (1): 1–31.

Germany, Kent B. 2011. *New Orleans after the Promises: Poverty, Citizenship, and the Search for the Great Society*. University of Georgia Press.

Gessen, Masha. 2017. "Al Franken's Resignation and the Selective Force of #MeToo." *New Yorker*, December 7, 2017. https://www.newyorker.com/news/our-columnists/al-fran ken-resignation-and-the-selective-force-of-metoo.

Gittell, Marilyn, Kathe Newman, Janice Bockmeyer, and Robert Lindsay. 1998. "Expand- ing Civic Opportunity: Urban Empowerment Zones." *Urban Affairs Review* 33 (4): 530–58.

Glaeser, Edward L., Joseph Gyourko, and Raven Saks. 2005. "Why Is Manhattan So Ex- pensive? Regulation and the Rise in Housing Prices." *Journal of Law and Economics* 48 (2): 331–69.

Goehring, Benjamin, and Kenneth Lowande. 2024. "Public Responses to Unilateral Poli- cymaking." *Journal of Experimental Political Science*, OnlineFirst, April, 1–13.

Goodman, Christopher B., and Megan E Hatch. 2023. "State Preemption and Affordable Housing Policy." *Urban Studies* 60 (6): 1048–65.

Gotham, Kevin Fox. 2000. "Urban Space, Restrictive Covenants and the Origins of Racial Residential Segregation in a US City, 1900–50." *International Journal of Urban and Regional Research* 24 (3): 616–33.

———. 2002. *Race, Real Estate, and Uneven Development: The Kansas City Experience, 1900–2000*. SUNY Press.

Grant, Keneshia. 2019. *The Great Migration and the Democratic Party: Black Voters and the Realignment of American Politics in the 20th Century*. Temple University Press.

Green, Donald P., Dara Z. Strolovitch, and Janelle Wong. 1998. "Defended Neighbor- hoods, Integration, and Racially Motivated Crime." *American Journal of Sociology* 104 (2): 372–403.

Green, Elna C. 1997. *Southern Strategies: Southern Women and the Woman Suffrage Ques- tion*. University of North Carolina Press.

Green, Rodney D., and Jillian Aldebron. 2019. "In Search of Police Accountability: Civilian Review Boards and Department of Justice Intervention." *Phylon (1960-)* 56 (1): 111–33.

Gregory, Michelle. 1996. "Anatomy of a Neighborhood Plan: An Analysis of Current Practice." In *Modernizing State Planning Statutes*. American Planning Association Neigh- borhood Collaborative Planning Symposium.

Gross, Zenith, and Alan Reitman. 1966. "Police Power and Citizens' Rights: The Case for an Independent Police Review Board." American Civil Liberties Union.

Grumbach, Jacob M., and Alexander Sahn. 2020. "Race and Representation in Campaign Finance." *American Political Science Review* 114 (1): 206–21.

Grumbach, Jacob M., Alexander Sahn, and Sarah Staszak. 2020. "Gender, Race, and In- tersectionality in Campaign Finance." *Political Behavior* 44:319–340.

Guarneros-Meza, Valeria. 2009. "Mexican Urban Governance: How Old and New Insti- tutions Coexist and Interact." *International Journal of Urban and Regional Research* 33 (2): 463–82.

Guinier, Lani. 1991. "The Triumph of Tokenism: The Voting Rights Act and the Theory of Black Electoral Success." *Michigan Law Review* 89 (5): 1077–154.

Gullett, Gayle. 1995. "Women Progressives and the Politics of Americanization in California, 1915–1920." *Pacific Historical Review* 64 (1): 71–94.

Gutmann, Amy, and Dennis Thompson. 1998. *Democracy and Disagreement*. Harvard University Press.

Gyourko, Joseph, Albert Saiz, and Anita A. Summers. 2007. "A New Measure of the Local Regulatory Environment for Housing Markets: The Wharton Residential Land Use Regulatory Index." *Urban Studies* 45 (3), 693–729.

Haas, Edward F. 1988. *Political Leadership in a Southern City: New Orleans in the Progressive Era, 1896–1902*. McGinty Publications.

———. 1998. "Political Continuity in the Crescent City: Toward an Interpretation of New Orleans Politics, 1874–1986." *Louisiana History: Journal of the Louisiana Historical Association* 39 (1): 5–18.

———. 2014. *Mayor Victor H. Schiro: New Orleans in Transition, 1961–1970*. University Press of Mississippi.

Habermas, Jürgen. 1984. *The Theory of Communicative Action*. Vol. 2. Beacon Press.

Hallman, Howard. 1974. *Neighborhood Government in a Metropolitan Setting*. SAGE.

Hammer, David. 2021. "FBI Raids Sewerage & Water Board Hours after WWL-TV Investigation." *WWLTV*, November 9, 2021. https://www.wwltv.com/article/news/investigations/david-hammer/fbi-raid-new-orleans-sewerage-water-board/289-7f05e993-f5b9-4794-ac9e-c241573c470e.

———. 2023. "Orleans 911 Chief Tyrell Morris Resigns after Crashing Taxpayer-Funded Car." *nola.com*, June 26, 2023. https://www.nola.com/news/orleans-911-chief-tyrell-morris-resigns-after-crashing-taxpayer-funded-car/article_fa571b3a-1463-11ee-b71c-932dac4f1f86.html.

Hanlon, Bernadette. 2009. "A Typology of Inner-Ring Suburbs: Class, Race, and Ethnicity in U.S. Suburbia." *City & Community* 8 (3): 221–46.

Hannagan, Rebecca J., and Christopher W. Larimer. 2010. "Does Gender Composition Affect Group Decision Outcomes? Evidence from a Laboratory Experiment." *Political Behavior* 32 (1): 51–67.

Hannagan, Rebecca J., Christopher W. Larimer, and Matthew V. Hibbing. 2017. "Sex Differences, Personality, and Ideology: A Deeper Investigation via Contexts in a Study of Local Politics." *Politics, Groups, and Identities* 4 (4): 561–78.

Hansen, Debra Gold, Karen F. Gracy, and Sheri D. Irvin. 1999. "At the Pleasure of the Board: Women Librarians and the Los Angeles Public Library, 1880–1905." *Libraries & Culture* 34 (4): 311–46.

Harden, Kendal. 2016. "Exposure to Police Brutality Allows for Transparency and Accountability of Law Enforcement." *John Marshall Journal of Information Technology & Privacy Law*, 33:75–100.

Hardy, Eric. 2004. "The New Order Has Arrived: Dutch Morial, Reform, and the Sewerage and Water Board of New Orleans, 1980–1981." Master's thesis, University of New Orleans.

Harris, Allison P., Hannah L. Walker, and Laurel Eckhouse. 2020. "No Justice, No Peace: Political Science Perspectives on the American Carceral State." *Journal of Race, Ethnicity, and Politics* 5 (3): 427–49.

Hatch, Megan E. 2017. "Statutory Protection for Renters: Classification of State Landlord–Tenant Policy Approaches." *Housing Policy Debate* 27 (1): 98–119.

Hayes, Matthew, and Matthew V. Hibbing. 2017. "The Symbolic Benefits of Descriptive and Substantive Representation." *Political Behavior* 39 (1): 31–50.

Hays, Samuel P. 1964. "The Politics of Reform in Municipal Government in the Progressive Era." *Pacific Northwest Quarterly* 55 (4): 157–69.

Hayter, Julian. 2017. *The Dream Is Lost: Voting Rights and the Politics of Race in Richmond, Virginia.* University of Kentucky Press.

Heath, Roseanna, Leslie A. Schwindt-Bayer, and Michelle M. Taylor-Robinson. 2005. "Women on the Sidelines: Women's Representation on Committees in Latin American Legislatures." *American Journal of Political Science* 49 (2): 420–36.

Hebert, Scott, Franklin James, Avis Vidal, Greg Mills, and Debbie Gruenstein. 2001. "Interim Assessment of the Empowerment Zones and Enterprise Communities (EZ/EC) Program: A Progress Report." U.S. Department of Housing and Urban Development.

Heldman, Caroline, Meredith Conroy, and Alissa R. Ackerman. 2018. *Sex and Gender in the 2016 Presidential Election.* ABC-CLIO.

Hendriks, Carolyn M., Annie Bolitho, and Chad Foulkes. 2013. "Localism and the Paradox of Devolution: Delegated Citizen Committees in Victoria, Australia." *Policy Studies* 34 (5–6): 575–91.

Herbers, John. 1985. "Mayors Bid Congress Amend Tax Proposal." *New York Times*, June 20, 1985.

Hero, Rodney E. 2000. *Faces of Inequality: Social Diversity in American Politics.* Oxford University Press.

Hero, Rodney E., and Caroline J. Tolbert. 1995. "Latinos and Substantive Representation in the U.S. House of Representatives: Direct, Indirect, or Nonexistent?" *American Journal of Political Science* 39 (3): 640–52.

———. 1996. "A Racial/Ethnic Diversity Interpretation of Politics and Policy in the States of the U.S." *American Journal of Political Science* 40 (3): 851–71.

Hertel-Fernandez, Alexander. 2014. "Who Passes Business's 'Model Bills'? Policy Capacity and Corporate Influence in U.S. State Politics." *Perspectives on Politics* 12 (3): 582–602.

———. 2019. *State Capture: How Conservative Activists, Big Businesses, and Wealthy Donors Reshaped the American States—and the Nation.* Oxford University Press.

Hinojosa, Magda, and Miki Caul Kittilson. 2020. *Seeing Women, Strengthening Democracy: How Women in Politics Foster Connected Citizens.* Oxford University Press.

Hirschman, Albert O. 1970. *Exit, Voice, and Loyalty: Responses to Decline in Firms, Organizations, and States.* Harvard University Press.

Hoang, Bai Linh, and Andrea Benjamin. 2023. "'Defund' or 'Refund' the Police?: City Council Responsiveness to the Black Lives Matter Protests." *Urban Affairs Review* 60 (1): 387–419.

Hodges, Ron, Eugenio Caperchione, Jan Van Helden, Christoph Reichard, and Daniela Sorrentino. 2022. "The Role of Scientific Expertise in COVID-19 Policy-Making: Evidence from Four European Countries." *Public Organization Review* 22 (2): 249–67.

Hollyer, James R., B. Peter Rosendorff, and James Raymond Vreeland. 2011. "Democracy and Transparency." *Journal of Politics* 73 (4): 1191–1205.

Holman, Mirya R. 2014. "Sex and the City: Female Leaders and Spending on Social Welfare Programs in U.S. Municipalities." *Journal of Urban Affairs* 36 (4): 701–15.

———. 2015. *Women in Politics in the American City.* Temple University Press.

———. 2017. "Women in Local Government: What We Know and Where We Go from Here." *State and Local Government Review* 49 (4): 285–96.

———. 2019. "Urban Fiscal Crises and City-State Relations in American Political Development." Paper presented at the 2018 Toronto Conference on Political Development, University Toronto, September 27, 2018.

Holman, Mirya R., Emily M. Farris, and Jane Lawrence Sumner. 2020. "Local Political Institutions and First-Mover Policy Responses to COVID-19." *Journal of Political Institutions and Political Economy* 1 (4): 523–41.

Holman, Mirya R., Lakshmi Iyer, and Christina Wolbrecht. 2022. "Organization, Ideology, and Access to Governing Power: How Suffrage Shifted the Membership of Local Political Institutions." Paper presented at the 2024 Workshop on Women's Suffrage; University of Oslo, Oslo, Norway, May 31–June 1, 2023.

———. 2023. "Where Do Women Govern? The Gendered Distribution of Local Power." Paper presented at the 2023 Annual Meeting of the American Political Science Association, Los Angeles, CA, August 31–September 3, 2023.

Holman, Mirya R., and Nathan P. Kalmoe. 2021a. "Partisanship in the #MeToo Era." *Perspectives on Politics* 22 (1), 44–61.

———. 2021b. "The Polls—Trends: Sexual Harassment." *Public Opinion Quarterly* 85 (2): 706–18.

Holman, Mirya R., and J. Celeste Lay. 2020. "How Katrina Shaped Trust and Efficacy in New Orleans." *The Forum* 18 (1): 117–30.

———. 2021. "Are You Picking Up What I Am Laying Down? Ideology in Low-Information Elections." *Urban Affairs Review* 57 (2): 315–41.

Holman, Mirya R., Jennifer L. Merolla, and Elizabeth J. Zechmeister. 2017. "Can Experience Overcome Stereotypes in Times of Terror Threat?" *Research & Politics* 4 (1).

Houghton, David G. 1988. "Citizen Advisory Boards: Autonomy and Effectiveness." *American Review of Public Administration* 18 (3): 283–96.

Howard, Amy L., and Thad Williamson. 2016. "Reframing Public Housing in Richmond, Virginia: Segregation, Resident Resistance and the Future of Redevelopment." *Cities* 57:33–39.

Hoy, Suellen. 1995. *Chasing Dirt: The American Pursuit of Cleanliness.* Oxford University Press.

Hunt, Kate, and Mike Gruszczynski. 2019. "The Ratification of CEDAW and the Liberalization of Abortion Laws." *Politics & Gender* 15 (4): 722–45.

Hutchins, Ethan. 2017. "Mayor Bynum Recommends Creation of African American Commission." *KTUL*, February 6, 2017. https://ktul.com/news/local/tulsa-commission-will-study-reparations-for-1921-race-massacre-victims-descendants.

IAFF. 2021. "Local 632 Wins Big Raises for New Orleans Fire Fighters." International Association of Fire Fighters, October 5, 2021. https://www.iaff.org/news/local-632-wins-big-raises-for-new-orleans-fire-fighters/.

Ifill, Sherrilyn A. 1997. "Judging the Judges: Racial Diversity, Impartiality and Representation on State Trial Courts." *Boston College Law Review* 39:95.

Ihlanfeldt, Keith R. 2004. "Exclusionary Land-Use Regulations within Suburban Communities: A Review of the Evidence and Policy Prescriptions." *Urban Studies* 41 (2): 261–83.

IPUMS. 1970. "Richmond, Virginia 1970." Integrated Public Use Microdata Series. https://usa.ipums.org/usa/resources/voliii/pubdocs/1970/Pop_Housing/Vol1/39204513p18ch01.pdf

Irvin, Renée A., and John Stansbury. 2004. "Citizen Participation in Decision Making: Is It Worth the Effort?" *Public Administration Review* 64 (1): 55–65.

Jacob, Suraj, John A. Scherpereel, and Melinda Adams. 2014. "Gender Norms and Women's Political Representation: A Global Analysis of Cabinets, 1979–2009." *Governance* 27 (2): 321–45.

Jacoby, Melissa B. 2014. "The Detroit Bankruptcy, Pre-Eligibility." *Fordham Urban Law Journal* 41:849–66.

Jones, Beverly W. 1982. "Mary Church Terrell and the National Association of Colored Women, 1896 to 1901." *Journal of Negro History* 67 (1): 20–33.

Jones, David. 2022. "Thieves Hit Seven Blocks in Lakeview, Break into City Councilman's Vehicle." *Fox8live*, April 20, 2022. https://www.fox8live.com/2022/04/20/thieves-hit -seven-blocks-lakeview-break-into-city-councilmans-vehicle/.

———. 2023. "Lakeview Residents Question Whether Extra Paid Security Is Being Properly Dispatched." *Fox8live*, April 20, 2023. https://www.fox8live.com/2023/04/20/lake view-residents-question-whether-extra-paid-security-is-being-properly-dispatched/.

Jones, L. H. 1896. "The Politician and the Public School: Indianapolis and Cleveland." *Atlantic Monthly Magazine*, June 1896.

Jordan, Bre. 2020. "Denouncing the Myth of Place-Based Subsidies as the Solution for Economically Distressed Communities: An Analysis of Opportunity Zones as a Subsidy for Low-Income Displacement." *Columbia Journal of Race and Law* 10 (1): 65–113.

Joyce, Patrick D. 2003. *No Fire Next Time: Black-Korean Conflicts and the Future of America's Cities*. Cornell University Press.

Joyce, Philip G., and Daniel R. Mullins. 1991. "The Changing Fiscal Structure of the State and Local Public Sector: The Impact of Tax and Expenditure Limitations." *Public Administration Review* 51 (3): 240–53.

Judd, Dennis R. 1979. *The Politics of American Cities*. Little, Brown.

Juenke, Eric Gonzalez, and Paru Shah. 2015. "Not the Usual Story: The Effect of Candidate Supply on Models of Latino Descriptive Representation." *Politics, Groups, and Identities* 3 (3): 438–53.

Kalmoe, Nathan P., Raymond J. Pingree, Brian Watson, Mingxiao Sui, Joshua Darr, and Kathleen Searles. 2018. "Crime News Effects and Democratic Accountability: Experimental Evidence from Repeated Exposure in a Multiweek Online Panel." *International Journal of Public Opinion Research* 31 (3): 506–27.

Kanthak, Kristin, and George A. Krause. 2010. "Valuing Diversity in Political Organizations: Gender and Token Minorities in the U.S. House of Representatives." *American Journal of Political Science* 54 (4): 839–54.

Karnig, Albert K. 1979. "Black Resources and City Council Representation." *Journal of Politics* 41 (1): 134–49.

Karpowitz, Christopher F., J. Quin Monson, and Jessica Robinson Preece. 2017. "How to Elect More Women: Gender and Candidate Success in a Field Experiment." *American Journal of Political Science* 61 (4): 927–43.

Kasakove, Sophie. 2020. "New Orleans Courts Suspend Residential Evictions in Response to Coronavirus Outbreak." *The Lens*, March 13, 2020.

Kassel, Lola. 1929. "A History of the Government of Los Angeles, 1781–1925." Master's thesis, Occidental College.

Kathlene, Lyn. 1994. "Power and Influence in State Legislative Policy-Making: The Interaction of Gender and Position in Committee Hearing Debates." *American Political Science Review* 88 (3): 560–76.

Katz, Michael B. 1986. *In the Shadow of the Poorhouse: A Social History of Welfare in America*. Basic Books.

Kerner Commission. 1968. "Report of The National Advisory Commission on Civil Disorders." U.S. Government Printing Office.

Khanna, Kabir, Kosuke Imai, and Hubert Jin. 2017. "Wru: Who Are You? Bayesian Prediction of Racial Category Using Surname and Geolocation." R Package. Version 0.9–10. https://github.com/Kosukeimai/Wru.

Kimani, Abraham Carter. 2012. "Mothers of the City: The Phyllis Wheatley Club and Home, the Great Migration, and Communal Family in Black Chicago, 1910–1930." PhD diss., University of California, Los Angeles.

King, Desmond S., and Rogers M. Smith. 2005. "Racial Orders in American Political Development." *American Political Science Review* 99 (1): 75–92.

King, Kevin. 2015. "Effectively Implementing Civilian Oversight Boards to Ensure Police Accountability and Strengthen Police-Community Relations." *Hastings Race & Poverty* Law Journal 12:91–120.

King, Noel. 2021. "A Brief History of How Racism Shaped Interstate Highways." *NPR*, April 7, 2021. https://www.npr.org/2021/04/07/984784455/a-brief-history-of-how-ra cism-shaped-interstate-highways.

Kingdon, John W. 1984. *Agendas, Alternatives, and Public Policies*. Little, Brown.

King-Meadows, Tyson, and Thomas F. Schaller. 2007. *Devolution and Black State Legislators: Challenges and Choices in the Twenty-First Century*. SUNY Press.

Kirkland, Patricia A. 2020. "Mayoral Candidates, Social Class, and Representation in American Cities." *Journal of Political Institutions and Political Economy* 1 (1): 105–36.

———. 2022. "Representation in American Cities: Who Runs for Mayor and Who Wins?" *Urban Affairs Review* 58 (3): 635–70.

Klar, Samara, and Alexandra McCoy. 2021. "The #MeToo Movement and Attitudes toward President Trump in the Wake of a Sexual Misconduct Allegation." *Politics, Groups and Identities* 10 (5): 837–46.

Klüver, Heike, and Iñaki Sagarzazu. 2013. "Ideological Congruency and Decision-Making Speed: The Effect of Partisanship across European Union Institutions." *European Union Politics* 14 (3): 388–407.

Knack, Ruth. 1996. "The Real Story behind the Standard Planning and Zoning Acts of the 1920s." *Land Use Law & Zoning Digest* 48 (2): 3–9.

Knupfer, Anne M., and Leonard Silk. 1997. *Toward a Tenderer Humanity and a Nobler Womanhood: African American Women's Clubs in Turn-of-the-Century Chicago*. NYU Press.

Koelble, Thomas A. 1995. "The New Institutionalism in Political Science and Sociology." *Comparative Politics* 27 (2): 231–43.

Kopecký, Petr, Jan-hinrik Meyer Sahling, Francisco Panizza, Gerardo Scherlis, Christian Schuster, and Maria Spirova. 2016. "Party Patronage in Contemporary Democracies: Results from an Expert Survey in 22 Countries from Five Regions." *European Journal of Political Research* 55 (2): 416–31.

Kraft, Patrick W., and Benjamin J. Newman. 2023. "Complaints about Police Misconduct Have Adverse Effects for Black Civilians." *Political Science Research and Methods* 12 (3): 1–24.

Krell, Matthew Reid. 2016. "Fear-Driven Donations: Campaign Contributions as Mechanisms for Entrenching White Supremacy." *Social Science Quarterly* 97 (5): 1119–29.

Krishnamurthy, Arvind. 2023. "Handcuffed: The Limited Effects of Civilian Oversight on Police Behavior." Working Paper, Ohio State University, Criminal Justice Research Center. https://cjrc.osu.edu/events/handcuffed-design-limited-effects-civilian-oversight -agencies-police-behavior.

Kroll, Andy. 2021. "Meet the Undercover Anti-Fascists." *Rolling Stone*, February 14, 2021.

Krook, Mona Lena, and Diana Z. O'Brien. 2012. "All the President's Men? The Appointment of Female Cabinet Ministers Worldwide." *Journal of Politics* 74 (3): 840–55.

Kruse, Kevin M. 2005. "The Politics of Race and Public Space: Desegregation, Privatization, and the Tax Revolt in Atlanta." *Journal of Urban History* 31 (5): 610–33.

———. 2013. *White Flight: Atlanta and the Making of Modern Conservatism*. Princeton University Press.

Kuhlman, Martin. 1994. "The Civil Rights Movement in Texas: Desegregation of Public Accommodations, 1950–1964." PhD diss., Texas Tech University.

Lacey, Amy. 2017. "Hidden History: Eleanor Parker Sheppard, Richmond's First Female Mayor." *WRIC*, May 31, 2017. https://www.wric.com/news/hidden-history-eleanor -parker-sheppard-richmonds-first-female-mayor/.

Lageson, Sarah Esther. 2022. "Criminal Record Stigma and Surveillance in the Digital Age." *Annual Review of Criminology* 5 (1): 67–90.

Lassiter, Matthew D. 2013. *The Silent Majority: Suburban Politics in the Sunbelt South*. Princeton University Press.

Lay, J. Celeste. 2022. *Public Schools, Private Governance: Education Reform and Democracy in New Orleans*. Temple University Press.

Lee, Myunghee, and Amanda Murdie. 2020. "The Global Diffusion of #MeToo Movement." *Politics & Gender* 17 (4), 827–55.

Leifheit, Kathryn M., Sabriya L. Linton, Julia Raifman, Gabriel L. Schwartz, Emily A. Benfer, Frederick J. Zimmerman, and Craig Evan Pollack. 2021. "Expiring Eviction Moratoriums and COVID-19 Incidence and Mortality." *American Journal of Epidemiology* 190 (12): 2503–10.

Leland, Suzanne, Jacqueline Chattopadhyay, Cherie Maestas, and Jaclyn Piatak. 2021. "Policy Venue Preference and Relative Trust in Government in Federal Systems." *Governance* 34 (2): 373–93.

Lens, Michael C., and Paavo Monkkonen. 2016. "Do Strict Land Use Regulations Make Metropolitan Areas More Segregated by Income?" *Journal of the American Planning Association* 82 (1): 6–21.

Lerner, Gerda. 1974. "Early Community Work of Black Club Women." *Journal of Negro History* 59 (2): 158–67.

Leung, Lillian, Peter Hepburn, James Hendrickson, and Matthew Desmond. 2023. "No Safe Harbor: Eviction Filing in Public Housing." *Social Service Review* 97 (3): 456–97.

Levi, Margaret, Audrey Sacks, and Tom Tyler. 2009. "Conceptualizing Legitimacy, Measuring Legitimating Beliefs." *American Behavioral Scientist* 53 (3): 354–75.

Levin, Benjamin. 2020. "Imagining the Progressive Prosecutor." *Minnesota Law Review* 105: 1415.

Levin, Kevin M. 2020. "Richmond's Confederate Monuments Were Used to Sell a Segregated Neighborhood." *Atlantic*, June 11, 2020. https://www.theatlantic.com/ideas/archive /2020/06/its-not-just-the-monuments/612940/.

Lewis, Tiffany. 2011. "Municipal Housekeeping in the American West: Bertha Knight Landes's Entrance into Politics." *Rhetoric & Public Affairs* 14 (3): 465–91.

Lewthwaite, Stephanie. 2009. *Race, Place, and Reform in Mexican Los Angeles: A Transnational Perspective, 1890–1940*. University of Arizona Press.

Lincoln Institute of Land Policy. 2020. "Fiscally Standardized Cities Database." Lincoln Institute of Land Policy. https://www.lincolninst.edu/data/fiscally-standardized-cities/.

Lippincott, Jordan. 2022. "New Orleans PCAB President Calls Leaders to Action amid Crime Spike." *WGNO*, January 26, 2022. https://wgno.com/news/local/new-orleans -pcab-president-calls-leaders-to-action-amid-crime-spike.

Lipsky, Michael. 1969. *Protest in City Politics: Rent Strikes, Housing, and the Power of the Poor*. Rand McNally.

Littlejohn, Edward J. 1981. "The Cries of the Wounded: A History of Police Misconduct in Detroit." *University of Detroit Journal of Urban Law* 59:177–219.

Locke, Hubert. 1967. "Police Brutality and Civilian Review Boards: A Second Look." *Journal of Urban Law* 44 (4): 625–34.

Loewen, James. 2005. *Sundown Towns: A Hidden Dimension of American Racism*. The New Press.

Logan, John R., and Harvey Luskin Molotch. 1987. *Urban Fortunes: The Political Economy of Place*. University of California Press.

Louisiana State Bar Association. 1922. *Proceedings of the Louisiana Bar Association*. Montgomery-Andree Print Company.

Lowery, David, and Lee Sigelman. 1981. "Understanding the Tax Revolt: Eight Explanations." *American Political Science Review* 75 (4): 963–74.

Lowndes, Vivien. 2001. "Rescuing Aunt Sally: Taking Institutional Theory Seriously in Urban Politics." *Urban Studies* 38 (11): 1953–71.

Lowndes, Vivien, and Mark Roberts. 2013. *Why Institutions Matter: The New Institutionalism in Political Science*. Bloomsbury Publishing.

Lucas, Jack. 2016. *Fields of Authority: Special Purpose Governance in Ontario, 1815–2015*. University of Toronto Press.

Lupton, Ellen, and J. Abbott Miller. 1996. *The Bathroom, the Kitchen, and the Aesthetics of Waste*. Princeton Architectural Press.

Luskin, Robert C., James S. Fishkin, and Roger Jowell. 2002. "Considered Opinions: Deliberative Polling in Britain." *British Journal of Political Science* 32 (3): 455–87.

Lusvardi, Amber Nicole. 2022. "The End of the Child Bride: Social Movements and State Policymaking on Underage Marriage." PhD diss., Purdue University.

Lynn, Frances M., and Jack D. Kartez. 1995. "The Redemption of Citizen Advisory Committees: A Perspective from Critical Theory." In *Fairness and Competence in Citizen Participation: Evaluating Models for Environmental Discourse*, edited by Ortwin Renn, Thomas Wehler, and Peter Wiedemann, 87–101. Springer Netherlands.

Macdonald, John, and Robert J. Stokes. 2006. "Race, Social Capital, and Trust in the Police." *Urban Affairs Review* 41 (3): 358–75.

MacLean, Nancy. 1995. *Behind the Mask of Chivalry: The Making of the Second Ku Klux Klan*. Oxford University Press.

MacManus, Susan. 1981. "A City's First Female Officeholder: 'Coattails' for Future Female Officeholders?" *Western Political Science Quarterly* 34 (1): 88–99.

———. 1992. "How to Get More Women in Office: The Perspectives of Local Elected Officials." *Urban Affairs Quarterly* 28:159–70.

Mahoney, James. 2000. "Path Dependence in Historical Sociology." *Theory and Society* 29 (4): 507–48.

Maldonado, Charles. 2023. "Nearly the entire board is made up of city officials who report directly to the mayor. One of the exceptions is Brobson Lutz's seat. And Lutz has long been the sole source of dissent on the board." Twitter [X], July 5, 2023. https://twitter.com/Maldonado_CB/status/1676704054100017153.

Malone, Aaron. 2018. "(Im)Mobile and (Un)Successful? A Policy Mobilities Approach to New Orleans's Residential Security Taxing Districts." *Environment and Planning C: Politics and Space* 37 (1): 102–18.

———. 2019. "Why New Orleans' Residential Security Districts May Be Undermining Public Safety." *USAPP* (blog). December 4, 2019. https://blogs.lse.ac.uk/usappblog/2019/12/04/why-new-orleans-residential-security-districts-may-be-undermining-public-safety/.

Mansbridge, Jane J. 1983. *Beyond Adversary Democracy*. University of Chicago Press.

———. 1999. "Should Blacks Represent Blacks and Women Represent Women? A Contingent 'Yes.'" *Journal of Politics* 61 (3): 628–57.

Marcus, Nancy C. 2016. "From Edward to Eric Garner and Beyond: The Importance of Constitutional Limitations on Lethal Use of Force in Police Reform." *Duke Journal of Constitutional Law & Public Policy* 12:53.

Martinez-Ebers, Valerie, and Brian Calfano. 2020. *Human Relations Commissions.* Columbia University Press.

Maryland Historical Magazine. 1962. "Baltimore's Interracial History."

Massey, Douglas S., and Nancy A. Denton. 1988. "The Dimensions of Residential Segregation." *Social Forces* 67 (2): 281–315.

Maynard, Guy. 2016. "Just People Like Us." *Oregon Humanities*, April 11, 2016. https://www.oregonhumanities.org/rll/magazine/root-spring-2016/just-people-like-us/.

McBain, Howard Lee. 1917. "The Delegation of Legislative Power to Cities." *Political Science Quarterly* 32 (2): 276–95.

McBrayer, Markie, and Robert Lucas Williams. 2022. "The Second Sex in the Second District: The Policy Effects of Electing Women to County Government." *Political Research Quarterly* 76 (2): 825–40.

McCabe, Barbara Coyle, Richard C. Feiock, James C. Clingermayer, and Christopher Stream. 2008. "Turnover among City Managers: The Role of Political and Economic Change." *Public Administration Review* 68 (2): 380–86.

McCammon, Holly. 2003. "'Out of the Parlors and into the Streets': The Changing Tactical Repertoire of the U.S. Women's Suffrage Movements." *Social Forces* 81 (3): 787–818.

McConnell, Michael W., and Randal C. Picker. 1993. "When Cities Go Broke: A Conceptual Introduction to Municipal Bankruptcy." *University of Chicago Law Review* 60:425–95.

McDermott, Rose. 2011. "Internal and External Validity." *Cambridge Handbook of Experimental Political Science.* Cambridge University Press.

McGregor, Shannon C., Rachel R. Mourão, and Logan Molyneux. 2017. "Twitter as a Tool for and Object of Political and Electoral Activity: Considering Electoral Context and Variance among Actors." *Journal of Information Technology & Politics* 14 (2): 154–67.

McNamara, Kevin. 2023. "What's Next for Josephine County without New Homelessness Funding?" *KTVL*, April 11, 2023. https://m.ktvl.com/news/local/gallery/whats-next-for-josephine-county-without-new-homelessness-funding-governor-kotek-state-emergency-oregon-legislation-budget-human-services-grants-pass?photo=1.

McNitt, Andrew D. 2011. "Big City Mayors: Political Specialization and Business Domination in the 19th and 20th Centuries." *Journal of Urban Affairs* 33 (4): 431–49.

McQueen, Shannon. 2021. "Pipeline or Pipedream: Gender Balance Legislation's Effect on Women's Presence in State Government." *State Politics & Policy Quarterly* 21 (3): 243–65.

McRae, Elizabeth Gillespie. 2018. *Mothers of Massive Resistance: White Women and the Politics of White Supremacy.* Oxford University Press.

Mead, Joseph. 2024. "Yes: the Question before the Supreme Court Is whether a Person Who Is Homeless and Involuntarily without Shelter Can Be Punished for Sleeping Outside with a Blanket." Bluesky Social, April 17, 2024. https://bsky.app/profile/josephwmead.bsky.social/post/3kqdxbl3u2k2g.

Meier, Kenneth J., and Kendall D. Funk. 2016. "Women and Public Administration in a Comparative Perspective." *Administration & Society* 49 (1): 121–42.

Meijer, Albert Jacob. 2003. "Transparent Government: Parliamentary and Legal Accountability in an Information Age." *Information Polity* 8 (1,2): 67–78.

Mele, Christopher. 2013. "Neoliberalism, Race and the Redefining of Urban Redevelopment." *International Journal of Urban and Regional Research* 37 (2): 598–617.

Melosi, Martin V. 2008. *The Sanitary City: Environmental Services in Urban America from Colonial Times to the Present.* University of Pittsburgh Press.

Merolla, Jennifer L., and Elizabeth Zechmeister. 2009. "Terrorist Threat, Leadership, and the Vote: Evidence from Three Experiments." *Political Behavior* 31 (4): 575–601.

———. 2013. "Evaluating Political Leaders in Times of Terror and Economic Threat: The Conditioning Influence of Politician Partisanship." *Journal of Politics* 75 (3): 599–612.

Merritt, Sharyne. 1977. "Winners and Losers: Sex Differences in Municipal Elections." *American Journal of Political Science* 21 (4): 731–43.

Meyer, Stephen Grant. 2000. *As Long as They Don't Move Next Door: Segregation and Racial Conflict in American Neighborhoods.* Rowman & Littlefield.

Mezey, Susan Gluck. 1978. "Women and Representation: The Case of Hawaii." *Journal of Politics* 40 (2): 369–85.

Michener, Jamila. 2020. "Power from the Margins: Grassroots Mobilization and Urban Expansions of Civil Legal Rights." *Urban Affairs Review* 56 (5): 1390–1422.

Miller, David R., and Andrew J. Reeves. 2017. "Attitudes toward Delegation to Presidential Commissions." *Presidential Studies Quarterly* 47 (3): 495–516.

Mitchell, Jerry. 2001. "Business Improvement Districts and the 'New' Revitalization of Downtown." *Economic Development Quarterly* 15 (2): 115–23.

Mohl, Raymond A. 2001. "Whitening Miami: Race, Housing, and Government Policy in Twentieth-Century Dade County." *Florida Historical Quarterly* 79 (3): 319–45.

Molotch, Harvey Luskin. 1972. *Managed Integration: Dilemmas of Doing Good in the City.* University of California Press.

———. 1976. "The City as a Growth Machine: Toward a Political Economy of Place." *American Journal of Sociology* 82 (2): 309–32.

Moniz, Philip, and Christopher Wlezien. 2020. "Issue Salience and Political Decisions." In *Oxford Research Encyclopedia of Politics.* Oxford University Press.

Moore, Dorothea. 1906. "The Work of the Women's Clubs in California." *Annals of the American Academy of Political and Social Science* 28 (2): 59–62.

Moore, Leonard N. 2010. *Black Rage in New Orleans: Police Brutality and African American Activism from World War II to Hurricane Katrina.* LSU Press.

Mordechay, Kfir. 2014. "Vast Changes and an Uneven Future: Racial and Regional Inequality in Southern California." The Civil Rights Project. https://www.civilrightspro ject.ucla.edu/research/metro-and-regional-inequalities/lasanti-project-los-angeles -san-diego-tijuana/vast-changes-and-an-uneasy-future-racial-and-regional-inequality -in-southern-california/mordechayi-uneasy-future-lasantai-2014.pdf.

Morris, Kevin T., and Kelsey Shoub. 2023. "Contested Killings: The Mobilizing Effects of Community Contact with Police Violence." *American Political Science Review* 118 (1): 458–74.

Mossberger, Karen, and Gary Stoker. 2001. "The Evolution of Urban Regime Theory: The Challenges of Conceptualization." *Urban Affairs Review* 36:810–35.

Mozzone, Katherine. 2020. "New Orleans Firefighters Union and City Leaders Negotiating Contract amid Recent Conflict." *Fox8live*, March 7, 2020. https://www.fox8live .com/2020/03/07/new-orleans-firefighters-union-city-leaders-negotiating-contract -amidst-recent-conflict/.

Muddiman, Ashley, Shannon C. McGregor, and Natalie Jomini Stroud. 2019. "(Re)Claiming Our Expertise: Parsing Large Text Corpora with Manually Validated and Organic Dictionaries." *Political Communication* 36 (2): 214–26.

Mullen, Lincoln, Cameron Blevins, and Ben Schmidt. 2015. "Gender: Predict Gender from Names Using Historical Data." R Package Version 0.5 1.

Mullin, Megan. 2008. "The Conditional Effect of Specialized Governance on Public Policy." *American Journal of Political Science* 52 (1): 125–41.

———. 2009. *Governing the Tap: Special District Governance and the New Local Politics of Water*. MIT Press.

Myers, Ben. 2023a. "New Orleans S&WB Refuses to Comply with Parts of Billing Law." *Times Picayune*, April 20, 2023. https://www.nola.com/news/politics/new-orleans-swb -refuses-to-comply-with-parts-of-billing-law/article_c732f118-dfcd-11ed-bf0e-5bd6 4f4e1fec.html.

———. 2023b. "NOPD Officer Accused of Affair with Mayor LaToya Cantrell Was Paid to Attend HANO Meetings." *Times Picayune*, March 16, 2023. https://www.nola.com /news/politics/nopd-officer-accused-of-affair-with-mayor-latoya-cantrell-was -paid-to-attend-hano-meetings/article_f385a72a-c451-11ed-810d-4b48941628bc .html.

NACOLE. 2023. "Community Oversight Paves the Road to Police Accountability." National Association for Civilian Oversight of Law Enforcement. https://www.nacole.org /community_oversight_paves_the_road_to_police_accountability.

NAEH. 2023. "State of Homelessness: 2023 Edition." National Alliance to End Homelessness. https://endhomelessness.org/homelessness-in-america/homelessness-statistics /state-of-homelessness/.

Nall, Gail. 2004. "Louise C. Morel, The Louisville Women's City Club, and Municipal Housekeeping in Louisville, 1917–1935." PhD diss., University of Louisville.

National Advisory Commission on Civil Disorders. 1968. "Report of the National Advisory Commission on Civil Disorders." Office of the President of the United States.

National Municipal League. 1916. "*A Model City Charter and Municipal Home Rule*, as Prepared by the Committee on Municipal Program of the National Municipal League." National Municipal League.

NBC 4. 2020. NBC 4 New York/Marist Poll, Question 12, 31117554.00011. Marist College Institute for Public Opinion. Cornell University, Roper Center for Public Opinion Research, 2020, Survey question. https://doi.org/10.25940/ROPER-31117554.

NBC Los Angeles. 2023. "LA Planning Commission to Vote on Proposal to Fast-Track Affordable Housing." *NBC Los Angeles*, November 16, 2023. https://www.nbclosangeles .com/news/local/la-planning-commission-to-vote-on-proposal-to-fast-track-afford able-housing/3270143/.

Nellis, Eric, and Anne Decker Cecere. 2006. *The Eighteenth-Century Records of the Boston Overseers of the Poor*. Colonial Society of Massachusetts.

Newton, Damien. 2011. "The Lorenzo Project in South L.A. Is Controversial, But Is It T.O.D." *Streetsblog Los Angeles*, January 20, 2011. https://la.streetsblog.org/2011/01/20 /the-lorenzo-project-in-south-l-a-is-controversial-but-is-it-t-o-d.

Nielsen, Ingrid, Zoe Robinson, and Russell Smyth. 2020. "Keep Your (Horse) Hair On? Experimental Evidence on the Effect of Exposure to Legitimising Symbols on Diffuse Support for the High Court." *Federal Law Review* 48 (3): 382–400.

Nightingale, Carl Husemoller. 2006. "The Transnational Contexts of Early Twentieth-Century American Urban Segregation." *Journal of Social History* 39 (3): 667–702.

Nuamah, Sally A. 2022. *Closed for Democracy: How Mass School Closure Undermines the Citizenship of Black Americans*. Cambridge University Press.

O'Brien, Diana Z. 2015. "Rising to the Top: Gender, Political Performance, and Party Leadership in Parliamentary Democracies." *American Journal of Political Science* 59 (4): 1022–39.

O'Brien, William E. 2012. "State Parks and Jim Crow in the Decade Before *Brown v. Board of Education*." *Geographical Review* 102 (2): 166–79.

———. 2015. *Landscapes of Exclusion: State Parks and Jim Crow in the American South*. University of Massachusetts Press.

Ocasio-Cortez, Alexandria @AOC. 2020. "A lot of ppl are asking abt policy solutions. Here are a few: 1. Ask your mayor and city council for strong Citizen Review Boards. 2. Budgets. They're powerful. Find your city's police budget. Compare that to the school & housing budget. More $ in fmr school-to-prison pipeline." Twitter [X], May 30, 2020. https://x.com/AOC/status/1266783358731931648.

Och, Malliga. 2018. "The Local Diffusion of International Human Rights Norms—Understanding the Cities for CEDAW Campaign." *International Feminist Journal of Politics* 20 (3): 425–43.

O'Connor, Shay. 2022. "'We'll Do It Ourselves': Lakeview Residents Add More Patrols in Their Neighborhood amid Crime Surge." *WDSU*, February 11, 2022. https://www.wdsu.com/article/well-do-it-ourselves-lakeview-residents-add-more-patrols-in-their-neighborhood-amid-crime-surge/39047327.

Oestreicher, Richard Jules. 1989. *Solidarity and Fragmentation: Working People and Class Consciousness in Detroit, 1875–1900*. University of Illinois Press.

Ofer, Udi. 2015. "Getting It Right: Building Effective Civilian Review Boards to Oversee Police." *Seton Hall Law Review* 46:1033–62.

O'Grady, Tom. 2019. "Careerists Versus Coal-Miners: Welfare Reforms and the Substantive Representation of Social Groups in the British Labour Party." *Comparative Political Studies* 52 (4): 544–78.

Oliveros, Virginia. 2021. *Patronage at Work: Public Jobs and Political Services in Argentina*. Cambridge University Press.

Olson, Mancur. 1965. *The Logic of Collective Action: Public Goods and the Theory of Groups*. Harvard University Press.

Olzak, Susan. 2021. "Does Protest Against Police Violence Matter? Evidence from U.S. Cities, 1990 through 2019." *American Sociological Review* 86 (6): 1066–99.

Ondercin, Heather L. 2022. "Location, Location, Location: How Electoral Opportunities Shape Women's Emergence as Candidates." *British Journal of Political Science* 52 (4): 1523–43.

Ong, Paul. 2020. "Systemic Racial Inequality and the COVID-19 Renter Crisis." Luskin Institute on Equality and Democracy. UCLA. https://challengeinequality.luskin.ucla.edu/2020/08/07/systemic-racial-inequality-covid-19-renter-crisis/.

Orren, Karen, and Stephen Skowronek. 2004. *The Search for American Political Development*. Cambridge University Press.

Ostrom, Elinor. 1999. "Institutional Rational Choice: An Assessment of the Institutional Analysis and Development Framework." In *Theories of the Policy Process*, 2nd ed., edited by Paul Sabatier. Routledge.

Ostrom, Vincent. 1953. *Water and Politics: A Study of Water Policies and Administration in the Development of Los Angeles*. Haynes Foundation.

Owens, Michael L., and Anna Gunderson. 2023. "Noncongruent Policymaking by Cities for Citizens with Criminal Records: Representation, Organizing, and 'Ban the Box.'" *Political Research Quarterly* 76 (2): 977–93.

Pachón, Mónica, and Gregg B. Johnson. 2016. "When's the Party (or Coalition)? Agenda-Setting in a Highly Fragmented, Decentralized Legislature." *Journal of Politics in Latin America* 8 (2): 71–100.

Pacific Outlook. 1909. "Expressions of Prominent Citizens on the Election Results." *Pacific Outlook*, December 11, 1909.

Palmer, Barbara, and Dennis Simon. 2010. *Breaking the Political Glass Ceiling: Women and Congressional Elections*. Routledge.

Panizza, Francisco, B. Guy Peters, and Conrado R. Ramos Larraburu. 2019. "Roles, Trust and Skills: A Typology of Patronage Appointments." *Public Administration* 97 (1): 147–61.

Parfitt, Jamie, and Colten Weekley. 2023. "Could an Oregon Court Case on Homeless Camp Bans Go to the US Supreme Court?" *KGW8*. August 5, 2023.

Parker, Joseph. 1998. *The Morrison Era: Reform Politics in New Orleans*. Pelican Press.

PBS. 2022. "Almost Half of New Orleans Residents Are Renters. Advocates Worry an Eviction Crisis Looms." *PBS NewsHour*. January 12, 2022. https://www.pbs.org/new shour/nation/almost-half-of-new-orleans-residents-are-renters-advocates-worry-an -eviction-crisis-looms.

Perlstein, Mike. 2023. "Embattled Orleans 911 Director Resigns 2 Months Early Citing 'Overwhelming Media Attention.'" *WWLTV*, July 10, 2023. https://www.wwltv.com /video/news/local/orleans/embattled-911-director-resigns-2-months-early-citing -overwhelming-media-attention/289-570ef4a2-bac9-46cc-a338-790f8baf6a68.

Peterson, Jon A. 1979. "The Impact of Sanitary Reform upon American Urban Planning, 1840–1890." *Journal of Social History* 13 (1): 83–103.

Peterson, Paul E. 1981. *City Limits*. University of Chicago Press.

Pew Research Center. 1985. *The People & the Press 1985 Survey*. Report Overview. https:// www.pewresearch.org/politics/1985/11/15/the-people-the-press/.

———. 2023. Pew American Trends Panel Poll, Question 53, 31120106.00056. Ipsos. Cornell University, Roper Center for Public Opinion Research, 2023. Web, January 18, 2023.

Pierson, Paul. 2000. "Not Just What, but When: Timing and Sequence in Political Processes." *Studies in American Political Development* 14 (1): 72–92.

Piliawsky, Monte. 1985. "The Impact of Black Mayors on the Black Community: The Case of New Orleans' Ernest Morial." *Review of Black Political Economy* 13 (4): 5–23.

Pincetl, Stephanie S. 2003. *Transforming California: A Political History of Land Use and Development*. Johns Hopkins University Press.

Piven, Frances Fox, and Richard A. Cloward. 1971. *Regulating the Poor: The Functions of Public Welfare*. Pantheon Books.

Plunkett, Harriette Merrick. 1885. *Women, Plumbers, and Doctors*. D. Appleton.

Portney, Kent E., and Jeffrey M. Berry. 2010. "Participation and the Pursuit of Sustainability in U.S. Cities." *Urban Affairs Review* 46 (1): 119–39.

Powell, Lawrence. 1999. "Reinventing Tradition: Liberty Place, Historical Memory, and Silk-stocking Vigilantism in New Orleans Politics." *Slavery & Abolition* 20 (1): 127–49.

Powell, Zachary A., Michele Bisaccia Meitl, and John L. Worrall. 2017. "Police Consent Decrees and Section 1983 Civil Rights Litigation." *Criminology & Public Policy* 16 (2): 575–605.

PPIC (Public Policy Institute of California). 2019. PPIC Statewide Survey, Question 9, 31119669.00008. Abt Associates. Cornell University, Roper Center for Public Opinion Research, 2019. Web, May 19, 2019.

Preece, Jessica Robinson. 2016. "Mind the Gender Gap: An Experiment on the Influence of Self-Efficacy on Political Interest." *Politics & Gender* 12 (1): 198–217.

Prenzler, Timothy. 2016. "Scandal, Inquiry and Reform: The Evolving Locus of Responsibility for Police Integrity." In *Civilian Oversight of Police: Advancing Accountability in Law Enforcement*, edited by Tim Prenzler and Garth den Heyer, 3–27. CRC Press.

Prenzler, Timothy, and Carol Ronken. 2001. "Models of Police Oversight: A Critique." *Policing and Society: An International Journal* 11 (2): 151–80.

Preston, Anne E., and Casey Ichniowski. 1991. "A National Perspective on the Nature and Effects of the Local Property Tax Revolt, 1976–1986." *National Tax Journal* 44 (2): 123–45.

Quigley, John, Steven Raphael, and Larry A. Rosenthal. 2004. "Local Land-Use Controls and Demographic Outcomes in a Booming Economy." *Urban Studies* 41 (2): 389–421.

Quintana, Dolores. 2023. "LA City Planning Commission Greenlights New Sawtelle District Multi-Family Development." WestsideToday.com, December 17, 2023. https://westsidetoday.com/2023/12/17/la-city-planning-commission-greenlights-new-saw telle-district-multi-family-development/.

Rampell, Catherine. 2018. "States Are Taking Action on #MeToo. Why Isn't Congress?" *Washington Post*, October 15, 2018. https://www.washingtonpost.com/opinions/states -are-taking-action-on-metoo-why-isnt-congress/2018/10/15/88b8fbf4-d0b3-11e8 -83d6-291fcead2ab1_story.html.

Ramphal, Bruce, Ryan Keen, Sakurako S. Okuzuno, Dennis Ojogho, and Natalie Slopen. 2023. "Evictions and Infant and Child Health Outcomes: A Systematic Review." *JAMA Network Open* 6 (4): e237612–e237612.

Randolph, Lewis A., and Gayle T. Tate. 2003. *Rights for a Season: The Politics of Race, Class, and Gender in Richmond, Virginia*. University of Tennessee Press.

Ranker, Luke. 2019a. "Fort Worth Official Accused of Sharing Racist Facebook Memes." *Fort Worth Star-Telegram*, July 3, 2019. https://www.star-telegram.com/news/local/fort -worth/article232189932.html.

———. 2019b. "Mayor Betsy Price on Fort Worth's Human Relation's Commission." *Fort Worth Star-Telegram*, July 2, 2019. https://www.star-telegram.com/latest-news/article 232222022.html.

Rast, Joel. 2001. "Manufacturing Industrial Decline: The Politics of Economic Change in Chicago, 1955–1998." *Journal of Urban Affairs* 23 (2): 175–90.

———. 2009. "Regime Building, Institution Building: Urban Renewal Policy in Chicago, 1946–1962." *Journal of Urban Affairs* 31 (2): 173–94.

Rawls, John. 2005. *Political Liberalism*. Columbia University Press.

Rebori, Marlene K. 2011. "Citizen Advisory Boards and Their Influence on Local Decision-Makers." *Community Development* 42 (1): 84–96.

Reckhow, Sarah. 2009. "The Distinct Patterns of Organized and Elected Representation of Racial and Ethnic Groups." *Urban Affairs Review* 45 (2): 188–217.

Reps, John William. 1965. *The Making of Urban America: A History of City Planning in the United States*. Princeton University Press.

Retzlaff, Rebecca. 2019. "Desegregation of City Parks and the Civil Rights Movement: The Case of Oak Park in Montgomery, Alabama." *Journal of Urban History* 47 (4): 715–752.

Reynolds, George Millar. 1936. *Machine Politics in New Orleans, 1897–1926*. Columbia University Press.

Rice, Bradley Robert. 2014. *Progressive Cities: The Commission Government Movement in America, 1901–1920*. University of Texas Press.

Rich, Michael J., and Robert P. Stoker. 2010. "Rethinking Empowerment: Evidence from Local Empowerment Zone Programs." *Urban Affairs Review* 45 (6): 775–96.

Riposa, Gerry. 1996. "From Enterprise Zones to Empowerment Zones: The Community Context of Urban Economic Development." *American Behavioral Scientist* 39 (5): 536–51.

Robinson, Zoe. 2012. "A Comparative Analysis of the Doctrinal Consequences of Interpretive Disagreement for Implied Constitutional Rights." *Washington University Global Studies Law Review* 11:93.

Rocco, Philip, Daniel Béland, and Alex Waddan. 2020. "Stuck in Neutral? Federalism, Policy Instruments, and Counter-Cyclical Responses to COVID-19 in the United States." *Policy and Society* 39 (3): 458–77.

Rocha Beardall, Theresa. 2022. "Police Legitimacy Regimes and the Suppression of Citizen Oversight in Response to Police Violence." *Criminology* 60 (4): 740–65.

Rogers, Kim Lacy. 1993. *Righteous Lives Narratives of the New Orleans Civil Rights Movement.* New York University Press.

Rolett, Burl. 2014. "City Makes Pricey Promises to Land Stone Brewing." *Richmond Biz-Sense,* October 9, 2014. https://richmondbizsense.com/2014/10/09/city-makes-pricey-promises-to-land-stone-brewing/.

Rosen, Christine Meisner. 2003. *The Limits of Power: Great Fires and the Process of City Growth in America.* Cambridge University Press.

Rosenbaum, Walter A. 1976. "The Paradoxes of Public Participation." *Administration & Society* 8 (3): 355–83.

Rosenberg, Daniel. 1988. *New Orleans Dockworkers: Race, Labor, and Unionism 1892–1923.* SUNY Press.

Rouault, Sophie. 2017. "Symbolic Policy Making for Gender Equality: Comparing the Use of Quotas for Civil Service and Corporate Boards in France and Germany." In *Gender and Family in European Economic Policy: Developments in the New Millennium,* edited by Diana Auth, Jutta Hergenhan, and Barbara Holland-Cunz, 43–62. Springer International Publishing.

Roychoudhury, Debanjan. 2023. "Police Violence in Black and White: A Critical Discourse Analysis of Newspaper Reporting on the Police Killings of Clifford Glover and Sean Bell in Jamaica, Queens, New York." *Du Bois Review: Social Science Research on Race* 20 (1): 111–41.

Runyan, Anne Sisson, and Rebecca Sanders. 2021. "Prospects for Realizing International Women's Rights Law Through Local Governance: The Case of Cities for CEDAW." *Human Rights Review* 22 (3): 303–25.

Russell, Annelise, Maggie Macdonald, and Whitney Hua. 2023. "Sit Still, Talk Pretty: Partisan Differences Among Women Candidates' Campaign Appeals." *Journal of Women, Politics & Policy* 44 (3): 354–70.

Russell, James. 2019. "UPDATE: No. 2: Steele Rejects Mayor's Call to Resign." *Dallas Voice,* July 2, 2019. https://dallasvoice.com/fort-worth-hrc-member-posts-transphobic-racist-right-wing-memes-on-fb/.

Rynbrandt, Linda J. 1999. *Caroline Bartlett Crane and Progressive Reform: Social Housekeeping as Sociology.* Taylor & Francis.

Salsich, Peter W. 2000. "Grassroots Consensus Building and Collaborative Planning." *Washington University Journal of Law and Policy* 3:709–42.

Saltzstein, Grace Hall. 1986. "Female Mayors and Women in Municipal Jobs." *American Journal of Political Science* 30 (1): 140–64.

———. 1989. "Black Mayors and Police Policies." *Journal of Politics* 51 (3): 525–44.

Sanbonmatsu, Kira. 2006. "Gender Pools and Puzzles: Charting a Path to the Legislature." *Politics & Gender* 1 (03): 387–400.

Sanbonmatsu, Kira, and Kelly Dittmar. 2020. "Are You Ready to Run? Campaign Trainings and Women's Candidacies in New Jersey." In *Good Reasons to Run: Women and Political Candidacy,* edited by Shauna L. Shames, Rachel Bernhard, Mirya R. Holman, and Dawn Langan Teele. Temple University Press.

Sances, Michael W. 2023. "Defund My Police? The Effect of George Floyd's Murder on Support for Local Police Budgets." *Journal of Politics* 85 (3): 1156–60.

Sapiro, Virginia. 1983. *The Political Integration of Women: Roles, Socialization, and Politics*. University of Illinois Press.

Schaffner, Brian F., Jesse H. Rhodes, and Raymond J. La Raja. 2020. *Hometown Inequality: Race, Class, and Representation in American Local Politics*. Cambridge University Press.

Schattschneider, Elmer Eric. 1975. *The Semisovereign People: A Realist's View of Democracy in America*. Reprint edition. Dryden Press.

Schiesl, Martin J. 1975. "Progressive Reform in Los Angeles under Mayor Alexander, 1909–1913." *California Historical Quarterly* 54 (1): 37–56.

———. 1980. *The Politics of Efficiency: Municipal Administration and Reform in America, 1880–1920*. University of California Press.

Schneller, John. 2016. "Electrical Power: Its Advent and Role in Revitalizing and Expanding New Orleans 1880–1915." Master's thesis, University of New Orleans.

Schudson, Michael. 2015. *The Rise of the Right to Know*. Harvard University Press.

———. 2020. "The Shortcomings of Transparency for Democracy." *American Behavioral Scientist* 64 (11): 1670–78.

Schwartz, Gabriel L., and Jaquelyn L. Jahn. 2020. "Mapping Fatal Police Violence across US Metropolitan Areas: Overall Rates and Racial/Ethnic Inequities, 2013–2017." *PloS ONE* 15 (6): e0229686.

Schwindt-Bayer, Leslie A. 2010. *Political Power and Women's Representation in Latin America*. Oxford University Press.

Scott, Mel. 1971. *American City Planning since 1890: A History Commemorating the Fiftieth Anniversary of the American Institute of Planners*. University of California Press.

Sears, David O., and Jack Citrin. 1982. *Tax Revolt: Something for Nothing in California*. Harvard University Press.

Seehafer News. 2021. "Milwaukee City Attorney Says Anti-Harassment Policy Doesn't Apply to Him." *Seehafer News*, April 29, 2021. https://www.seehafernews.com/2021/04/29/milwaukee-city-attorney-says-anti-harassment-policy-doesnt-apply-to-him/.

Sernett, Milton C. 1997. *Bound for the Promised Land: African American Religion and the Great Migration*. Duke University Press.

Shah, Paru. 2014. "It Takes a Black Candidate: A Supply-Side Theory of Minority Representation." *Political Research Quarterly* 67 (2): 266–79.

Shah, Paru R., Melissa J. Marschall, and Anirudh V. S. Ruhil. 2013. "Are We There Yet? The Voting Rights Act and Black Representation on City Councils, 1981–2006." *Journal of Politics* 75 (4): 993–1008.

Shapiro, Ian. 1999. "Enough of Deliberation: Politics Is About Interests and Power." In *Deliberative Politics: Essays on Democracy and Disagreement*, edited by Stephen Macedo, 31–39. Oxford University Press.

Sharara, Fablina, Eve E. Wool, Gregory J. Bertolacci, Nicole Davis Weaver, Shelley Balassyano, and Ismaeel Yunusa. 2021. "Fatal Police Violence by Race and State in the USA, 1980–2019: A Network Meta-Regression." *Lancet* 398 (10307): P1239.

Sharp, Steven. 2023. "Affordable Housing Streamlining Ordinance Clears City Planning Commission." *Urbanize—Los Angeles*, November 20, 2023. https://la.urbanize.city/post/city-planning-commission-upholds-approval-mixed-use-project-7115-van-nuys-boulevard.

Shefter, Martin. 1977. "New York City's Fiscal Crisis—The Politics of Inflation and Retrenchment." *Public Interest* 48 (Summer): 98–127.

———. 1992. *Political Crisis Fiscal Crisis*. Columbia University Press.

Shurlle, Swain. 1996. "Women and Philanthropy in Colonial and Post-Colonial Australia." *Voluntas: International Journal of Voluntary and Nonprofit Organizations* 7 (4): 428–43.

Sills, Stephen J., and Bruce A. Rich. 2021. "Housing Instability and Public Health: Implications of the Eviction Moratoria during the COVID-19 Pandemic." *North Carolina Medical Journal* 82 (4): 271–75.

Silva, Andrea, Diego Esparza, Valerie Martinez-Ebers, and Regina Branton. 2022. "Perceived Police Performance, Racial Experiences, and Trust in Local Government." *Politics, Groups, and Identities* 10 (3): 343–66.

Silva, Andrea, and Carrie Skulley. 2019. "Always Running: Candidate Emergence among Women of Color over Time." *Political Research Quarterly* 72 (2): 342–59.

Silver, Christopher. 1984. *Twentieth-Century Richmond: Planning, Politics, and Race.* University of Tennessee Press.

———. 1988. "The Changing Face of Neighborhoods in Memphis and Richmond, 1940–1985." In *Shades of the Sunbelt: Essays on Ethnicity, Race, and the Urban South*, edited by Randall M. Miller and George Pozzetta. Greenwood Press.

Simon, Richard. 1993. "Alpheus Hodges: A Name to Remember for Obscure Reasons." *Los Angeles Times*, March 15, 1993.

Sivulka, Juliann. 1999. "From Domestic to Municipal Housekeeper: The Influence of the Sanitary Reform Movement on Changing Women's Roles in America, 1860–1920." *Journal of American Culture* 22 (4): 1.

Smydra, David F. 1993. "The Detroit Board of Police Commissioners: Historical and Policy Context." Citizens Research Council of Michigan.

Solowiej, Lisa A., Wendy L. Martinek, and Thomas L. Brunell. 2005. "Partisan Politics: The Impact of Party in the Confirmation of Minority and Female Federal Court Nominees." *Party Politics* 11 (5): 557–77.

Sonenshein, Raphael. 2006. "Los Angeles: Structure of a City Government." League of Women Voters of Los Angeles. https://my.lwv.org/sites/default/files/leagues/los-angeles/structureofacity.pdf.

Sorensen, Martin Selsoe. 2020. "Copenhagen Mayor Resigns Amid #MeToo Wave in Denmark." *New York Times*, October 22, 2020. https://www.nytimes.com/2020/10/22/world/europe/copenhagen-mayor-metoo-denmark.html.

Spain, Daphne. 2016. *Constructive Feminism: Women's Spaces and Women's Rights in the American City.* Cornell University Press.

Spencer, Martin E. 1970. "Weber on Legitimate Norms and Authority." *British Journal of Sociology* 21 (2): 123–34.

Spencer-Wood, Suzanne M. 1994. "Turn of the Century Women's Organizations, Urban Design, and the Origin of the American Playground Movement." *Landscape Journal* 13 (2): 124–37.

Stach, Patricia Burgess. 1989. "Real Estate Development and Urban Form: Roadblocks in the Path to Residential Exclusivity." *Business History Review* 63 (2): 356–83.

Statutes of California. 1925. California State Printing Office.

Stauffer, Katelyn E. 2021. "Public Perceptions of Women's Inclusion and Feelings of Political Efficacy." *American Political Science Review* 115 (4): 1226–41.

Steffens, Lincoln. 1904. *The Shame of the Cities.* McClure, Phillips.

Stein, Michael Isaac. 2020. "With City Personnel Cuts Looming, Cantrell Quietly Moved to Replace Civil Service Commission Chair." *The Lens*, October 19, 2020. https://thelensnola.org/2020/10/19/with-city-personnel-cuts-looming-cantrell-quietly-moved-to-replace-civil-service-commission-chair/.

———. 2023a. "Firefighters Union, without Contract since 2012, Says Negotiations Stalled with Cantrell Admin." *Verite News*, April 12, 2023. https://veritenews.org/2023/04/12/firefighters-union-without-contract-since-2012/.

———. 2023b. "Payroll Fraud and a 'Secret Sex Room': Troubling Allegations at New Orleans S&WB." *Fox8News*, June 26, 2023. https://www.fox8live.com/2023/06/26/pay roll-fraud-secret-sex-room-troubling-allegations-new-orleans-swb/.

———. 2023c. "Scathing New Report Calls for Overhaul of Sewerage & Water Board's Structure." *Louisiana Illuminator*, May 21, 2023. https://lailluminator.com/2023/05/21 /scathing-new-report-calls-for-overhaul-of-sewerage-water-boards-structure/.

Steinhauer, Jennifer. 2010. "The Ebell Club, a Women's Social Club, Tries to Remain Relevant in Los Angeles." *New York Times*, August 9, 2010. https://www.nytimes.com /2010/08/10/us/10ebell.html.

Stewart, Alva A. 1999. "The Why, When and How of Women Mayors." *American City and County* 114 (8): 59–60.

Stewart, Debra W. 1980. "Institutionalization of Female Participation at the Local Level." *Women & Politics* 1 (1): 37–63.

Stivers, Camilla. 1990. "The Public Agency as Polis: Active Citizenship in the Administrative State." *Administration & Society* 22 (1): 86–105.

Stone, Clarence N. 1980. "Systemic Power in Community Decision Making: A Restatement of Stratification Theory." *American Political Science Review* 74 (4): 978–90.

———. 1989. *Regime Politics: Governing Atlanta, 1946–1988. Studies in Government and Public Policy*. University of Kansas Press.

———. 1996. "Urban Political Machines: Taking Stock." *PS: Political Science & Politics* 29 (3): 446–50.

Strange, John H. 1972a. "Citizen Participation in Community Action and Model Cities Programs." *Public Administration Review* 32:655–69.

———. 1972b. "Community Action in North Carolina: Maximum Feasible Misunderstanding? Mistake? Or Magic Formula?" *Publius* 2 (2): 51–73.

Street Renaming Commission. 2021. "New Orleans City Council Street Renaming Commission Final Report." https://nolaccsrc.org/NOCCSRC-FinalReport.pdf.

Subbaraman, Nidhi. 2019. "New Orleans Has Been Hiding an Alarming Report about Lead in the City's Water." *Buzzfeed News*, November 4, 2019. https://www.buzzfeed news.com/article/nidhisubbaraman/new-orleans-lead-water-hidden-report.

Sullivan, John L. 1973. "Political Correlates of Social, Economic, and Religious Diversity in the American States." *Journal of Politics* 35 (1): 70–84.

Sumner, Jane Lawrence, Emily M. Farris, and Mirya R. Holman. 2020. "Crowdsourcing Reliable Local Data." *Political Analysis* 28 (2): 244–62.

———. 2021. "Annual Comprehensive Financial Report." Sewerage and Water Board of New Orleans. https://www.swbno.org/Reports/Financial.

———. 2022. "Energy New Orleans, Sewerage and Water Board Break Ground on West Power Complex, Phase I," press release, December 5, 2022. https://www.swbno.org /PressReleases/Details/4720.

Swers, Michele L. 2013. *Women in the Club: Gender and Policy Making in the Senate*. University of Chicago Press.

Tam Cho, Wendy K. 2003. "Contagion Effects and Ethnic Contribution Networks." *American Journal of Political Science* 47 (2): 368–87.

Tao, Jie, and Brian Collins. 2024. "De-Funding the Police or Re-Funding the Police: Do Public Safety Special Districts Impact Public Safety Expenditures and Crime?" Paper presented at the Southern Political Science Association Conference, New Orleans, LA.

Tausanovitch, Chris, and Christopher Warshaw. 2013. "Measuring Constituent Policy Preferences in Congress, State Legislatures, and Cities." *The Journal of Politics* 75 (2): 330–42.

Teele, Dawn Langan. 2018. "How the West Was Won: Competition, Mobilization, and Women's Enfranchisement in the United States." *Journal of Politics* 80 (2): 442–61.

———. 2024. "The Political Geography of the Gender Gap." *The Journal of Politics* 86 (2): 428–42.

Terjesen, Siri, Ruth Sealy, and Val Singh. 2009. "Women Directors on Corporate Boards: A Review and Research Agenda." *Corporate Governance: An International Review* 17 (3): 320–37.

Thomas, Karen Kruse. 2016. *Health and Humanity: A History of the Johns Hopkins Bloomberg School of Public Health, 1935–1985.* Johns Hopkins University Press.

Thompson, A. C. 2017. "Police Stood By as Mayhem Mounted in Charlottesville." *ProPublica*, August 12, 2017. https://www.propublica.org/article/police-stood-by-as-may hem-mounted-in-charlottesville.

Tiebout, Charles M. 1956. "A Pure Theory of Local Expenditures." *Journal of Political Economy* 64 (5): 416–24.

Tocqueville, Alexis de. 2006 [1835]. *Democracy in America* (Volumes 1 and 2, Unabridged). Harper Collins.

Toll, Seymour I. 1969. *Zoned American.* Grossman Publishers.

Tolley, Erin, Randy Besco, and Semra Sevi. 2022. "Who Controls the Purse Strings? A Longitudinal Study of Gender and Donations in Canadian Politics." *Politics & Gender* 18 (1): 244–72.

Troesken, Werner, and Randall Walsh. 2019. "Collective Action, White Flight, and the Origins of Racial Zoning Laws." *Journal of Law, Economics, and Organization* 35 (2): 289–318.

Trotter, Joe W. 1995. "African Americans in the City: 'The Industrial Era, 1900–1950.'" *Journal of Urban History* 21 (4): 438–57.

Trounstine, Jessica. 2006. "Dominant Regimes and the Demise of Urban Democracy." *Journal of Politics* 68 (4): 879–93.

———. 2008. *Political Monopolies in American Cities: The Rise and Fall of Bosses and Reformers.* University of Chicago Press.

———. 2009. "All Politics Is Local: The Reemergence of the Study of City Politics." *Perspectives on Politics* 7 (3): 611–18.

———. 2011. "Evidence of a Local Incumbency Advantage." *Legislative Studies Quarterly* 36 (2): 255–80.

———. 2013. "Turnout and Incumbency in Local Elections." *Urban Affairs Review* 49 (2): 167–89.

———. 2018. *Segregation by Design Local Politics and Inequality in American Cities.* Cambridge University Press.

Truong, Thanh. 2021. "New Orleans Firefighters Call for a Living Wage." *WWLTV*, June 6, 2021. https://www.wwltv.com/article/news/local/orleans/new-orleans-firefighters -call-for-a-living-wage/289-c7e9dec4-0e7a-4f72-a879-fee1aca6a560.

Turnbull, Craig. 2009. *An American Urban Residential Landscape, 1890–1920.* Cambria Press.

Turner, F. C. 1972. "The Case for Highway Planning." *Transportation Law Journal* 4 (2): 167–76.

Tyler, Pamela. 2009. *Silk Stockings and Ballot Boxes: Women and Politics in New Orleans, 1920–1963.* University of Georgia Press.

Tyler, Tom R. 2006. "Psychological Perspectives on Legitimacy and Legitimation." *Annual Review of Psychology* 57 (1): 375–400.

U.S. Census Bureau. 2012. "Growth in Urban Population Outpaces Rest of Nation, Census Bureau Reports," press release, March 26, 2023. https://www.census.gov/newsroom/releases/archives/2010_census/cb12-50.html.

U.S. Department of Housing and Urban Development. 1968. "The Model Cities Program: Questions and Answers." https://ia902200.us.archive.org/29/items/modelcitiesprogr00unit/modelcitiesprogr00unit.pdf.

U.S. Small Business Administration. 2020. "What Is the 504 Loan Program?" https://www.sba.gov/funding-programs/loans/504-loans.

Valdini, Melody E. 2019. *The Inclusion Calculation*. Oxford University Press.

Vedlitz, Arnold. 2010. "Moving Forward: Charting the Future of Civil Service in New Orleans." PhD diss., Texas A&M University, Bush School of Government and Public Service.

Vernon's. 1950. *Vernon's Texas Statutes: 1950s Supplement*. Vernon Law Book Company.

Villanueva-Marquez, Victoria. 2021. "Why, Despite Public Outcry, Delray Still Plans to End Lease with Old School Square." *Palm Beach Post*, August 2021. https://www.palmbeachpost.com/story/news/local/delray/2021/08/18/despite-public-outcry-delray-to-end-lease-with-old-school-square/.

Voelkel, Jan Gerrit, and Robb Willer. 2019. "Resolving the Progressive Paradox: Conservative Value Framing of Progressive Economic Policies Increases Candidate Support." SSRN Working Paper.

Walensky, Rochelle. 2021. "Temporary Halt in Residential Evictions in Communities with Substantial or High Levels of Community Transmission of Covid-19 to Prevent the Further Spread of COVID-19." Centers for Disease Control and Prevention. https://stacks.cdc.gov/view/cdc/108498/cdc_108498_DS1.pdf.

Walker, Hannah L. 2020. "Targeted: The Mobilizing Effect of Perceptions of Unfair Policing Practices." *Journal of Politics* 82 (1): 119–34.

Walker, Samuel. 1977. *A Critical History of Police Reform*. Lexington Books.

Wallace, Clare. 1934. "William Henry Pierce." County of Los Angeles Public Library Local History Collection Biography. https://dbase1.lapl.org/webpics/calindex/documents/07/518084.pdf.

Walters, Lawrence C., James Aydelotte, and Jessica Miller. 2000. "Putting More Public in Policy Analysis." *Public Administration Review* 60 (4): 349–59.

Wang, Yu. 2023. "Topic Classification for Political Texts with Pretrained Language Models." *Political Analysis* 31 (4): 662–68.

Warken, Philip W. 1969. "A History of the National Resources Planning Board, 1933–1943." PhD diss., The Ohio State University.

Warshaw, Christopher. 2019. "Local Elections and Representation in the United States." *Annual Review of Political Science* 22 (1): 461–79.

Washnis, George J. 1973. "Model Cities Impact on Better Communities." Report for the Congress of the United States, House Committee on Banking and Currency. U.S. Government Printing Office.

Wasow, Omar. 2020. "Agenda Seeding: How 1960s Black Protests Moved Elites, Public Opinion and Voting." *American Political Science Review* 114 (3): 638–59.

WDSU Digital Team.. 2021. "New Orleans Jail Regresses on Consent Decree Compliance, Feds Say." *WDSU*, October 11, 2021. https://www.wdsu.com/article/new-orleans-jail-regresses-on-consent-decree-compliance-feds-say/37928872.

Weatherford, M. Stephen. 1992. "Measuring Political Legitimacy." *American Political Science Review* 86 (1): 149–66.

Weaver, Timothy. 2016. *Blazing the Neoliberal Trail: Urban Political Development in the United States and the United Kingdom.* University of Pennsylvania Press.

———. 2018. "By Design or by Default: Varieties of Neoliberal Urban Development." *Urban Affairs Review* 54 (2): 234–66.

———. 2021. "Market Privilege: The Place of Neoliberalism in American Political Development." *Studies in American Political Development* 35 (1): 104–26.

Weber, Bret A., and Amanda Wallace. 2012. "Revealing the Empowerment Revolution: A Literature Review of the Model Cities Program." *Journal of Urban History* 38 (1): 173–92.

Weeks, Ana Catalano. 2018. "Why Are Gender Quota Laws Adopted by Men? The Role of Inter- and Intraparty Competition." *Comparative Political Studies* 51 (14): 1935–73.

———. 2022. *Making Gender Salient: From Gender Quota Laws to Policy.* Cambridge University Press.

Wenham, Clare, Julia Smith, and Rosemary Morgan. 2020. "COVID-19: The Gendered Impacts of the Outbreak." *Lancet* 395 (10227): 846–48.

WGNO. 2023. "Legal Fallout in Officer Vappie Internal Investigation." *WGNO*, March 16, 2023. https://wgno.com/news/local/legal-fallout-in-officer-vappie-internal-investigation/.

Wike, Richard, Laura Silver, and Alexandra Castillo. 2019. "Why People Are Dissatisfied with How Democracy Is Working." Pew Research Center.

Wilkinson, Missy. 2022. "Accountant Imprisoned 3½ Years for Taking $1 Million from New Orleans Firefighters Fund." *NOLA.com*, July 13, 2022. https://www.nola.com/news/crime_police/accountant-imprisoned-3-years-for-taking-1-million-from-new-orleans-firefighters-fund/article_f7ec0af4-02df-11ed-88e2-839689808cfc.html.

Williams, Robert W. 1961. "Martin Behrman and New Orleans Civic Development, 1904–1920." *Louisiana History: Journal of the Louisiana Historical Association* 2 (4): 373–400.

Willison, Charley E. 2021. *Ungoverned and Out of Sight: Public Health and the Political Crisis of Homelessness in the United States.* Oxford University Press.

Willison, Charley E., Denise Lillvis, Amanda Mauri, and Phillip M. Singer. 2021. "Technically Accessible, Practically Ineligible: The Effects of Medicaid Expansion Implementation on Chronic Homelessness." *Journal of Health Politics, Policy and Law* 46 (6): 1019–52.

Willison, Charley E., Naquia Unwala, Phillip M. Singer, Timothy B. Creedon, Brian Mullin, and Benjamin Lê Cook. 2023. "Persistent Disparities: Trends in Rates of Sheltered Homelessness Across Demographic Subgroups in the USA." *Journal of Racial and Ethnic Health Disparities* 11 (1): 326–38.

Wilson, Erika K. 2019. "The New White Flight." *Duke Journal of Constitutional Law & Public Policy* 14:233–84.

Wilz, Kelly. 2016. "Bernie Bros and Woman Cards: Rhetorics of Sexism, Misogyny, and Constructed Masculinity in the 2016 Election." *Women's Studies in Communication* 39 (4): 357–60.

Winling, LaDale C., and Todd M. Michney. 2021. "The Roots of Redlining: Academic, Governmental, and Professional Networks in the Making of the New Deal Lending Regime." *Journal of American History* 108 (1): 42–69.

Witt, Matthew. 1999. "The Origins and Evolution of Conflict in Portland's Neighborhood Association System: A Case Study of North Portland's District Coalition Board." *Administrative Theory & Praxis* 21 (1): 62–75.

Wolbrecht, Christina. 2000. *The Politics of Women's Rights: Parties, Positions, and Change.* Princeton University Press.

Wolbrecht, Christina, and J. Kevin Corder. 2019. *A Century of Votes for Women: American Elections Since Suffrage.* Cambridge University Press.

Wolf, Michael Allan. 1990. "Enterprise Zones: A Decade of Diversity." *Economic Development Quarterly* 4 (1): 3–14.

Wolman, Harold, and David Spitzley. 1996. "The Politics of Local Economic Development." *Economic Development Quarterly* 10 (2): 115–50.

Wu, Henry H., Ryan J. Gallagher, Thayer Alshaabi, Jane L. Adams, Joshua R. Minot, Michael V. Arnold, Brooke Foucault Welles, Randall Harp, Peter Sheridan Dodds, and Christopher M. Danforth. 2023. "Say Their Names: Resurgence in the Collective Attention toward Black Victims of Fatal Police Violence Following the Death of George Floyd." *PLoS ONE* 18 (1): e0279225.

Wyman, Roger E. 1974. "Middle-Class Voters and Progressive Reform: The Conflict of Class and Culture." *American Political Science Review* 68 (2): 488–504.

Yang, Kaifeng, and Kathe Callahan. 2007. "Citizen Involvement Efforts and Bureaucratic Responsiveness: Participatory Values, Stakeholder Pressures, and Administrative Practicality." *Public Administration Review* 67 (2): 249–64.

Yang, Kaifeng, and Sanjay K. Pandey. 2011. "Further Dissecting the Black Box of Citizen Participation: When Does Citizen Involvement Lead to Good Outcomes?" *Public Administration Review* 71 (6): 880–92.

Yoder, Jesse. 2020. "Does Property Ownership Lead to Participation in Local Politics? Evidence from Property Records and Meeting Minutes." *American Political Science Review* 114 (4): 1213–29.

Zhang, Lu. 2012. "Board Demographic Diversity, Independence, and Corporate Social Performance." *Corporate Governance: The International Journal of Business in Society* 12 (5): 686–700.

Zhang, Yahong, and Min-Hyu Kim. 2018. "Do Public Corruption Convictions Influence Citizens' Trust in Government? The Answer Might Not Be a Simple Yes or No." *American Review of Public Administration* 48 (7): 685–98.

Zhang, Yahong, and Yuguo Liao. 2011. "Participatory Budgeting in Local Government: Evidence from New Jersey Municipalities." *Public Performance & Management Review* 35 (2): 281–302.

Zurik, Lee, and Dannah Sauer. 2022. "NOPD Investigating Officer Frequently Inside Cantrell's City-Owned Apartment." *Fox8live*, November 11, 2022. https://www.fox8live.com/2022/11/10/zurik-nopd-investigating-officer-frequently-inside-cantrells-city-owned-apartment/.

Index

Mirya R. Holman is a Professor in the Hobby School of Public Affairs at the University of Houston, author of *Women in Politics in the American City* (Temple), and coauthor of *The Power of the Badge: Sheriffs and Inequality in the United States.*

www.ingramcontent.com/pod-product-compliance
Lightning Source LLC
Chambersburg PA
CBHW070357270326
41926CB00014B/2590